Parenting Teens
with Love and Logic

Parenting Teens with Love and Logic

Preparing Adolescents for Responsible Adulthood

UPDATED AND EXPANDED EDITION

Foster Cline, MD and Jim Fay

NAVPRESS

NAVPRESS⚫.

NavPress is the publishing ministry of The Navigators, an international Christian organization and leader in personal spiritual development. NavPress is committed to helping people grow spiritually and enjoy lives of meaning and hope through personal and group resources that are biblically rooted, culturally relevant, and highly practical.

For a free catalog go to www.NavPress.com
or call 1.800.366.7788 in the United States or 1.800.839.4769 in Canada.

© 1992, 2006 by Foster Cline, MD and Jim Fay

ISBN-13: 978-1-57683-930-0

Cover design by: Kirk DouPonce, DogEaredDesign.com
Cover photo by: Jupiter Images and Getty Images
Creative Team: Terry Behimer, Amy Spencer, Cara Iverson, Darla Hightower, Arvid Wallen, Laura Spray

First edition text was written by Tom Morton.
Second edition was prepared by Rick Killian, Killian Creative, Boulder, Colorado, www.killiancreative.com.

All Scripture quotations are from the *New Revised Standard Version Bible,* © 1989, Division of Christian Education of the National Council of the Churches of Christ in the United States of America. Used by permission. All rights reserved.

Some of the anecdotal illustrations in this book are true to life and are included with the permission of the persons involved. All other illustrations are composites of real situations, and any resemblance to people living or dead is purely coincidental.

Library of Congress Cataloging-in-Publication Data

Cline, Foster.
  Parenting teens with love and logic : preparing adolescents for responsible adulthood / Foster W. Cline and Jim Fay.-- Updated and expanded ed.
     p. cm.
  Rev. ed. of: Parenting teens with love & logic. c1992.
  Includes bibliographical references and index.
  ISBN 1-57683-930-3
  1. Parent and teenager. 2. Teenagers--Family relationships. 3. Adolescent psychology.
  I. Fay, Jim. II. Cline, Foster. Parenting teens with love & logic. III. Title.
  HQ799.15.C55 2006
  649'.125--dc22
                            2005037528

Printed in the United States of America
6 7 8 9 10 11 / 12 11 10 09

To all the parents and children (including our own!)
who were my teachers, and to my wife, Hermie, who gave support.

—Foster

To my wife, Shirley,
whose love, support, and wisdom have always been
a source of motivation and strength.

—Jim

Trust, with confirmation

Contents

Foreword to the Second Edition

We have been gratified to see the response that the world has given *Parenting with Love and Logic* and *Parenting Teens with Love and Logic*. Since these books were first published in 1990 and 1992, they have had twenty-six and seventeen printings respectively and have been translated into eight languages. Parents on six continents—all except Antarctica—have effectively embraced Love and Logic concepts. During these years since the first edition, we have happily collected success stories of parents who excitedly and proudly told us of raising their children with choices, consequences, and empathy, as taught in *Parenting Teens with Love and Logic*.

While sales have continued to increase, it is apparent that the world has changed in many ways since the books were written. In those days, there was no instant messaging, no talking to strangers in chat rooms, no computer games. There was less premature sex, less violent behavior, and fewer parents struggling as singles to raise teens.

Yet whether parents are relating to their children about a game of pool or about a violent video game, whether they are concerned about their children's knickers being above the knees or about their children's noses and lips being pierced, good parenting boils down to loving and effective parent-child relationships and communication that engender respect and self-discipline, no matter the generation.

Our goal in this second edition has not changed, but we have added information on how parents can specifically handle the new challenges our children face. This new information includes real-life examples of effective communication with teens.

We thank the parents who have told us how the principles here have helped them raise children equipped to make good decisions and who are loving, responsible, and fun to be around. We also thank those who have given us ideas and suggestions, some of which have been included in this edition.

Foster Cline and Jim Fay
March 2006

Introduction

Parents whose children are now turning thirteen know that kids face far greater challenges than they did just a generation ago. Risky behaviors such as binge drinking, drug use, and premature sexual activity are more rampant than ever in our high schools, and children are experimenting with them at younger ages. Research tells us that the levels of clinical depression in high schools now are similar to what they were in mental health institutions in the 1950s (roughly one in four show such symptoms). Add to that the greater availability and greater potency of drugs such as marijuana and methamphetamine, the rampant increase of sexually transmitted infections among youth, and the increased isolation of our kids from caring adults for a number of cultural reasons, and it is easy to see that our children are facing many difficult and even life-and-death decisions earlier in life.

That means parents are also facing far greater challenges than we did just a few short years ago.

Most parents learn parenting simply by doing it. We feel joy and relief when our children learn how to live and grow on their own. We feel the sting of disappointment when an approach fails. We suffer dread when it looks like our children—despite our best efforts—somehow aren't going to "turn out right."

This kind of trial-and-error parenting can be pretty nerve-wracking in light of the consequences looming over our kids' lives.

Do you find yourself wondering whether you're doing the right things to equip your kids for the challenges they're facing? Do you wonder how to equip yourself for the challenges *you're* facing?

Take heart. You're not alone. Parenting is a challenge—and an opportunity—for anyone with teenagers. It doesn't matter what kind of batting average you've been maintaining so far; adolescence can be a whole new ball game.

We (Foster and Jim) have watched our own children grow through adolescence, and we have dealt with thousands of other parents and teens through our respective professions of psychiatry and education. We have some coaching tips we're convinced will help you.

The Love and Logic Approach

We offer an approach called "Parenting with Love and Logic." We spelled it out in an earlier book by that name. You may have read it, learned its principles, and applied them to your children.

If you haven't read *Parenting with Love and Logic*, you might find it helpful to get ahold of a copy, especially to read the first part, although we will cover many of those same principles from a different perspective in this book specifically about teens. If you have read *Parenting with Love and Logic*, you've got a good jump on the material here. When you come to sections you're familiar with, read them as a refresher course in Love and Logic parenting, or simply skim through them.

Why do we call our approach "Love and Logic parenting"? The first half, *love*, is essential to parenting. As you will learn, however, *love* does not mean hovering around your teens to protect them from all the rocks flung at them by the world. Nor does *love* mean tolerating outlandish, disrespectful, or illegal behavior. Rather, *love means maintaining a healthy relationship with our teens, empowering them to make their own decisions, to live with their own mistakes, and to grow through the consequences.*

The second half of our approach, *logic*, centers on the consequences themselves. Most decisions and mistakes lead to logical consequences. And those consequences, when accompanied by empathy — compassion for the disappointment, frustration, and pain that teens experience — will drive home lessons powerfully enough to change a teen's thinking for a lifetime. In other words, *logic allows our kids to figure out for themselves the cause-and-effect patterns of how their decisions and behaviors lead to certain consequences; it allows them to know that we love, support, and feel empathy for them in their situations but will not bail them out; and it allows responsibility to develop in them as they work through their difficulties and solve their problems for themselves.*

Using Love and Logic doesn't mean we transfer all of our answers or values to our teens. Instead we help place them in situations where they can discover answers and values on their own.

Who Is an Adolescent?

Although this book is called *Parenting Teens with Love and Logic*, it is actually about parenting adolescents. The definition of *teen* is clear: A teen is someone who exists between his or her thirteenth and twentieth birthday. *Adolescent* is a bit more ambiguous. An adolescent can be packaged as a child of ten. Or as an adult of forty, living with his parents and acting fourteen. Or as a man married to a woman who plays the role of mother to a husband acting seventeen.

So how do you know if your child is an adolescent and that the examples and advice given in this book apply to your situation? For our purposes, an adolescent is a person who (1) is newly dealing with intense physical and social changes, (2) has the ability (whether or not it is used) to figure out how to express himself or herself, and (3) is capable of making productive, healthy decisions—hormones or no.

This definition incorporates important conditions, and this book will be most helpful if all three conditions are met.

An adolescent is experiencing life's most intense changes. These adjustments include changes in appearance and in bodily urges. An adolescent also knows that within a relatively short time, he or she will be living in a different place, with different expectations, with new people, expressing himself or herself in new ways.

In early adolescence our children begin to develop the ability to think like adults, taking the great leap from concrete thinking to understanding metaphors and similes. They are able to weigh abstract concepts, and they wonder if the means really do justify the ends. Let's look at an example. A parent asks his or her child, "What does it mean that people in glass houses shouldn't throw stones?" If the child answers about glass breaking, then he or she is a concrete thinker. If the child says something along the lines of, "You better be careful before you say something about someone else when the same thing could be said about you," then he or she is an abstract thinker.

The ability of our adolescents to see cause-and-effect relationships, to apply situational ethics, to put things into an adult perspective, and to recognize parental and societal shortcomings has the potential to cause all sorts of tension between us and our children. These changes may make rebellion more likely, but they also make deep and delightful parent-child relationships possible.

It's not an easy job to parent children who are reaching the threshold of adulthood, coping with an updated brain, experiencing new feelings, and immersing themselves in new experiences. Parenting styles that vary from demanding and controlling to permissive and over-accommodating may be marginally effective with younger children, but they are doomed to failure when used with adolescents. It is therefore our privilege—and blessing, really—to offer the philosophy, tools, and techniques that will help you parent your adolescent toward responsible adulthood.

How This Book Is Organized

This book is written in three sections. Part 1 adapts concepts from *Parenting with Love and Logic* and discusses applying them specifically to teenagers. In it we discuss effective and ineffective parenting styles. We also explain how teens deal with self-esteem, control, decisions, and consequences, and how parents meet the consequences of their teens' decisions with empathy. These concepts lay the foundation for effectively parenting teens.

In part 2 we explore development in teens: how children grow from childhood into adolescence (and how parents go through growth phases with them!) and how they react to internal as well as external change. We conclude this section with practical guidelines and encouragement for parents on how to raise responsible teenagers.

In part 3 we get down to nuts-and-bolts specifics. We offer thirty-nine Love and Logic "pearls" dealing with everyday problems and issues most parents will face during their children's teenage years. Although these strategy nuggets are short and to the point, they should be read only after the principles in the first two parts of the book have been studied and understood.

We believe that Love and Logic parenting works, or we wouldn't have written this book. More than three decades of research, teaching, refining its methods, and seeing it work time and again have made us confident of its effectiveness. But no parenting system works perfectly every time. Over the years, we have emphasized key factors that keep the bond of our relationship with our teens strong. We have added techniques that neutralize arguments and have made various other changes. As the years have passed, we have discovered no other system as effective as Love and Logic for building adolescents into responsible adults.

Actually, Love and Logic parenting is not so much a system as an attitude. When it's applied in the context of a healthy relationship with our teens, this attitude will free them to grow in maturity as they grow in years. It will teach them to think, to decide, and to live with their decisions. They will learn responsibility as we learn to live with less control and make peace with our own abilities and shortcomings. As our children grow older and wiser, we'll gain not just a more mature child, but a lifelong adult friend as well.

Not all teens are alike, of course. Children who seemed so similar when they were younger than age eleven develop in much different ways in their teenage years. No book on teenagers can anticipate every physical change or every outside influence.

Therefore, in this book we assume that although teens share basic similarities, each family has its own kind of child. One teen's rebellion is another teen's independence. The closeness and quality of the parent-child relationship will vary from one family to another. And some kids are just plain different.

Another assumption we're making is that the principles in this book will not be abused. A how-to book, especially one that offers advice on a matter as sensitive as parenting teenagers, can often be misused. For example, just because we believe that teens should live with the consequences of their decisions in no way implies that parents should look the other way if their children are involved in life-threatening acts such as playing with loaded weapons. Adolescents are still under our guardianship because they still need loving guides and consultants as they face the challenges of their times.

We also assume that parents who read this book are caring and loving people. Abusive parents could use these principles and possibly cause harm to their teen. Unfortunately, most parents who are abusive don't recognize or acknowledge it. Parents who suspect that they may be abusive should seek professional advice.

We believe parents face no greater challenge—and have no greater opportunity—than to guide their children through the teen years so they grow to enjoy productive, happy, and responsible adult lives. We believe that this book will help parents meet that challenge and rejoice in that opportunity. It's never too late to start parenting the Love and Logic way.

Part 1

Love and Logic Parents Grow Up

1

Teenagers 101: Welcome to Parenting Graduate School

Jake had never been what you'd call bad, but as he grew into the teen years, he wasn't what you'd call good either. He was sort of a not-nice, mister-in-between type of adolescent. At sixteen Jake was moody and detached from his parents. He wasn't in-your-face rebellious but simply preferred to respond to his folks as he would any other dust mote that floated through the house. That is, he really didn't relate to his parents unless he wanted something. When at home, he would retire moodily to his room.

For a parent, sometimes being ignored can be even more painful than putting up with overtly negative nasty-isms. "It's not that we didn't deserve it," Jake's mother, Tammy, recounted.

> We had always given Jake pretty much what he wanted. We rescued him from his own mistakes and worked hard to give him all the material things that Gary and I never had. We knocked ourselves out trying to please that kid, so, of course, he had no respect for us at all. Probably just being around us reminded him unconsciously of whom he had internalized as a role model. We didn't understand all that back in those days. Gary calls them the pre-Love and Logic WJDGI days—meaning "'We just didn't get it.
>
> Gary and I had just finished our first Love and Logic class, and we were down in the dumps. Here we were with this

noncommunicative and aloof human being that we ourselves had created. We were going through the if-only-we-had-found-Love-and-Logic-ten-years-ago routine, feeling kind of hopeless, when God and luck brought us a critical "significant learning opportunity" that helped snap everything around and get us going in a great new direction.

I arrived home from work and received a call from a Sergeant Robert Kenner. He said that some kid they had picked up had copped a plea and had fingered Jake as being one of a twosome that had tried to rip off a few watches from Wal-Mart. It was Jake's friend Chris, who had been identified on video surveillance and preferred to share the glory. No honor among thieves, you know.

Sergeant Kenner said he'd be dropping by the house. I think Jake knew from my end of the conversation what the call had been about, and I know he expected the usual WJDGI routine, "Oh, woe is us" with hand-wringing angst from me and rage from his dad. But by then a new day had started to dawn, and I said, "That was an interesting call. The cops will be here shortly. Good luck, Jake. I'm curious to know how you will handle it."

Right then and there, as I looked at the utter surprise and consternation on his face, I felt this overwhelming joy screaming inside me, saying, "You did it! You did it!" That was a milestone for this hovering mother and made the class worth every penny.

When Sergeant Kenner arrived, he had a long talk with Jake. I reveled in staying out of it and feeding the dog, who had been a lot more responsive than Jake had been recently. Kenner said he was taking Jake downtown, and I merely said, "I understand," instead of variations on "Oh no!" or "How long?" or "Oh dear!" or "When can I pick him up?" Jake looked absolutely horror struck at my simply "understanding" the situation.

As Kenner prepared to take Jake, resplendent in cuffs, to the squad car, I asked if I could talk to him alone, and he said yes. When he came back, I asked him how long he might keep Jake, and he said he couldn't keep him long. Jake was a juvenile and they couldn't hold him on this first offense, but he would like to take him down and get fingerprints.

I asked him if he could *not* let Jake know that he couldn't be kept in a cell—or even put in one! Would he help me with a plan? Yes, he would. We cooked up all the details together there in the kitchen. As we talked about how we would handle it, I could see this officer looking at me appreciatively, like I was some kind of great mom or something! Wow, that was new! Nobody had ever accused me of *that* before.

Sergeant Kenner left with Jake, who was sitting forlornly in the back of the squad car with lights flashing and siren wailing, and we put the plan into action. [Kenner] phoned me on his cell phone on the way downtown to the city jail and activated the speaker on the phone so Jake could hear our conversation. As prearranged, [he] said, "You can come down and pick Jake up in a couple hours."

I said, "Gee, officer, I'm sorry, but I have other things to do."

"So, when *can* you pick him up?"

"Well, not today, *that's* for sure."

"Lady, we don't have any room in juvie, so he'll have to be in the adult cells, and we're tight on room there too. We're packed with pedophiles and sex abusers who are in lock-up right now."

"Officer, you do whatever you need to do, but I just don't have time today."

"Lady, do you know what could happen?!"

"Officer, I'm not the one who ripped off Wal-Mart. Jake made some poor choices and needs to handle the consequences, but he's tough, officer. I'm sure he'll be just fine." At that point I heard Jake actually starting to wail in the background, "Mom, pick me up." That's when this great officer disconnected, saying, "Okay, lady, but don't say I didn't warn you."

They could hold Jake only for three hours so that's when I went down to the jail. They pulled Jake off a wooden bench where he had been sitting the whole time, and he literally ran toward me and threw his arms around me. "Thank you, Mom!

Thank you, Mom!" I hadn't been hugged like that for years. Then he started to weep.

It was the beginning of a whole new life with Jake. Truly, since that day, he has treated us with respect, been responsible, and is almost always fun to be around, but I can't give him *all* the credit. We've changed too. I know we now come through a lot less critical and more accepting—but not always *approving*—on some things. Now we are massively consequential rather than "ranting, raving, and rescuing."

A Disturbing Call

Sandy and Alan Frank surveyed the dinner table. The silver, china, lighted tapers, and platters were decked out to a turn. They nodded to their guests—colleagues from Alan's law firm—and all sat down to what promised to be a perfect evening of home entertaining.

Alan and Sandy could count on a quiet evening; their teenage son Ryan was out on a date. Despite their outward ease with their guests, though, these parents harbored anxiety about their increasingly wayward son.

That anxiety wound into a knot when the phone rang during dessert. Sandy answered the phone and called for Alan with a trembling voice. Ryan and Desiree were being held at the sheriff's office. They had both been drinking, so Ryan—in a gesture of chivalrous cowardice—let Desiree drive. She drove the car over a curb, conveniently across the street from the police station, and shredded a tire. Both got tickets. The officer wanted to know when Alan and Sandy could come by to bail them out.

Sandy's worst fears were realized. Her eighteen-year-old had formally embarked on a life of crime. Her face pale, she groped her way back to the table. When her guests asked what was wrong, she responded with a flat, this-happens-all-the-time voice, "Oh, the sheriff's department called and said they are detaining Ryan."

Alan, still on the phone, decided then and there to change his parenting style. He and Sandy had recently attended a seminar on parenting with Love and Logic and realized they needed to do some things differently.

Instead of coming to Ryan's rescue or getting nasty as they used to do, Alan decided to let Ryan learn some responsibility and grow up.

"We're not coming down to the station to pick up Ryan," he told the officer.

"Well, Mr. Frank, if you don't pick him up, I'll have to lock him up."

"Well, officer, whatever it takes."

Alan, sporting a nervous grin, returned to the dining room just as Sandy was clearing the table. She was fumbling for a polite way to end the evening, escort her guests to the door, and then drive to the station to bail out Ryan. Alan walked in, tossed a pack of cards on the table, and said, "Let's play Hearts." He pulled the stunned Sandy aside, smiled, and said, "Let's not spoil a nice evening."

Who's in Charge Here?

For years, Ryan had appeared headed for a life of irresponsibility. He lived like a slob and had increasingly resisted his parents' badgering about his sloppy appearance, grungy clothes, messy room, and that "infernal music" thudding through the walls.

At thirteen, Ryan simply "forgot" to do his chores.

The older he grew, the more defiant he became. At seventeen, he started drinking even on school nights and experimenting with drugs, both of which were murder on his grades. He went out with girls running with the wrong crowd, such as Desiree, telling his dad, "She comes from a broken home and needs me as a counselor," prompting Alan to counter sarcastically, "Just what kind of counseling techniques are you using?"

Ryan had long since blown off the hallowed family tradition of kissing his parents good-night. Now they were lucky if he just yelled through their master bedroom door, "I'm home."

Alan responded to Ryan's moral slide by losing his temper and yelling. "You smell like a fermentation vat!" he would greet his son after a night out. Or "You have the social traits of a bum!"

Sandy would mutter aloud, "I know this is a kid I wouldn't take off the shelf myself."

Ryan, of course, just sneered. He had his parents emotionally eating out of his hand, and he knew it.

They knew it too. But they felt helpless to reassert control.

Then Alan and Sandy attended a seminar that introduced them to the Love and Logic parenting approach. They learned that parents should take care of themselves first, let their children own their own problems, and allow them to live with the consequences of their decisions.

A Change of Tactics

After the guests from Alan's law firm had gone home, Alan and Sandy had another opportunity to apply those principles. At 11:00 p.m., while they were lying awake wondering if they had done the right thing, the phone rang.

"Yes, who is it?" Alan answered.

"Dad!" came Ryan's urgent voice over the phone. "Dad, it's pretty bad down here."

"Hey, pal, is it really that bad?" Alan went on the offensive. "Let's agree that if I get thrown into the hoosegow, *you* won't rescue *me*."

That was too much for the rattled Ryan. "Okay, be that way!" he shouted, and slammed down the phone.

The phone rang fifteen minutes later. This time Sandy answered.

"Mrs. Frank? This is Julie. I'm a counselor at the detention center. Mrs. Frank, I'm so proud of you and your husband. Ryan is just fine. You'd be surprised at how many parents come down here and bail their kids out. Parents like you deserve a medal."

Alan and Sandy held off the next day as well, but Desiree's mother bailed out the two teens. Sandy was dreading the coming confrontation. However, Ryan didn't come home right away. He delayed his return in fear of his parents' anger.

When Ryan did arrive home, he was surprised to find that his parents weren't mad at him. His arrest was his responsibility, they communicated. They weren't going to berate him, but they weren't going to rescue him either.

This response defused any anger or defensiveness on Ryan's part. Now that he knew the situation was his responsibility, he was open to doing something about it.

Ryan told his parents that he would need to earn money to reimburse

Desiree's mom for bail, to get the car out of impound, to tow it to a garage, and to have a new tire put on. "This is the most expensive date I've ever been on," he exclaimed.

Sandy was amazed at Ryan's respectful and responsible response. "After that experience, we never used the rant-and-rave method again with the kids," she commented.

Rather than becoming a derelict, Ryan went on to college and eventually graduate school. He became a social worker worrying about getting grants to make the world a better place. Alan describes him as a "picture of social responsibility."

Sandy now says, "It's easy for us to forget that adolescence is a phase for the teen and for us too. But if you use the right techniques, it shortens the bad phases."

Learning Responsibility

Lori, the mother of fourteen-year-old Abby, had been looking forward to the evening for some time. After preparing to go out, she went to the closet to grab the $389 leather coat she had just bought, excited about wearing it for the first time. The coat wasn't there.

Lori immediately knew where it was. Abby was about her size and had been getting into the habit of borrowing her things without asking.

Later that evening, Lori waited up for her daughter, stewing in anger. When Abby got home, she did indeed have the coat on — and there was paint on the sleeve.

"Abby," her mother began, "how could you have done such a thing! You know I just bought that coat."

"Oh, Mom, it's not a big deal."

"Not a big deal! I just bought that coat, and now there's paint on the sleeve."

"That wasn't my fault. It was an accident. Besides, if you weren't so stingy and ever bought me anything nice for myself, I wouldn't have to borrow your stuff to wear."

At that, Lori was ready to hit the roof, but she had been taking a Love and Logic class and knew she was too emotional to deal with the situation at that moment. "Abby," she said, mustering her self-control, "I love you too much to argue with you, and I am in no state to solve this right now, but you wore the jacket without permission and you are going to have to find a solution for this. Let's go to bed and we can discuss it again later. Let me know what you figure out."

Later the next day, Lori again approached her daughter about the coat. "Have you thought about what you are going to do?"

"Oh, I don't know. Can't you just ground me or something?"

"Well, that wouldn't really solve the problem, would it?"

"I guess not."

"Would you like me to give you some options?"

"I guess so, okay."

"Well, you could buy a new coat."

"How much did it cost?"

"Three hundred and eighty-nine dollars."

"I can't do that! I don't have that kind of money."

"Okay, well, you could just blow it off."

"Oh, I couldn't do that. You'd never forget what happened and never let me forget it either."

"Well, you are right there. Another option would be to take it to a leather expert and see what they could do to get the paint off."

Abby chose that option and found that for thirty-five dollars the cleaner would try to get the paint off the jacket, but would not guarantee the work. When she offered to give Lori the thirty-five dollars to make it even, Lori again refused and handed the problem back to her daughter. Ultimately, Abby would have to find a solution on her own, whether it was to try the cleaners or hold a garage sale of her own things to pay for the jacket.

It is better for a fourteen-year-old to learn fiscal responsibility by "going bankrupt" at that age rather then when she is older and has others relying on her. Either way, Abby would provide the solution.

The Times They Are a'Changin'

Tammy, Gary, Sandy, Alan, and Lori all received a graduate-level education in parenting through their experiences. Their previous "schooling" hadn't prepared them for the intensity of the joys, sorrows, and dilemmas they faced daily and sometimes hourly with a teenager—from relationships, to jobs, to fashion, to loud music, to broken hearts, to broken laws.

Parents of teenagers invariably find out—if they haven't found out already—what these five parents learned: *Children change*. And what a change!

Just a few years ago, we were changing diapers, reinforcing basic manners, ferrying kids here and there, assisting them with homework, watching them play. Sure, we lost our temper at times, and sometimes even felt that we were losing our mind. And yes, there were the inevitable and seemingly endless challenges to our parental authority. But even through the hard lessons, we were still the parents. Our children were still within our control.

But then along came a phase change that sent us scrambling back for more education: a graduate course in "Teenagers."

All of a sudden, our kids didn't look the same anymore. Benny used to be satisfied with double-knee jeans and a T-shirt. Jocelyn used to let Mom buy her clothes. Now Ben Junior wears jeans with holes—and not just at the knees—and Jocelyn has a close personal relationship with every clothing clerk at the mall. Sometimes they dress as if every day were Halloween. These kids are going through bodily transformations that we think no doctor's ever heard of. Ben Junior towers above Dad and can lift Mom off the floor with one hand. Jocelyn looks good—too good—in skin-tight, midriff-baring clothes.

Fact is, children go through more physical changes in five years of adolescence than at any other time during their lives:

- Their brains change so they can think abstractly. They may question your faith, and they're not too sure they believe in you either.
- Their hormones rage as never before, and they are susceptible to everything from incredible growth spurts to extreme mood swings.
- Their bodies produce more oil, making their faces break out and sending them into emotional tailspins over zits.
- And, in case you forgot, they become fertile.

Modern parents face a number of challenges. Children seem to be maturing at younger ages, and societal influences are bombarding families and teens at warp speed, with incredible and sometimes catastrophic effects.

These social upheavals have scattered families in their wake — chief among them the "traditional" family of a working father, homemaking mother, and children, which is found in less than one in four households today.[1] This is old news to most of us. But what we really have trouble comprehending is the extent of the revolution in teen life. Consider:

- Homicide and suicide are the second and third leading causes of death among those 15 to 24, behind unintentional injuries.
- Of unintentional injuries leading to death, traffic accidents account for most of them,[2] and roughly 29 percent of accidents for 15- to 20-year-olds involve a driver who had been drinking.[3]
- In 2002 and 2003, more than one in five persons aged 16 to 20 reported that they had driven in the past year while under the influence of alcohol or illicit drugs.[4]
- According to the 2003 Youth Risk Behavior Survey done by the Center for Disease Control, one in ten (9.9 percent) had tried marijuana before the age of 13, while 22.4 percent were using it. (And 5.8 percent were smoking it at school.)
- More than one in four teens (28.3 percent) is currently involved in binge drinking.
- Of those surveyed, 3.3 percent had tried heroin, 6.1 percent had used steroids, 7.6 percent had tried methamphetamines, 8.7 percent had tried cocaine, 11.1 percent had tried ecstasy, and 12.1 percent had tried some form of inhalant.
- More than one out of every four (28.7 percent) had been offered, sold, or given an illegal drug on school property.
- Nearly half (46.7 percent) lost their virginity before graduating from high school (this statistic does not include those active in oral or anal intercourse, a trend that is growing among today's youth; most of them believe these do not cause them to lose their virginity).[5]

- An estimated 9.1 million new cases of sexually transmitted infections (STIs) occur every year among youth ages 15 to 24. While this age group accounts for about a quarter of those sexually active, it represents nearly half of the new STIs each year.[6]
- An unacceptable number of teens will drop out of high school.
- The percentage of children living with both their birth parents continues to decline as the divorce rate hovers at 50 percent for all marriages.
- Unless major economic change occurs, this generation of teenagers will be the first since the Depression to have a lower standard of living than their parents.

But family and societal changes are just the outside view. Complicating matters tremendously are the changes on the inside—what teens experience as they live through their own personal development.

Braving the Challenges of the Millennial Generation

As you watch your children enter the brave new world of twenty-first-century adolescence, you can feel the sting of their volatile emotional reactions to this inner upheaval.

Being a teenager is an out-of-body experience—out of a child's body and into an adult's, or somewhere in between. A teenager may look like an adult while acting like a two-year-old, as determined to establish their own identity as a defiant toddler. Naturally, we're concerned. Are they ready to handle the real world that waits beyond the safety of our protective care? And just as naturally, our teens grow more self-involved, questioning, and peer-oriented. They assimilate into a subculture, adopting distinctive dress and hairstyles, along with music and language that often offends adult ears.

All this is grounded in a deep personal struggle with identity and self-worth. "Who am I?" is more than a throwaway line from television shows and rock songs: it is the central question in teens' transition from dependence to independence.

But our teens can seem like aliens compared to the children we used to know. We wonder if other parents could possibly have as many sleepless nights worrying about their teenagers. Some of us wonder if our children and our marriages will survive.

Faced with this loss of control, we wonder, "What's wrong with me? Did my folks feel the same way about me when I was a teenager?"

What did your folks do? After all, it wasn't so long ago that you were cruising Main Street, singing along with Steppenwolf or *Thriller*, tasting your first cigarettes and beer, skipping church, breaking curfew, and even getting grounded on occasion. Did your folks wonder if you would ever grow up and become a responsible adult? Yup, they did! But you made it.

Now fast-forward several frames. *You* are the parent of teenagers, and you hope in the few years left before they fly the coop that somehow they'll learn how to make decisions in the real world.

"The real world"—now there's a phrase to make us shudder. The pressures and influences everywhere today were practically unheard of in ours or our parents' day. We're tempted to sink into despair as we watch our children face life-and-death decisions long before they're on their own. Drugs, alcohol, premarital sex, and especially depression and suicide confront teens and even much younger children frequently. These pressures can overload parents as much as teens, perhaps even more so, especially if they're trying to parent just like their parents did a generation earlier.

For example, when Jim's parents said, "Jump," he thought they could actually make him do it. Teens today know that parents simply don't have that my-word-is-the-law-in-this-house control because of the social, cultural, and technological revolutions since World War II. They know they have a right to be treated with respect and dignity, not auto-cratic control.

Now teens say to themselves, "I'm not sure my parents are right in what they're asking me to do and how they're asking me to do it. And my friends are saying that I don't have to put up with that." They are strug-gling to find their own way. No wonder parents are stressed finding ways to work with their teenagers. And teens are stressed trying to figure out how to live with their parents. We're all braving a new world.

A Reason for Hope

Is there any hope? We believe the answer is a resounding yes.

We all hope that we can raise our children in such a way that by the time they turn eighteen we can be friends, right? We look forward to meeting them on common ground as adults. But what does this mean?

Well, we know what we expect from our adult friends. We assume they will talk and act responsibly, think clearly, play with us when we want to have fun, be serious for the tough times of life, and leave us alone when we need privacy.

Why can't we expect the same from our teens?

You're probably thinking, *You must be talking about somebody else's teens. Mine just walked in at 4:00 a.m. She won't even be coherent until tomorrow afternoon. The only reason she would pay attention to my expectations is to figure out how to frustrate them.*

But we *are* talking about your teen. The principles we lay out in this book are relevant across the board—from shrinking violets to rebels without a cause. We're going to teach you how to apply them in the task of helping your teens become responsible adults.

Parenting requires not only commitment and hard work but also the right skills. Love and Logic techniques are particularly well suited to the teen years because they emphasize good communication and a consultant approach. These fit well with the emerging independence of the typical teen. And best of all, Love and Logic parents are building friendships with their children that should last a lifetime.

Love and Logic is a win-win philosophy. Presuming genetics and social situations are stable, parents win because they love in a healthy way and establish effective control over their teens. They don't need to resort to the anger, lectures, threats, and repeated warnings that will haunt teens along the path to adulthood. They also avoid the anger and frustration that just works to feed misbehavior. Teens win because they learn responsibility and the logic of life by solving their own problems. They acquire the necessary tools for coping with "the real world."

We offer this philosophy because, although teens' fundamental needs are the same as they have been in past generations and across cultures, the influences and pressures on them are radically different.

Today's challenges require a new approach to parenting teens more than ever before.

2

Love and Logic Parenting: Will It Work with Teenagers?

While putting some laundry away, Amy stumbled onto her son's stash of marijuana by accident. "I was so shocked," she later said. "I just didn't know what to do. My day was ruined. I was depressed beyond anything I can explain."

She knew she needed to confront the issue, but she didn't know what to do or say. Because she had removed the drugs from Mark's room, she knew she either had to put them back in the same place or had to talk to him soon; he would know they had been discovered.

Amy's inclination was to return the bag to its original place so she would have time to talk to someone who could give her advice. However, before she could act, Mark returned to the house and walked in on her while she had the bag in her hand.

Needless to say, they were both shocked. There she stood in the kitchen with drugs. Mark stuttered out something that sounded like "It's not what you think, Mom. That's not my weed. I'm just holding it for a friend."

Amy managed to respond with "I've heard that one before, and it doesn't matter. Drugs are not allowed in this house. I'm going to have to do something about this."

"What, Mom?"

"I don't have the slightest idea. This is such a disappointment. This is so serious. I'm going to have to think about this for a while. Take this bag and do something with it. I'm so upset I have to go to my room. I'll talk to you another time."

Amy agonized for the rest of the day, talked with some of her friends, and called one of the counselors at the high school. At the end of this time she still didn't know what to do. She just became more upset about the situation.

Mark came to the dinner table, but he could not look at his mom. There was silence throughout the meal. When dinner was over, he offered to do the dishes. Amy realized this was a little unusual. He usually took off to escape to his computer. She later said, "I think he was trying to do a little damage control and soften me up."

While Mark worked with the dishes he asked again, "You haven't told me what you're going to do about that problem. What's going on?"

Amy's response was, "I've thought of nothing else since I found your stash, but I don't have any idea what to do. It's been horribly upsetting to me. I have to tell you that I'm so unhappy I can't even put it into words."

She continued, "The thing that saddens me the most is that I know at your age I can no longer protect you from your bad decisions. I can't stand between your bad decisions and what the world has to offer for those decisions. So I guess your bad decisions are just going to have to be your bad decisions and the consequences for those decisions will have to be your consequences. You are the one who will have to deal with them, and my heart will ache for you."

She went on to tell him she wasn't going to do anything about the marijuana other than tell him it could never be in her house.

Amy went to bed a heartbroken person. She couldn't sleep, so she got up and went into the living room to try to read. Before long Mark came to her with the bag of marijuana.

"Mom, I'm going to bury this stuff in the back yard."

"Why? I told you I was not going to punish you."

"Mom, when you told me you could no longer stand between my bad decisions and what the consequences might be, that really scared me. If you're not going to worry about that, I decided I'm going to have to."

Standing on Their Own Two Feet

Remember how eager we were to see our children walk for the first time? We hovered over each one, armed with a camcorder, recording baby's first step for all time.

Then once they were off, they were off and running—full tilt. They ran around the kitchen, shaving it close around corners. They ran around the house, always veering toward the head of the stairs. They ran across the yard and down the block, with grown-ups in hot pursuit.

We were proud, if not a little terrified, to see how quickly they became mobile and demanded to go their own way.

Now they're teenagers. Have they finally slowed down? Just long enough to ask us for driver's education lessons and the keys to the family car. They're off and running once again—as they shift the car into reverse and head down the driveway. But they're not just driving out of the garage. They're about to drive out of our lives. As they disappear with a puff of exhaust blowing back our way, we hope they have the smarts and responsibility to make it on their own.

How should parents use these last few years to prepare their teens for leaving home? How do we prepare them to live as independent adults?

No parenting strategy is foolproof. However, we believe that wise application of Love and Logic principles will increase the odds of raising responsible teenagers who will leave home competent to face life on their own.

But before we present an overview of the Love and Logic way, first let's look at two familiar parenting styles that almost guarantee gray hair—or no hair at all—before teens drive away that last time.

Helicopter Parents

Helicopters are exciting because they make a lot of wind, noise, and vibration, and they don't go very fast (except for jet-powered attack helicopters; which we will discuss later). Their place in the world is to hover, rescue, and protect. Emergency response teams couldn't function without them.

But what if the helicopter hovers overhead when there's no emergency? Then it's a problem.

When parents insist on hovering overhead to provide constant protection, it's a nuisance. It can even hinder normal life. We call those who use this approach "helicopter parents." They stay close by in order to rescue their children whenever a problem arises.

To get a good look at helicopter parents, just visit your local middle or high school. You'll see them hovering in and out the front door, carrying field-trip permission slips, homework assignments, band or orchestra instruments, and coats. Helicopter parents watch for their beloved offspring to send up a signal flare, and then they swoop in to shield their children from teachers, playmates, and other apparently hostile elements. Unfortunately, they also shield their children from any of the significant learning opportunities offered; helicopter parents accept the worry for consequences their children should be shouldering themselves. You'll hear the principal muttering under his breath, "Wow! How long did it take the kid to train his parents to do stuff like that?"

Other moms and dads sometimes regard helicopter parents as model citizens. After all, look at how involved they are. They're on every committee and seem to be at school more than some of the teachers. They seem so caring. They're always "there" for their kids. Besides, the dangers are real, so kids need rescuing, right?

But if you look just under the surface, you'll discover that helicopter parents often do things for their kids because of the way they—the parents—feel. Out of "love" or guilt, they will refrain from imposing or allowing consequences, because they feel uncomfortable with consequences. When their children hurt, they bail them out—because *they* hurt too.

Helicopter parents behave the way they do because they confuse love, protection, and caring. Each of these concepts is good, but they aren't synonymous with each other.

Helicopter parents won't allow their children to fail. If their kids fail, they mistakenly reason, it means they are uncaring and unloving parents. Rescuing parents often rescue out of their own needs. They unconsciously enjoy healing another's hurts. They are parents who need to be needed, not parents who want to be wanted.

Children who are raised with the "love" of helicopter parents will turn into helicopters themselves. But some day they will run out of fuel and crash in their personal lives. Why? Because their learning opportunities were stolen from them in the name of love.

These kids keep breaking the speed limit because they know Dad will pay the fine, or they engage in promiscuous sex because Mom paid for the birth control pills. A few years later, they flunk out of college, mishandle what little money they have, or meander about "getting their heads together." The real world, these young adults discover, doesn't offer a grand helicopter parent in the sky to heal their diseases, pay for their bounced checks, save them from irresponsible people, or literally bail them out of jail.

The Evolution of the Helicopter Parent: The Jet-Powered Attack Model

When we first wrote this book, helicopter parents seemed to be worried only about rescuing their kids from crisis situations. In the midst of the prosperity of the 1990s a new type emerged that no longer just rescued and defended, but also flew in with guns blazing and missiles locked in to attack anyone who held their child accountable for his or her actions.

We have come to call them the "jet-powered attack model" of the helicopter parent. These parents are obsessed with the desire to create a perfect life for their kids. This life is one in which the children never have to face struggles, inconveniences, discomforts, or disappointments. It is a life in which the children can be launched into adulthood with the best of credentials possible because they have never faced defeat, even if it meant someone else doing most of the work or making sure the rules were bent just the right way so they could win.

The adolescent children of jet-powered attack helicopter parents look great on paper. Their middle and high school transcripts show high grades, extracurricular activities and awards, and special honors — most of which were never really earned. These teens' mistakes are swept under the carpet, and awards are earned with little or no effort on their part. We have often heard their parents say, "It's a competitive world out there, and I want my kids to have every advantage. What they do when they are young should not hold them back later."

In their zeal to protect their young, these parents swoop down on any person, school, or agency that they see as a threat to their children's impeccable credentials. Armed with verbal smart bombs, they are quick to blast away at anyone who sets high standards for behavior, morality, or achievement that may cause their children to take responsibility for themselves.

Declaring their child a victim is a favorite tactical maneuver designed to send school personnel or social workers diving into the trenches for protection. The constant barrage of attack helicopter parents wears down teachers and school administrators.

It is horribly disappointing to watch children learn to blame others for their lack of success instead of becoming people who reach goals through determination and hard work. We daily hear about the jet-powered attack helicopter parents who are not satisfied with just protecting their children, but even prefer to destroy the infrastructure of the very agencies that are dedicated to nurturing their children into educated, responsible, moral human beings.

The company that hires a child of such parents won't be easily intimidated by parental pressure in the face of substandard performance. A perfect image and spotless school transcript are poor substitutes for character and the attitude that achievement comes through struggle and perseverance. The workforce of tomorrow—and to a great extent, many of those starting work today—are in for a rude awakening when they realize that "going to work" means just that, and that they won't be able to call their parents in to chew their bosses out because their promotion went to someone more willing to put in the elbow grease and apply themselves to learning the skills needed to get the job done.

Drill Sergeant Parents

Drill sergeants are impressive because, like helicopters, they make a lot of noise, stir things up, and create incredible and immediate motivation in their listeners. They're forthright and definite: "Do it or you're grounded!" they bark.

If we were drill sergeants and had to take you to war with us, there might be a time when we'd have to say, "We're going up the hill after that machine-gun nest!" The last thing we'd need to hear from you is, "But wait a minute, sarge! People have been hurt in situations like this. We all want to take a vote." In such times of crisis, democracy can be deadly slow. What is needed is action, and action *right now.*

Drill sergeants have a place in our world. But their style is no way to run a country—or a household.

If you're not at war, raising teens by barking orders at them isn't effective. In fact, it can *cause* war. We know this because many of us grew up with drill sergeant parents. And, by the way, that probably was the best way for a parent to handle things back then, because the whole culture believed that children must submit without protest to their parents. In those days children were expected to grow up obediently, grow up through discipline, become company people, and follow orders in adulthood. They were expected to fit in more than think for themselves.

That was okay for back then. Such "blind obedience" was admirable in an age when a person could expect to have one job for life. The world was less complex, and roles were well defined.

Jim remembers never criticizing his dad for saying to him, "I don't care how you feel about it—you get it done *now!*" When Jim grew up, however, he vowed never to be like that. But he became more like his father in his early parenting days than he ever could have imagined.

It's a hard habit to break. Drill sergeant parents feel that the more they bark control, the better their children will be in the long run. These parents are on a power trip. They assume, "These kids will be disciplined. They'll know how to act right."

Although the drill sergeant style seems so much different from the helicopter style, the results are the same. Children of drill sergeant parents don't know how to make decisions. They've been ordered around all their lives, listening to voices coming from outside their heads. When they move into adolescence and try to shout out their parents' voices, they have no internal voice of their own. So they begin to listen to other voices outside their heads—and those voices come from their peers.

Drill sergeants frequently use punishment as a consequence of their children's mistakes. However, the real world largely doesn't operate by punishment. Unless they break the law and get convicted, adults don't get grounded when they mess up in life. If they do experience some kind of punishment for their actions, they seldom pause for self-examination. Resentment is the more common reaction.

Drill sergeant parents eventually discover that when they punish their teens they provide them with a great escape valve: an escape from the consequences of their actions. Their teens never have to think when they're punished. All they do is seethe with resentment because parents are doing their thinking for them.

The real world doesn't operate on punishment. It operates on consequences. If we do a consistently lousy job at work, our boss doesn't take away our DVD player. He fires us—and boy, do we think of solutions then! In other words, we start saying, "I have to think for myself."

Sometimes these two parenting styles, helicopters and drill sergeants, provide a cover for emotional distance from children. The family may live in the same house, eat at the same table, and ride in the same car, but they might as well be on different planets. Family members are often blind to the problem because they're not even aware it exists. If they did have some vague sense of something being wrong, most likely they wouldn't be able to articulate it anyway.

When these families do interact on rare occasions, the parents fall into either the helicopter or the drill sergeant style of relating to their children. It's either "Oh, hon, you know we love you and will do anything for you," or "Don't get emotional around me, buster! You do as you're told."

The Laissez-Faire Parent

Another kind of parenting worth mentioning here in passing is what we call the "laissez-faire parent." These are parents who let their children raise themselves, all by themselves.

Some have bought into the theory that children are born with the ability to govern themselves—if given the time and opportunity—and will eventually grow into successful, creative people if the parent would just stay out of the way and not interfere.

Others believe that they should be their children's best friend, never holding them accountable for anything and making sure they are always happy and have what they want (for example, the "fun mom" in the movie *Mean Girls*). They believe that preserving this type of relationship is more important than teaching their children about self-discipline or character.

Others feel guilty for working out of the home and spending so little time with their kids. Rather than holding their children accountable for their actions, they simply let them run free, believing that responsibility will rub off on their children during "quality time."

Still others have trouble holding their adolescents responsible for acting the same way they did when they hit their teen years. The common argument is, "Well, I drove fast, tried marijuana, drank a little too much, and I turned out okay. They will too." They believe this despite the fact that many of their peers did not and that those same behaviors are much more risky today.

Still others just don't know what to do anymore, so they have given up trying.

We would like to emphasize that this is not truly a parenting type, but an abdication of parenting responsibilities. As we like to say, "If children were meant to run the home, they would have been born larger."

The Consultant Parent

Helicopters can't hover forever. Eventually, drill sergeants go hoarse. And laissez-faire parents do nothing. Allow us to introduce a better alternative, which works well throughout life but is especially effective with teenagers: the consultant parenting style.

In adolescence, an important change takes place in thinking ability. Children move from being concrete thinkers to having what noted child psychologist Jean Piaget called "formal operations," or abstract thinking. As this important change in cognition happens, parents must adjust the way they parent to meet the needs of the new thought processes happening in their children. Recent studies shows that teenage brain development is ongoing and very active. This research seems to indicate that patterns developed in the years between ages twelve and twenty-five are more likely to affect brain wiring—and thus future behavior patterns—than at any other time. (We will discuss this development at greater length in chapter 6.)

Younger children think concretely and need thoughtful guidance and sometimes firm limits. However, teens often resent guidelines and rebel at firm limits because they've grown to think differently. While their brains are drawn to pure emotion and extreme thrills, they also have the ability to reason abstractly and, given the chance, escape the basic animal-like reactions of the amygdala—or "emotional brain," if you will—and work more on developing the reasoning skills of the higher and more advanced parts of their brains.

Teens read the rescue message from helicopter parents as "You're fragile and can't make it without me." And they pick up on the do-as-I-tell-you message from drill sergeant parents who covertly communicate, "You can't think for yourself, so I'll do it for you." They see the "whatever will be, will be" approach of laissez-faire parents as not caring about them or not being of any help in setting boundaries in which they can feel safely.

For many parents, setting limits turns into issuing commands. They back up those limits and rules with more commands—heavily spiced with sternness and anger—and when those fail they resort to punishment. Typically, teens respond to these commands and punishments with irresponsibility, resistance, and rebellion.

Parents trained in Love and Logic avoid the helicopter, drill sergeant, and laissez-faire mentalities by instead using a consultant style. They ask questions and offer choices. Instead of telling their children what to do, they put the burden of decision-making on their kids' shoulders. They establish options within safe limits.

Parents can prepare their children for the real world by shaping family life to reflect the realities their children will soon be facing on their own. Therefore, we can look to how consultants operate in other fields in order to enrich our understanding of a consultant parenting style.

Business Consultants

Businesses often hire specialized consultants to provide an outside perspective on a particular problem the company is facing. The company hires consultants for their expertise, not to tell the firm how to operate. In fact, the management of most businesses would fire a consultant who tried to order them around.

Consultants don't dictate, they advise. They say things like "I'm wondering if it would be more effective for you to . . ." This posture actually has great advantages, because consultants aren't responsible for whether their clients take their advice. If the client doesn't like the consultant's advice, the client doesn't have to listen to it anymore.

And consultants are not responsible for what happens if their clients do or do not take their advice. If a company loses money after following a consultant's recommendation, the loss isn't taken out of the consultant's pocket. Worst case, the consultant gets fired and loses referrals.

Therefore, as consultants give up authority, they happily give up the responsibility that accompanies it. That's an advantage!

Therapists and Guidance Counselors

A consulting example from another field is the therapist or the school guidance counselor. Here again, the consultant is sought out by the client.

Although young children do not decide on their own to consult a counselor (it's a rare eight-year-old who says, "Mommy, I need a therapist"), most teens are able to recognize their own needs. Many of them will voluntarily and eagerly seek help from a guidance counselor or therapist.

Like business consultants, guidance counselors and therapists don't give orders. They don't ground anybody. They rarely get mad and shout at their clients. They seldom perform rescue missions, and they don't allow themselves to be manipulated or abused. But they do offer lots of empathy and understanding.

On the other hand, clients expect their counselors to be chock full of good ideas. Therapists and counselors are responsible for offering their own points of view while exploring those of their clients. They use paraphrasing and thoughtful silences. They may often look quizzical in response to what they're hearing. They may wonder aloud about possible alternatives.

But paramount to what therapists and counselors do for their clients is their attitude. Most therapists feel that their clients are captains of their own ships of fate. They understand that their clients have made mistakes in the past and will most likely make mistakes in the future.

Most therapists hope that their clients will listen to them but do not require it. They show great concern but are fairly slow to rescue. In fact, by law, therapists are allowed to provide rescue by breaking confidentiality only when persons are physically endangering themselves or others. That's a pretty narrow restriction!

Parents as Consultants

As children grow into adolescence, it is understandably difficult for many parents to make the shift from being a guide, or even a benevolent dictator, into becoming a consultant.

One of the biggest transitions is from "you" language to "I" language. Parents who have become consultants recognize that it's no longer helpful to send "you" messages such as, "You'd better get your homework done now." Instead, effective consultant parents use "I" messages that speak to their own wonderings, musings, and possible predictions:

- "I'm wondering if graduating from high school isn't important to you."
- "I'm wondering if you feel upset with the choices you are making."
- "I'm curious about the feelings you're having that are leading you to the choices you're making."

These types of comments are far different from "You'd better get that done this week if you want a grade for that paper."

Sadly, however, some parents of teens are still in the guide mode rather than the consultant mode. When confronted with their child's mistakes, they send the message, "What am *I* going to do now about *your* problem?" Regrettably, the guide parent takes on the teen's responsibility, which usurps the teen's ownership of his or her own problem.

Consultants also ask a lot of questions. Questions showing curiosity and interest are powerful tools to use with adolescents. Orders and demands often don't work at all. Thoughtful, curious questions force thinking and often lead teens to find new and exciting answers that would never have occurred without the question.

Most therapists rely primarily on questions. It has been said that counselors have good answers and therapists have good questions. And which do you think most people appreciate? Probably the questions. They certainly pay more for a good therapist than a good counselor.

Questions encourage your teen's thoughts and exploration. Demands, lectures, ultimatums, and shared concerns may not. It's all too easy for a teen to respond to a worried mom by simply saying, "Don't worry, Mom," while not thinking at all about the dangers of the situation. But when a mom wonders aloud, "How will you handle it if the cops arrive at Jeanette's home and the parents aren't there and there has been underage drinking?" suddenly your teen has to come up with an answer.

Questions asked with bitterness and accusation are ineffective. When teens feel they are on the witness stand, they plead the Fifth — so to speak — and shut up. But when questions are asked with curiosity and honest interest, most teens will open up.

Almost any statement can be turned into a question. Here are some tips on how to use questions successfully as a consultant parent:

- Don't tell your child what you expect. Ask, "What do I expect from you?" Discuss it. Not "I expect you to behave like . . ." but "Honey, how do I expect you to handle it?"

- Not "I don't want you to have friends over when I'm not here," but "If you had friends over when I'm not here, and something turned up missing, who'd be blamed? How would you pay for that?"

- Don't expect answers to questions when your teen is in the heat of his or her anger or pain. At that point, it's best to allow breathing room, to express love and high expectations, and to come back to the issue later.

- When a teen doesn't answer and the adult asks more questions, it puts the child in control of the situation. When your child refuses to reply, don't make the mistake of demanding an answer. Instead of asking another question, simply say, "I can see why that's so difficult to answer. You might want to think about it for later."

There's a world of difference between a controlling, demanding parent and an empathetic, consultant parent. Teens need parents who consult while giving empathy and allowing consequences. Typically, teens respond to commands and punishments with irresponsibility, resistance, and rebellion. However, we can expect even rebellious teens to live up to certain expectations within our home. For instance, parents can expect their teens

- to be respectful to everyone in the home, including guests
- not to bring drugs into the home or anywhere on the property
- to contribute to the household upkeep by doing chores
- to ask permission to wear another family member's clothes or to use the family vehicle

Some parenting authorities call these "limits." For clarity, we label them "expectations." If necessary, parents can physically limit younger children, but it's more difficult to limit an adolescent or another adult in the traditional way "limit" is used: as a mandate that must be followed. However, we can give *expectations*, and when the expectations are not met, we can show or feel disappointment and then respond in a way that takes good care of our own needs.

Expectations are most effective not when made as statements, but when explored, with questions: "What do you think would be our response if we found drugs in the home?" or "How do you think the police would respond if we reported drugs in our home?"

The Love and Logic Way

We believe that one of the supreme goals of parenting is to raise responsible children—children who have been equipped with tools that will enable them to make wise choices throughout life.

The Love and Logic parenting style is based on a handful of core principles. Each principle is packed with underlying concepts and attitudes. They all work toward a simple method of raising children and helping teens become responsible and independent. We will explain the first four in greater detail in chapter 3, and the rest in chapter 4.

The following overview briefly summarizes the ideas that u͏ ͏͏͏ this unique win-win approach for parents and their children.

Responsible Teens Feel Good About Themselves

Self-esteem doesn't just "happen" by making teens feel good or happy. It begins when children assert their independence and try to show their families and the world that they are their own persons. When they accomplish things through their own sweat and smarts, they grow in self-confidence, but superficial trappings — looks, clothes, and a positive attitude — don't ensure that a teen will have a healthy self-concept. Teens develop this healthy self-concept through handling responsibility. In turn, they learn best when they feel good about themselves.

Responsibility Is Caught, Not Taught

Responsibility isn't something that a parent passes on to a teen by lectures, threats, or intimidation. Instead responsibility and the self-esteem that goes along with it are passed on through covert messages that allow teens to build their character on their strengths. We must give teens opportunities to make decisions, as well as mistakes.

Teens Should Own Their Problems and Their Solutions

Here is an alternative to helicopter parents who constantly rescue their children from misfortunes and mistakes, and to drill sergeant parents who dress down their teens for goofing up: Guide your teen to finding a solution to his or her own problem. Love and Logic consultant parents help their teens through life by offering choices, suggesting possible solutions to problems, and choosing to share control in the process.

Neutralizing Teen Arguing Keeps the Focus on Them

Perhaps one the most important principles of Love and Logic is, "Neutralize all arguing." Arguments give your children the opportunity to throw reason out the window and to see how many of your hot buttons they can push. When you both operate in the heat of emotion, the result will inevitably be lose-lose.

Gaining Control Through Choices

It's only natural for parents to want to control their teens, but they must resist that natural urge to keep all of the control for themselves if they want their teens to mature—and if they want to keep their sanity. Instead of viewing adolescence as a protracted conflict over control, why not loosen up a bit? The most effective parents are those who thoughtfully surrender control they don't have anyway by offering choices to their teens.

Setting Limits Through Thinking Words

Love and Logic parents offer choices by using thinking words, not fighting words. They state what they will offer or allow; they don't dictate to their teen what to do. However, thinking word choices must also be enforceable, so never issue choices you can't follow through on (for example, statements like "Calm down right now or you can walk the rest of the fifty miles home" are as ineffective as they are conscientiously unenforceable). Thinking words make teens do the work to figure out the problem, while parents stand aside to see how their children perform.

Empathy Plus Consequences Equals Success

When teens falter, Love and Logic parents face the greatest obstacle and the greatest opportunity in watching their teen grow up. Instead of giving in to the temptation to rescue or get angry at the teen, Love and Logic parents empathize with their teen and allow the logical consequences of the mistake to sink in. Locking in such empathy and then allowing the consequences drives home the lesson that the parent loves the teen, but the teen needs to learn how the real world operates.

Consequences Don't Have to Be Immediate

Too often parents feel pressured to come up with a consequence for a teen's action on the spot and at the peak of their anger. In the process we lose the ability both to develop responsibility in the teen and to help our son or daughter find the best solutions. It's okay to say, "You don't have to tell me how you are going to solve this situation right now. Let's both do some thinking about it and we will talk again later." Then call your spouse, friends, teachers, counselors, and ministers and try to come up with the best way to handle the situation. Don't worry; the last thing your teen is liable to do is forget.

Building a Lifelong Relationship

These parenting techniques aren't just to help you work out the rough spots of raising teenagers. The goal is to guide your teen to live a responsible, productive, and happy life. By allowing your teen to achieve independence, you watch an adult blossom. And that adult, who happens to be your child, can then become your friend. And how much stronger will that relationship be if you take the anger, repeated lectures, threats, and ultimatums out of your interactions and instead act as a loving, empathetic consultant to them as they solve their own problems?

These principles form the basis for parenting teenagers with Love and Logic. We will explain them in greater detail in the next two chapters, before we explore the special issues unique to teenagers.

3

Back to the Basics, Part One: Training Teens to Act Responsibly

Stephanie was angrily trying to convince the registrar that she should be allowed to enroll in a class that had been closed. When her efforts appeared futile, she pulled out her cell phone and dialed her mother at home. Handing the phone to the registrar, she demanded, "Here! Talk to my mother. She will straighten this out."

As bizarre as this sounds, it is not an unusual occurrence on today's campuses. Many young adults who are now away from home are incapable of making decisions or solving problems themselves.

In a recent newspaper article, a former vice president of student affairs, was quoted as saying, "The cell phone is the world's longest umbilical cord." Some colleges report that new-student orientation is starting to resemble that of kindergarten, where more parents than students are in attendance.

This scenario speaks to a major change we have seen over the past generation. Many young adults are leaving home with little practice in figuring things out for themselves and then acting responsibly.

We worry that young people like Stephanie, who don't believe they can solve everyday problems, will have little ability to take care of themselves. It is not difficult to predict how she might handle decisions about sex, binge drinking, and spending.

How could Stephanie have found herself suddenly launched into the adult world with such limited skills? Obviously, she believed that her mother cared for her and wanted her to be successful. Her mother was the one who chose the university Stephanie would attend, successfully picked the perfect roommate, chose her classes, and bought her books. Were those not the actions of a loving parent who wanted the best for her offspring?

Let's look at how children have been emotionally crippled and led to believe they are dependent on the judgments of others.

Many of today's parents want the best for their children. They don't want them to be disappointed, frustrated, or uncomfortable. They don't want their children to have to struggle like they once did. They want to feel like good parents. But they don't realize that they are robbing their children of the very skills they will need to succeed when they finally fly away from the nest. What will Stephanie's next stunt be? Will she dial her mom, hand the phone to her boss, and then expect Mom to explain to him why she should get a raise rather than be fired?

Love and Logic parenting is built on a group of principles that can be applied to children of any age for training them to act responsibly and to be able to handle their own problems. In this and the following chapter we present these building blocks with special applications to teenagers, so by the time they are sixteen or seventeen, they are able to make their own decisions, find their way in the world, and become the kind of adults you would want as your friends.

Basic Self-Concept — Who Am I?

John's best buddy came up to him at lunch and said, "Hey, John, I've got this really great stuff. Let's go smoke some of it behind the school."

"Sure, why not?" John replied. No "Just Say No" campaign had ever bothered him.

But John's dad — who wasn't even there — bothered John. *Boy*, he said to himself, *if I do that, my dad will really get mad*. And what's the next thing John said to himself? *Oh, he'll never find out*.

Teens are full of bravado, swagger, threats, intimidation, and voices — loud voices coming from outside their heads. But even in the best of situations, teens naturally suffer many problems with self-concept and doubt.

For all his supposed independence, John had a crummy way of making a decision. When sensible teens are asked to do drugs, they say to themselves, *Hey, I wonder how this is going to affect me?*

Teens struggle with many things in their lives that they don't understand. It's natural for them to go through some pretty shaky times, but those pass. What's important is that they gain a strong self-concept that will not only get them through tomorrow, but also give them stability for the future as well.

Travis, for instance, doesn't have the stability that his parents do, with their marriage, house, and cars. He doesn't know who he is yet, but he's working like crazy to find out. So he spends a lot of time away from home at Brandon's, comparing ratty jeans and earrings and proving to himself that he's not just an extension of his home. He spends increasing time listening to Brandon to show that he's not always listening to the folks. It doesn't occur to Travis that he's still listening to somebody *outside* his head; it's just that now the voice is more often Brandon's than his parents'.

Adolescent identity crises occur when teens are trying to make the right choices but they can't figure out whether it's because they want to or because it makes their parents happy. This is the classic adolescent identity crisis that James Dean immortalized in *Rebel Without a Cause.*

Self-Concept Struggles in Adolescence

Self-concept is often at its lowest ebb during the teenage years because so many things are happening that are very difficult to understand.

Every time teens look at their bodies, for example, they end up disappointed. There's something wrong with their hair. Their friends dress better than they do. Their body shape is too big or too small. They keep asking themselves, *What does a normal teenager look like? How does a normal teenager act?*

These questions drive teens crazy, continually throwing their self-concept into doubt. And wise parents know that teens' fears about themselves are often at their height just when they're acting the most sure of themselves.

What happens with friendships during those times? "Gee, my friend liked me yesterday but now he hates me." "The girls used to include me until I started hanging out with so-and-so." The cliques change constantly.

More important than appearances or friendships, however, are the life-and-death issues confronting teens on a daily basis. Abuse at home, drugs, and thoughts of suicide push and pull on them. If their self-concept isn't secure, they could stumble—with fatal results.

Tracking the Causes of Damaged Self-Concept

Problems with self-concept often start in the first year or two of life. Most parents don't intentionally damage their child's self-concept, but it can happen in many ways:

- excessive criticism
- overprotection and/or overindulgence
- neglect
- perfectionism
- genetics and/or prenatal factors
- excessive or inadequate control
- pushing children into formal learning before they're ready
- comparing children to others who are better achievers
- failure to allow children to own their own rewards and disappointments
- conditional love
- allowing children to be disrespectful
- failure of parents to provide an adequate model of taking good care of oneself
- learning disabilities
- emotional problems
- lack of early bonding

When you read this list of what can damage self-concept, you may wonder how good a parent you've been. No one bats a thousand—we've all made some mistakes. But you do have a choice about what you will do with the future. You can decide which attitudes will make you happiest and which will make your child—now a teenager—happiest.

Minute-to-Minute Self-Concept Building
Teens look to us for positive or negative affirmations, and they store them in their memory banks. The perceptions gained from these parental messages actually become their reality. Here are some tips on raising the odds for success as we exercise our responsibility to build the self-concept of our teens:

- Provide both stated and unstated messages that show you have unconditional love.
- Model your own healthy self-concept to your teens by taking care of yourself as much as you take care of them.
- Provide both stated and unstated messages that say, "I value you."
- Provide both stated and unstated messages that say, "You can think."
- Provide both stated and unstated messages that say, "You have control."
- Provide opportunities for teens to struggle through and own their decisions and responsibilities.

Three ways to show love are eye contact, touch, and smiles. In combination with each other, they're dynamite. The way we listen to teens also greatly affects how loved they feel and how much they love us.

We'd like to be able to help our kids, but ironically, this strong desire to help and care for other people can become our worst enemy in caring for our teens. If this desire leads to overprotection, it will thwart opportunities for them to learn responsibility.

The Three Voices of Self-Concept
Self-concept is like a three-legged table. If all three aspects of self-concept are not in place, it is wobbly. These three legs are like three voices. Teens with a strong self-concept have all three voices in their ear.

The first voice says, "I'm loved by the magic people in my life" — the significant other people. We're all magic people in the lives of teens.

The second voice says, "I have just as many skills as I need for a person my age. I can compete in the classroom. I can compete at home.

I can compete out on the street. I can compete in sports. I can compete anywhere with people my age. I'm okay."

The third voice says, "I can take control of my life. I can take responsibility and make decisions for myself, and here's the important part: I can live with the consequences of my decisions or actions."

Love and Logic Principle: Responsible Teens Feel Good About Themselves

Although we talk about self-concept, we do not concentrate on terms like *self-esteem* and *self-image*. You won't find any Love and Logic program designed to raise self-esteem in your child.

Don't get us wrong. We want your children to have high self-esteem. But they don't get high self-esteem or a good self-image by concentrating on developing it. In fact, if you ask the parents of a teenager with a great self-image how much they concentrate on it and talk about it, they will probably look a little confused and say something like "Well, gee. We don't ever talk about it, now that you mention it."

Self-esteem and self-image are outgrowths of the way a home operates. When a child is encouraged through consequences to make wise choices and productive decisions, a positive self-image will follow. Love and Logic parents don't concentrate on "talking nice" but on being straightforward, encouraging, empathetic, and thoughtful.

Take, for instance, sixteen-year-old Jeff who sleeps late, accomplishes little, and is disrespectful to his parents. Some books might encourage the parents to talk nicely to him about the way he feels about himself. And that may be important. Counseling also may be an option to explore. However, parents can use Love and Logic techniques to involve Jeff in coming up with responsible choices and consequences that they themselves are willing to live with.

Responsibility isn't something that a parent passes on to a teen by lectures, threats, or intimidation. Responsibility and its companion, self-concept, are passed on through covert messages that allow teens to build their character on their strengths. As we give teens opportunities to make decisions, we must also allow them to make mistakes. However, this philosophy does not define giving children responsibility as letting them get away with unacceptable behavior. Parents have a right to expect responsible behavior from their children.

This philosophy also says that adults and teens grow by building on their strengths. But that isn't the way many of us grew up. When Jim went to school, if a teacher had asked him, "Hey, Jimmy, what are you good at?" he would have said, "I don't know." And if the teacher pressed him, "Well, who does know?" then he would have answered, "Well, my teacher, my mother. They're supposed to know things like that."

But what if they came in and said, "Hey, Jimmy, what are your weaknesses?" Boy, there was no one else who was such an expert on that. He could rattle those things off because his teachers and parents felt that before he could learn anything, he had to realize how weak he was. For example, every time he turned around, his mother was saying, "Jim, your speech is sloppy. Watch your Ms, Ps, and Bs." But this ongoing critique didn't really help him—and I'm pretty sure it was no different from anybody else growing up around that time.

Let's help teens become aware of their strengths and build from there. This doesn't mean that we should ignore their weaknesses, but just that we are not majoring in them at the expense of their strengths. They can and should be working on them as well. The rule of thumb here is, I will never require myself or one of my children to work on more than one weakness at a time.

Covert Messages

The strongest messages we pick up from people are the implied ones, not the actual words that are said. When we imply to teens that they can handle a situation, they handle it. When we imply to them that they can't handle it, they don't. When we send teens a subconscious message that they can think, their self-concept improves. If teens receive enough of those good messages, they learn to like themselves.

The connection can be put in terms of a self-fulfilling prophecy: "I don't become what *you* think I can, and I don't become what *I* think I can. I become what *I think you think* I can."

Have you ever had a boss, a friend, or a teacher who thought you were the greatest thing going? How did you perform around that person? Did you make weekly appointments to go in and say, "Now, wait a minute. I'm not as good as you think I am"? Or did you find yourself living up to those expectations? Have you ever been around a person who thought you were the scum of the earth? How did that affect your responses?

A lot of our parenting work centers on how we can imply to teens—that is, without directly saying it—that we know they're going to handle whatever life hands them. Then we must trust them to do it and allow that self-fulfilling prophecy to do its work.

Just as there are parents who imply that a teen is either great or scum, there are two kinds of teens too.

Sonya wakes up in the morning, marches into the bathroom, and says to the mirror, "Hey, look at that babe. She's all right. I like that woman, and I bet other people are going to like her too."

Now switch to Hannah. She wakes up in the morning, drags herself over to the mirror, and mumbles to herself, "Oh, no, look at that. I don't like what I see. And I'll bet other people don't like her either."

Which of those teens causes problems at home or in school? Hannah, of course. She looks at herself and pronounces, "I'm bad." What comes next? "Bad teens should be punished. So how come nobody punishes me?" Then she hooks somebody into it: "I'll do something bad, and if they don't punish me, I'll do something worse." When she finally gets punished she can say, "See? I'm bad, and I should be punished."

Which covert messages do you want to send? The ones that prompt your teen to respond, "Oh, yeah? Make me do it," or the ones that invite your teen to comply, and feel good about it?

Love and Logic Principle:
Responsibility Is Caught, Not Taught

Parents have this much in common with God: We can give our children considerable freedom, just as God gave it to all humans—his supreme creation. This means freedom to goof up as well as get it right. Failure and success are two sides of the same coin.

For children to make their own decisions they sometimes have to assert independence by consciously choosing to fail. Paradoxically, parents who try to ensure their children's successes often raise unsuccessful children.

One thing we definitely cannot make teens do is "be responsible." Responsibility cannot be taught; it must be caught. The hardest lessons to learn involve the things we're told we must do. To help our children gain responsibility we must offer them opportunities to be responsible, rather than order them to do what we think is responsible.

"Rules" as such don't do much for building responsibility, because rules and regulations vary from job to job, institution to institution. Sometimes there are no rules at all—or only dumb rules.

In his travels as a speaker, Foster heard about one university that laid down a new rule a few years ago: "No sex in the coed dorms." That's a dumb rule. Most of us feel that sex should not be allowed in any of the dorms.

But let's say Jerry enters Behemoth Western University. He's eighteen years old and always has done what Mom and Dad told him to do. When he hits campus he thinks, *Gosh, I've never seen so many beautiful girls in my life.* He calls his folks after the first week and says, "Hey, Mom and Dad! These girls here are awesome! I'm going out with one to a party tomorrow night."

Now guess what happens. Mom and Dad—speaking long-distance—try to enforce the university's "no-sex-in-the-coed-dorms" rule: "Jerry, just where are you going to be tonight? Will there be any drugs there? When are you going to be back in your room? We want you back at twelve, and we don't mean one minute past twelve."

"Sure Mom, sure Dad," Jerry assures them. "I'll be good, just like you told me to." Maybe he even means it.

Come midnight when the beer is passed around, Jerry has a choice to make. He can listen to the memories of his parents or yield to the encouragement of his buddies and the girl tugging on his arm. But Jerry has never had the choice of listening to himself and making up his own mind.

Honestly now, do "no-sex-in-the-coed-dorm" rules make any sense at all? Of course not.

The only way any meaningful, mature behavior happens is when it springs from within our teen's character—and character is formed through learning to make decisions and learning to live with their consequences. We parents were able to get away with making choices for our children when they were young and didn't necessarily need to feel the sting of the consequences from their bad choices. That may have been easy for us as parents then, but if we keep it up it's not going to be easy for our teens when they confront life-and-death decisions almost unheard of a generation or two ago.

Tragically, for many teens the first real decisions they make are foolish choices about cars, sex, or behavior on the job. If they'd never had the opportunity to make decisions and own the consequences before, it really doesn't matter what they learned in driver's education or health classes because they never learned responsibility.

Responsibility is caught when parents share control with their teens. We can encourage teenagers to think for themselves while we help their self-concept stay intact. When teens think on their own, they make choices and learn to live with the consequences. If those consequences mean that they learn life's lessons the hard way, we can provide an equal amount of empathy or sadness to go along with it. That drives the pain of the consequence home so that they never forget the lesson—and never have to make that mistake again.

Shortly after Jerry went to the campus party, his loving parents were called. Jerry, it seems, had gotten into trouble. Not only was he arrested for public intoxication, it happened as he was escorting the girl—whose name he had quickly forgotten—out of his dorm at three the next morning.

Now it's the parents' turn to make a decision:

They can yell at Jerry, "We told you to be behave yourself, but you didn't listen! We're really mad at you! It'll cost us fifty dollars for your court costs and the fine for being drunk in public."

Or they can realize that Jerry is on his own now and must make his own decisions: "Well, son, we're truly sorry about what happened. We know that you really needed that money to buy some schoolbooks instead of pay that fine, but we're sure you can find a part-time job in the evenings to make it up."

Few teens really want to stay teenagers forever. They want to grow up and assert their independence, even if they show it in superficial ways. They've got the clothes, the swagger, and the answers. So let them act independent, and then let them live with what they've decided. In a few very short years, they won't have you to bail them out when they total the car, argue with their spouse, or squander the rent money for their apartment. Why wait?

Lessons always cost more tomorrow than they do today, so the earlier our adolescents are allowed to face the consequences of their decisions and learn from them, the better.

Some of us wait because of deeply ingrained patterns of parenting from that long-ago era when our sixteen-year-old hell-raiser was just a cute little devilish imp. We wanted to do everything humanly possible for our little one. But what got us into trouble was *how* we showed our "love"—often as protectionism.

Parents who don't know any better tend to fall into the helicopter and drill sergeant parenting styles that we've already seen don't work.

Love and Logic Principle: Let Teens Own Their Problems and Their Solutions

Love and Logic consultant parents help teens through life by offering choices and sharing control in the process, all the while building on their teens' healthy self-concept. They let teens own their problems as well as their solutions.

Building a strong self-concept is the first of three things we can do with teens so when they reach the age of temptation, we've got a chance that they're not going to abuse drugs and alcohol or engage in other risky behaviors.

The second thing we can do is to help teens learn how to make decisions. We do this in part by letting them own the responsibility—including the good feelings as well as the disappointments—of those decisions, planting in their consciousness this idea: "The quality of my life depends on the decisions I make."

Third, we can make it clear who owns the responsibility for a particular problem. If parents don't draw clear lines of demarcation when they're called for, they and their teenagers are in for a lot of grief.

Let the teens own their own problems, their own feelings, their own disappointments, their own rewards. One of the worst things we can do is give teens the message that they shouldn't do something because the logical consequence of their action is to make adults mad. First, that encourages them to shape their actions according to the voices outside their heads. And second, it can reinforce an immature rebellion in some teens who will go out of their way to make adults mad. Either way, they don't own the situation.

For example, let's say your daughter is out driving the family car and she's tempted to show off for her friends. Should she be thinking, "Boy, if I crash this car, my dad's really going to be mad"? Is that how a mature teen would react?

If she's a sensible young woman on her way to healthy independence, that's not what she'll be thinking. Instead she will say to herself, "Gee, if I crash this car, I'm going to splatter us all over the highway. Guess I better be careful."

It's the teen's responsibility to own the problem and find a solution. But that's not always as easy as it sounds, because we're tempted to rush in like a helicopter to protect our son or daughter from the real world. Or we march in like a drill sergeant, bark a few orders, and expect the teenage troops to fall into line unquestioningly. Those temptations must be resisted.

As a person in the helping profession of education, I (Jim) always felt tempted to solve my students' problems. So I had to train myself to do something different by using a key word: *bummer*. Whenever I used that word, it reminded me: "Jim, be careful. Don't solve the problem for him. Don't give him a solution. Don't give him advice, and don't be defensive. Let *him* do the thinking." And when the student hears "bummer," it sounds empathetic. "Gee, too bad. Bummer. I bet that feels lousy."

If we show that we understand how teens feel, we hand their feelings back to them — for *their* control, not ours.

Ownership of problems also flounders when we confuse praise with encouragement. Twenty years ago, public schools began using something called "positive reinforcement." That philosophy says that if we spend a lot of time telling teens how well they're doing, they will do better.

This approach works well with teens who see themselves as a "10" because they don't have to search for proof to back up their self-image. But how many teens in our classrooms or homes really consider themselves 10s?

We can encourage teens best by talking to them as adults. \
not build self-concept by telling them they're good. Teens with a poor self-image will simply discount it, and they'll probably end up worse off than if we'd said nothing.

One day teens are down; the next day they're up. It goes with the territory. We can help by criticizing them as little as possible and by refraining from telling them what they should be discovering for themselves. We want them to think for themselves, so we should be asking them questions instead of ordering them around. When they say they're going to do something stupid, we can respond, "Well, that's an option. You can do that. Have you ever thought of *this, this,* and *this?* We wish you well, and we'll still love you no matter what happens."

By talking to teens as if they were adults, we convey the strong message that we expect them to act like adults and take charge of things in their lives. But we certainly don't do this by lectures or threats.

Love and Logic Principle:
Neutralizing Teen Arguing Keeps the Focus on Them

We cannot state this plainly enough: Allowing or engaging in arguing will short-circuit any attempts to use Love and Logic techniques. Parents who argue or try to reason with their unreasonable teens are fighting a war of attrition. In the end, all they do is exhaust themselves and may eventually give up.

Obviously, when we hold teens responsible for their actions, their first remark is not going to be, "Gee, Mom, great parenting! Thanks so much for holding your ground to teach me this lesson." Instead they are going to be emotional—most likely angry—and they will stay in that state until they have some time to cool off. When angry, we use the most basic part of our brain, the amygdala or "emotional brain," and not the cortex, where analytical thought and reasoning takes place. When we argue with our teen in that state, the last thing he or she is going to do is be reasonable.

The best thing for a parent to do in a heated argument is to use a Love and Logic one-liner such as, "So, what did I say?" or "I love you too much to argue about that." Such a dialogue might go something like this one, in which Amanda is angry about not being able to go to a party:

AMANDA: You never let me do what I want.
MOM: I love you too much to argue about that. Let's talk about it when we've both cooled down.
AMANDA: But Carly always gets to do what she wants.
MOM: I love you too much to argue about that.
AMANDA: Yeah, that's 'cause you like her better.
MOM: So, what did I say?

This can't be condescending or sarcastic, but must always be expressed with empathy. Genuine empathy has an amazing ability to soak up emotions. It is best to use an empathetic statement that comes right from your heart, a statement that feels natural to you. It can even be the same one every time. If you want it to have a cumulative effect, also use the same facial expression and body language. Here are some examples of empathetic statements that work:

- "Oh no. I bet that feels terrible."
- "Wow. What a bummer."
- "I can't imagine how bad that feels."

And here are some examples of statements that frequently don't work as well:

- "I know how you feel."
- "I know just what you mean."
- "I understand."

As the parent, you must also focus on what is controllable by telling your teens what you *are going to do, not what* they *are going to do.* You are not going to argue, but you can't make them stop trying; you are going to talk with them about it later, but you can't make them have a definitive answer for you by then. You are going to control yourself, modeling for your teens the ability to resist useless bickering and compelling them to see that they need to take the consequences of the decisions they make.

In the next chapter, we'll examine how to speak to teens effectively through the following principles:

- gaining control through choices
- setting limits through thinking words
- the recipe for success: empathy with consequence
- building a relationship to last a lifetime

4

Back to the Basics, Part Two: Treating Teenagers as Responsible Adults

Fourteen-year-old Tina was angry and confused. Her mom, she said, treated her like she was either a two-year-old or an adult.

"Mom treats me okay when she's talking to me about my clothes, my friends, or my homework—those things are okay," Tina explained. "But when she's telling me if I can date or who can be my boyfriend, it's like I'm a little girl who doesn't know anything."

Tina's mom wasn't too happy either. "Tina acts like either a young lady or a two-year-old. I can't figure her out! She's so sweet when I ask how school is going, or when she shows off her new dress. But when we talk about those boys with the weird haircuts she likes, who I think are bad influences on her, she practically throws tantrums."

Tina and her mom were locked in a typical parental battle over control. On things the mom felt weren't too consequential, such as clothes, friends, and schoolwork, Tina was a young adult. But when it came to Tina's choice of boyfriends and dating, her mom treated her as if she were two. The more her mom pressed those issues, the more Tina rebelled, which is the same issue parents face with two-year-olds.

Love and Logic Principle: Gaining Control Through Choices

Have you, like Tina's mom, had a strong desire to enforce tighter rules with your teen? When you start to see your teen becoming independent, your natural tendency is to say, "I'd be a better parent if I could only control . . . "

But we have free will, and that means the right to make lots of decisions and live with the consequences. That's what makes human beings exciting. Wouldn't it be terrible if we could control our children's every move? Can you imagine the kind of people we'd have to live with when they grew up? At best, it would be awfully boring.

Would you like your teen to be reasonable, fun to be around, and responsible as well? Then *relax your grip*. Remember that your teen will be out in the adult world a few short years from now, so share control. The more control you relinquish now, the more they gain now. That's the self-control that they will use to make good decisions in establishing themselves as adults. The happiest teens are responsible teens who operate under real-world rules that inspire self-control rather than under parental rules and control that may encourage rebellion.

But *how* do we share control? Have you ever watched the classic scene of a parent trying to get absolute control and in the next split second the teen gets total control? What goes wrong?

In human interaction, there's a very fine line here. On one side of the line, the teens feel that they have some control. But on the other side of the line, they have none. Once we cross over onto the side where teens feel they have no control, that's when they suddenly decide to get it all.

For example, Dad warns his son, "You be home at midnight or else." The teen has no control over the situation. At that point, however, he can take total control by deciding to come home after midnight, and Dad must then react to him.

Achieving the Right Mix of Control

Psychologist Sylvia B. Rimm, PhD, states that people of all ages compare the amount of control they have in a relationship only to the amount of control they used to have, not to the amount they feel they should have. When control is increased over time, people are satisfied; when control is cut back, people are angry. Therefore, when parents relinquish control in increasing amounts, children—especially teenagers—are usually satisfied with the new levels of control they experience.

Rimm's analysis is called the V of love. The sides of the V represent firm limits within which the child may make decisions and live with the consequences. The bottom of the V represents birth, while the top represents the time when the child leaves home for adult life.[7] An example of relinquishing control may be giving toddlers the choice of white or chocolate milk; for teens, it may be the opportunity to decide when they will come home at night.

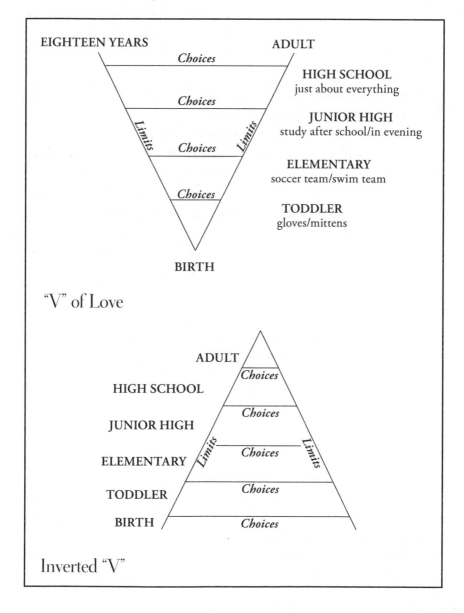

Unfortunately, many parents turn the V upside down. They treat their children like miniature adults right from the start, with all the privileges of adulthood granted immediately at birth. These children soon become tyrants. The parents don't control them; they control the parents, holding them hostage with temper tantrums and pouting. Tragically, many children who begin life with too much power lead unhappy lives as they grow older. Their misbehavior as teens forces the parents to keep clamping down on them, triggering anger and rebellion as rights and privileges are forcibly withdrawn. The unhappy teen then complains, "You're treating me like a five-year-old." And in many ways, that's true.

Rules for Control Battles

The Love and Logic approach to control says, "Don't be greedy. Never take any more control than you absolutely need to have." When the threat of a battle for control looms on the horizon, parents must ask themselves some questions, such as, "How much control do I absolutely need in this situation? More important than that, do I need to fight a control battle at all? Can my teen learn a valuable lesson if I offer advice or options instead?"

Love and Logic parents have learned that the more they relax, the easier it is to deal with control. We recommend three rules for control battles:

1. Avoid control battles at all costs.
2. If you are forced to have a control battle—on those rare occasions when it can't be avoided—then win at all costs.
3. Pick the issue carefully and deliberately without threatening to do so. Just do it.

When parents use these techniques, they don't have a battle. Instead they cause teens to think about their decisions.

When parents do get into control battles, teens are thinking about one thing: Who's going to win? They're especially good at picking battles that adults can't ever win: "What music are you going to forbid me to listen to? Who are you going to allow to be my boyfriend/girlfriend? When am I going to learn? See if you can make me talk. See if you can make me happy." These are common battlegrounds for parents and teens.

Whenever parents give teens an order that they can't enforce, they lose their teens' respect. Control battles over friends are a great example. If one of us says to a daughter, "Don't go out with that friend," or "I don't like those friends; don't hang around them," we're giving her an order that we can't make her follow. We're starting a battle we will inevitably lose. Why? Daughters (and sons) grow more independent as they enter adolescence, and choosing their own friends is one way of expressing that independence. No way will we be able to monitor this behavior twenty-four hours a day. Practically speaking, we couldn't enforce such a control battle even if we tried, so why not save the energy for one we can win?

But your teen might very well find that such a control battle is something she wants you to fight. Little children, not to mention teenagers, discover that they can bring great big adults to their knees with no effort whatsoever. All they need to do is trick the adults into fighting some kind of battle that could never be won in a million years. Then they keep the adults busy fighting that battle—and the adults have neither the time nor the energy left to fight the more important battles they could have won.

Not only that, but watching parents get angry and frustrated is great entertainment. Look at sitcoms: Almost all of the humor is based on watching frustrated authority figures try to control situations they can't.

There are, however, a few issues over which you must have control battles because they center around your self-respect as a parent. Choose these battles carefully, with every intention to win them. They include:

1. Parents must insist on respect from their children, even as their children deserve respect from their parents. When children are disrespectful of their parents, it lowers *their* self-image. Poor self-image in children begins with disrespect of parents.

2. Parents must exert control over basic conduct in family life. For example, if a teen is disturbing parents by smoking in the house, parents must model their self-respect and tell him or her to step outside. It's generally a mistake to get into a physical tussle with the teen, but parents can say in a firm we-mean-business voice, "We think you're making an unwise decision." They might not be able to remove the teen at that moment, but they must be able to establish that limit.

3. Parents must have control of the home environment. After all, the parents own the home. Sometimes teens bring whomever they wish into the home and act as if they own it. That's backward. Who owns the environment is an important concept. When the children grow up and have their own home, then they will have the right to make decisions in that environment.

Justin and his father used to get into continual battles around the stereo system. Justin would slip in a disc, turn it up loud, and his music would literally pound through the home. Then Justin's father would inevitably yell, over the din, "Turn that blankety-blank stereo down!" Passive-aggressively, Justin would take his time about complying and then sit and pout in a rebellious manner.

After attending a parenting seminar, Justin's father handled it differently. He waited for the microsecond when he and Justin were both in a great mood. Then he sat down with his son, put his arm around his shoulders (this action was so rare that it shocked Justin into focused awareness), and said, "You know, Justin, I understand how you love your music. And I admit I have a hard time enjoying it. So, I would really like you to keep the volume low when you play music on the stereo when Mom and I are home."

"Well, it seems unfair. You get to play your music up loud. This is my home too!" Justin answered.

"Justin," his father said lovingly, "you need to check the mortgage, find out whose home this is. This is my home, son. However, you get to live here. Someday, when you make the mortgage payments on your own home, I won't expect to bring over my disc and say, 'Hey, stuff this sucker into the machine and turn it up loud.' You know what I mean?"

Justin replied—a little resistant, but with dawning aware-ness—"Yeah, I guess that makes sense."

The father ended the conversation by saying, "I'll do my best not to feel too resentful of your music, and I would really appreciate your doing your best to keep down the decibels. Thanks a lot, Justin."

He gave his son a little squeeze around the shoulders and left. By his father's loving limits Justin was shocked into an awareness that the kids really *don't* own the home.

Try These Control Battles on for Size

Teens pick some interesting battles to wage, including, "See if you can make me talk." Good luck! I (Jim) remember a time when my second daughter was a teenager and the hours of energy I and she put into "Now I can see there's something wrong. Why don't you talk about it? What's the matter? You know you can talk to your mom or me. You know it's safe to talk to us." And the more I said "talk," the less she said because her silence put her in control.

Another battle teenagers love to engage us in concerns values: "See if you can make me have the same values you have." Again, lots of luck. The truth is that healthy teenagers, as a normal part of growing up, are constantly trying out some new value: "Would this be okay? Would that be okay?" They're experimenting with becoming adults.

This is why teens often make blunt statements such as, "School's not important." Then they stand back to watch their parents go crazy. It's not uncommon now for teens to come home and say, "I think anybody ought to be able to have sex with anybody they want—anytime, any-place. And it's nobody's business, especially their parents'."

Parents inevitably respond to statements like these by immediately trying to correct them: "Oh no, don't believe that, believe this. *This* will help, and *that* will help, and you can't do *any of these.*" The teen subconsciously revels in the parents' fumbling attempts to respond to his or her new values. Somewhere inside, the teen is saying, "Good luck! That will keep you busy for a while—so busy you won't have time to win some battles you could have won."

What's sad about this situation? These parents have just caused their teen to hold on for dear life to that particular value, because now that position is a way for the teen to establish who he or she is as an individual apart from them as the parents.

A better response is to allow teens to try on that new value. You can be sure they will come up with something else next week or next month.

But some parents can't let go of the anxiety: "What if my kid comes home and says something I don't agree with like, 'Socialism is a really great way to distribute wealth and create just societies'? How do I handle that?" Simple. Look at your teen, smile, and say, "Thanks for sharing that. I've always wondered how teenagers see that."

Let's play this out a little further and see what happens.

"But don't you see, Mom?" he continues. "Wouldn't it be wonderful if all the rich people could share their stuff with poor people?"

"Well, son," Mom responds, "that sounds interesting, but what if rich people don't want to go along with that?"

"Well, maybe people in power would have to force them to give up what they have."

"Oh, like you have your stereo. Dad and I don't have a stereo," Mom observes. "So we'd make you give us your stereo, right?"

Then Mom does a little of what we call referential speaking, in which parents refer to their values without forcing them on teens. She concludes, "That sure wouldn't work for us in our country, but I can understand how a teen might see it that way." This response forces teens to think, *Wait a minute! Mom's not playing the game right. She should be fighting over that.*

Parents often don't know this, but patience is one of the best qualities for enduring a values battle. Long before your teens turn thirty, they will wake up and discover that they hold many of the same values you do. So if they've had a good first eleven years of life, it really doesn't matter what they say about their values during the teenage years. By the time they're adults, they'll pretty well share yours.

A third big control battle with teens is, "See if you can make me learn." That only happens in families where the parents have made it very clear: "*We're* going to make you learn." When we throw down such a gauntlet, we inevitably create control battles about homework, grades, and extracurricular activities, and all the way to dating and curfews. Of course, we will lose those battles while our teens' grades are sliding, along with their respect for us as parents.

Love and Logic parents don't worry about making their teens learn. First, we know we can't control whether or not our teens study. Second, the grades are the teen's grades, not our grades. We have made it clear to our children that their success in school is their responsibility. The teens own their success, or they own their laziness and failures. When we give our teens control in the area of learning, they usually say to themselves, "Boy, if they're not going to worry about it, somebody had better worry—namely, me."

How to Offer Teens Choices

The most effective parents are always thoughtfully surrendering control by offering their teens choices, and those choices should always be within limits the parent can live with and enforce. This is the consultant parent way; we are there to advise, ask questions, and present options; then it is up to "the client" to decide the course of action.

The best time to give teens choices is when things are going well instead of waiting until things are falling apart. The pattern can be set as basically as "Would you like to have juice or milk?" when they are younger, and then continued later with, "Would you like to be home at 10:30 or 11:00 tonight?" You'll come out ahead if you give choices rather than orders. By giving their teen many choices when things are going well, effective parents create a type of "savings account" in their teen's mind, allowing him or her to feel—and actually be—in control. Then when things aren't going well, the parents can say, "Wait a minute, kid. It's my turn. I am going to make the choice on this one."

This technique can be compared to poker. Life is a game of poker in which parents hold all the aces. The parents lay down aces for major events in their teen's life such as learning to drive or going out with friends. But the parents can always say, "I call."

Have you ever looked into a teen's eyes while you're saying "Shut up!" or "Turn that stereo down"? What happens? They twinkle with anticipation, don't they? The teen says, "All right! Let's get it on. Here we go." In other words, any time we tell teens to do something we can't make them do, *we give them too much control.*

Here is where you must offer choices. Always start out very nicely with, "Would you rather . . . ?" "What would be best for you?" or "Feel free to . . ." You might say, "Feel free to make all the noise you want somewhere else," or "Feel free to stay here and be quiet. You decide."

Most creative teens will come up with a third choice, and you're not always going to like it, so brace yourself. That third choice often carries the response, "I live here. I've got rights. I can make noise because this is my house too."

No matter what third choice teens come up with, we must be ready with this rehearsed response: "What were the choices?" And the teen will say, "Yeah, but I—this isn't fair. My friends don't have to put up with that."

We say again in a steady, soft voice, "What were the choices?"

The teen says, "This is dumb!"

We say, "What were the choices?" Or another alternative, "What did I say?"—always in a nice tone.

Most normal teens, after they hear "What were the choices?" three or four times, will respond, "Give me a break, how long—what do I have to do to get away from this crazy adult?" In other words, we have the right to drive our teens crazy too!

Whenever you can, set your teen in a situation where he or she can't say no, but instead must make some kind of decision.

Love and Logic parents don't waste time saying, "You can't do this; you can't do that." Instead they say things like, "How are you going to handle it when . . . ?"

Some Tips on Choices

Don't turn choices into threats by telling your teen, "Choose my way—or else." Here's a supposed choice that is actually a thinly veiled threat: "You can either do your chores or lose your right to the car." That's no different from the boss saying, "Would you rather do that report today or get fired?" We must offer reasonable and realistic choices, not threats. For example:

- "Would you rather clean your room or mow the lawn so I'll have time to clean your room?"
- "Would you rather wash the car this morning or this afternoon?"
- "Do you want to negotiate a reasonable time to come home at night or not go out at all?"

Non-threatening choices, offered calmly, give teens a chance to take some control over their lives.

In summary, as we offer choices to our teens, we should remember five basic points:

1. Select only those choices that you as a parent like. Never offer one you like together with one you don't like, because instinctively teens will usually select the one you don't like.
2. Never give a choice unless you are willing to allow your teen to experience the consequences of that choice, even if you are the one who has to enforce those consequences.
3. Never give choices when the teen is in danger.
4. Never give choices unless you are willing to make the choice in the event the teen doesn't.
5. Pay careful attention to your delivery. Try to start your sentence with one of the following:

> "You're welcome to____ or ____ ."
> "Feel free to___or____ ."
> "Would you rather____ or ____?"
> "What would be best for you, _____or____?"

Love and Logic Principle:
Sharing Control Through Thinking Words

Remember helicopter and drill sergeant parents? When they talk to their teens, they either smother them with overprotection or hand down angry orders. (Laissez-faire parents just roll their eyes and walk away, doing nothing.) In either case, teens resent that sort of talk because it makes them feel like children. So it always sounds like fighting words to them.

Instead of the fighting words of helicopter and especially drill sergeant parents, Love and Logic parents use *thinking words*. They send the message to their teens, "You'd better think because the quality of your life has a lot to do with your decisions."

Teens are more likely to believe something that comes from inside their own heads. When they choose an option, they do the thinking, they make the choice, and the lesson sticks with them.

Consultant parents also take really good care of themselves in front of their teenagers when they're teaching them to think. The parents affirm, "If my kids are ever going to grow up to learn how to take care of themselves, they'd better see it in action."

As we discussed briefly at the end of the last chapter, we do this by telling teens what *we're* going to do, not what *they're* going to do. Telling teens what they're going to do is a waste of time and energy. They'll just get angry. Telling them what we're going to do interests them. That beats anger every time.

One of the best ways to help yourself in such situations is to use the phrase "no problem." That is, what you decide to do is "no problem" for you, but it might be a problem for your teen.

A woman wrote to us and told us the results of using "no problem":

> My kids think the phrase "no problem" has something to do with them. But it has something to do with me. It reminds me to use my techniques. So when the kids get upset, I say, "No problem, right?"
>
> The other thing I learned was never to tell the kid what to do. I tell him what *I'm* going to do.
>
> It really worked on my fourteen-year-old, Tony. For years, I'd had trouble with him every Saturday morning. I'd try to get him to clean up his room by saying to him, "I'm not driving you to your soccer game until you get that room cleaned; so do it *now*!" And he would always play brain drain on me.

"Brain drain" is trying to get an adult to do all the thinking, all the defending, and all the reasoning. As soon as the adult responds the teen just sits back and subconsciously says, "It won't work. You don't love me. You don't care." This woman explained to us:

> Well, Tony would always say things like, "You don't care if the team wins?" "What is the coach going to think?" "The other kids are really going to think that I let them down. You don't want me to let the other kids down, do you?"

I would always end up driving him to the game, screaming at him about the room, and being unhappy. I couldn't enjoy the game.

Eventually, she learned how to say "no problem" and discovered how to tell him what *she* would do, not what *he* had to do.

So I went to him and said, "Tony, I'm going to drive you to your game just as soon as you vacuum your room."

"Vacuuming is woman's work," he answered me. I had to actually hold on to the table while I said, "No problem, Tony."

"What do you mean, 'no problem'?"

"I just mean that I guess it isn't going to be a problem for me anymore." I went to the phone and called up a friend so that I wouldn't have to talk to him, because I didn't have any more answers.

Ten minutes later I heard the vacuum running. I really didn't recognize it at first because, you know, I've never heard it from a distance.

What I discovered through this was that before, when I was telling him what to do, he had something to fight. But when I told him what I was going to do instead, he was only confused. It's interesting and rewarding to watch fourteen-year-olds a bit confused and, at the same time, learning how to grow up.

Parents of teenagers know that teens fight commands, because they see an implied threat in them. They also know that some teens respond to threats and others don't.

"Fighting words" invite disobedience. Here are some examples:

- When we tell our teens what to do. ("Clean out the garage, *now!*")
- When we tell our teens what we will not allow. ("I won't let you hang out with those kids that smoke on the corner of the school campus.")
- When we tell our teens what we won't do for them. ("I'm not driving you to the dance until you finish your homework.")

When we issue these kinds of commands we're calling our teens to battles—mostly to ones we can't win.

Instead Love and Logic parents make statements with *thinking words*, telling our teens:

- What we will allow. ("Feel free to join us for the next meal as soon as the lawn is mowed.")
- What we will do. ("I'll be thrilled to give you a driving lesson as soon as you've straightened up the kitchen.")
- What we will provide. ("You may watch the TV show the rest of the family is watching, or you may wait until we're through and find something on another channel that pleases you more.")

When we give our children the right to make decisions, there is no anger for them to rebel against. Nobody's doing their thinking for them, and the limit is established.

Also, our choices must make real-world sense. As your teens edge closer to the time they'll fly the nest, it's important to stress, "Well, honey, that's the way the world works for me. First, I get my job done, then I get paid, then I eat. If it's good enough for me, guess who else it's good enough for?"

Gold or Garbage?

Is our word gold or garbage when we say, "Don't you look at me like that! And don't you talk to me like that! You get a civil tongue in your mouth!" Can you enforce these demands? No. So our word is garbage.

Are we expressing wishes or limits? Here we are expressing wishes because we're talking about you, and we can't control you. We can control only ourselves. If we want to set limits and turn our words into gold, we must absolutely talk about ourselves and what we would be glad to do.

Parents who turn their word into gold always talk about what they will offer, what they will allow, and what they will put up with. They seldom tell teens what to do.

"I'll be glad to listen to you when your voice is as soft as mine. Take your time. I'll see you later." Now, did this express a wish or a limit?

Did we have to raise our voice? Did we have to add on, "I mean it!"? We become very powerful when we talk about ourselves. In contrast, parents become powerless and impotent when they talk about what their adolescents have to do.

For example, a parent could say, "As long as you live in this house, you're not going to drink. Don't test me! I really mean it this time." It's a wish for the teen, isn't it? But instead we could say, "Would it be reasonable that if I don't have to worry about your using alcohol, then I wouldn't have to worry about your using the car when it's available? Have we got a deal? Put 'er there." Do we say this frowning or smiling? Smiling. Are we talking about something we can control or something we cannot control? Something we *can* control, of course.

Love and Logic Principle: Empathy and Sorrow Plus Consequences Equals Success

The old (and still popular) technique for control was anger, lectures, threats, and intimidation. The Love and Logic technique is equal parts of sorrow and consequence. If teens are going to learn anything, it is that they will one day have to live with their bad decisions. Love and Logic parents know firsthand that the best solution to any problem lives within the skin of the person who owns the problem.

For example, Phil's seventeen-year-old daughter, Tiffany, comes home with alcohol on her breath. Should Phil talk to her about it immediately or in the morning? Morning. With anger or sadness? Sadness. "Oh, I felt so sorry for you last night," Phil says the following morning. "I smelled alcohol on your breath. I'm starting to worry about you and alcohol. What would you guess about using the family car now?"

"I guess I might not get to use it," Tiffany replies.

"Good thinking," Phil replies.

Did Phil set a limit? Yes. Is Tiffany going to try to talk him out of it? Absolutely. Can she? No. Because no matter what Tiffany says, Phil can rely on the broken-record routine and always reply simply, "Probably so."

"But I won't do it again," Tiffany begs.

"Probably so."

"Well, all the other kids get to do it."

"Probably so."

"Well," says Tiffany, trying to draw her father into an argument, "so you've got a big problem over alcohol, Dad, and now I can't drive and I've got to look like a dork at school because——"

"Probably so."

"Well," she persists, "how am I supposed to get to work at the jewelry shop?"

Now Tiffany's trying to give her problem to her dad. If Phil gives her an answer, will she like it? No. It would be better for Phil to say, "I don't know. I was going to ask you the same thing."

"Well, I'll get fired!"

"Probably so."

Phil knows that if he gets angry with Tiffany, he will strip the consequences of her drinking of their power. By expressing anger he will insert himself into the process and impede the logic of the consequences from taking effect. By using "probably so" and keeping the focus on the effects of drinking and driving, Phil prevents Tiffany from focusing her anger on him. Instead, she is continually forced into facing the lesson taught by the consequences of her drinking.

Hurting from the Inside Out

Anger is an appealing emotion, especially when we're using it on our children. Punishment makes us feel so powerful. It makes us think we're in control. But as the children of drill sergeants will tell you, it doesn't work. When parents punish, they lose control over their teens. And the teens lose respect for their parents.

As a Love and Logic parent, Phil had learned to let Tiffany *hurt from the inside out*. He did this by allowing the natural consequences of her behavior to do the teaching. That way the consequence becomes the "bad guy" and Phil remained the "good guy."

Allowing consequences while expressing empathy is one of the toughest parts of Love and Logic parenting. It takes effort to resist the desire to yell at your son when he comes home late without phoning you. And it takes effort to resist the temptation to rescue your daughter by chewing out the school officials when she doesn't make the cheerleading squad.

But if you can be truly sorry with teens and offer suggestions for ways they can put their lives back together, you will teach them the value of struggling through their problems in order to find solutions. You will also build a friendship with them while you prepare them for the responsibilities of dealing with the real world.

Children who grow in responsibility also grow in self-esteem — a prerequisite for achievement in the real world. As self-esteem and self-confidence grow, youngsters are better able to make it once the parental ties are cut.

The greatest gift we can give our youth is the knowledge that with God's help they can always look to themselves first for the answers to their problems. Teens who come at life with the attitude "I can probably find my own solutions" become survivors. They have an edge in learning, relating to others, and making their way in the world.

Love and Logic Principle: Consequences Don't Have to Be Immediate

Another trap parents fall into is the feeling that unless we can give a response to our kids right away, they will forget and our actions will be of little effect. However true this is for rats, dogs, and other animals, it is often just the opposite with people. Have you ever made a promise to a two-year-old, forgotten it, but been reminded by the child when the right time came up? Toddlers don't forget. Neither do teens.

An immediate response is often an angry response, and the anger will override any effects that the consequences might have. Emotion draws teens like fire draws moths. That is one reason adolescents want their music louder, their thrills more exciting, and their conversations more intense. Ever watched a movie your kids said was "awesome" only to find that the plot made no sense and the storyline fell apart long before the climax? Teens will stay on for the ride because they never get out of their emotional brain into their thinking brain. They leave the theater "pumped" by the stunts and special effects; we leave confused by how the movie even got out of editing.

If we force our children to face consequences while we are angry, they won't see the logic of the decision. Instead they will focus on our anger. And instead of thinking about what they did to cause the problem, they will sulk about how mad we were, how unfair life is, and how justified their anger is in return. The focus remains on what the parent did, not on what the teen is going to do.

The best answer is often a delayed one. Delaying the answer gives everyone involved a chance to think and to find a solution. There is nothing wrong with saying to a middle-schooler, "Oh, that was a bad decision. I am going to have to do something about that. But not right now. I will get back to you on it. Try not to worry about it." Or to a high-schooler, "You know, this behavior really worries me. I don't feel good about it at all. But I have no idea what to say to you about it right now. Let's talk about it later."

Then, before you get back to them, work out your game plan. Talk with trusted advisors and devise responses to help your teens face their irresponsibility in a reasonable and logical way. Think about how they are going to respond and what they could do to unravel your plans. Plug the loopholes and fix the flaws in it. Then choose your own time for response, when everyone is calm, and spring it on them like a bolt of lightning out of the sky. That is one of the best ways to make sure they will never forget the lesson, and the object of their pondering will be the consequences of their decision, not your anger or unreasonableness.

Jan was faced with a dilemma. She had entered into an agreement with Josh, her seventeen-year-old son, that she would allow him to buy his own car, provided no other teenager rode with him until he was eighteen years old.

One of Jan's friends witnessed Josh driving with other kids in the car and reported it. Now that she had evidence that the agreement was broken, she was concerned about addressing this with her son.

Her concerns were related to several issues: Josh owned the car; Jan did not see the violation herself; and she had concerns about enforcing the agreement and basing it on the word of another adult.

She devised a plan that would begin with a discussion with Josh, followed by some action that enforced the agreement. The following is how such a conversation could go:

riding in cars

Back to the Basics, Part Two: Treating Teenagers as Responsible Adult.

JAN: Josh, you had someone riding with you. Our agreement was that you could have and drive the car, as long as there were no other kids riding with you during the first year. You broke our contract.

JOSH: I didn't have anyone else in the car. What do you mean?

JAN: Now we have a broken contract and a lie. That's making it worse.

JOSH: How do you know that? Who told you that? Have you been spying on me? Don't you trust me? I want to know who's been ratting me out.

JAN: I'm your parent. It's my job to know what's going on.

JOSH: But you didn't see me driving with other kids. This is so stupid!

JAN: Did our agreement say you couldn't have other riders, or did it say that you could have them as long as you didn't get caught?

JOSH: But, Mom, that rule was so lame in the first place. So what's the big deal anyway? What's a car for if you can't take your friends places? Besides, it's my car. I paid for it. You have no business telling me what I can do with it. None of my friends get treated like babies.

JAN: So I didn't hear the answer to my question. What was our agreement?

JOSH: I don't care about that stupid agreement. I paid for the car and you're not making any more rules about it. Get off my case.

JAN: Our agreement was that you could have and drive the car, as long as no other teens are with you. You broke the agreement and I'm going to have to do something about it.

JOSH: Well, you better not take my car. You can't do that. It's my property. I earned the money for it. You can just stuff your stupid rule. It's not like I'm driving drunk. I'm a good kid. I get good grades. It's not like I'm some low-life punk.

Josh's Defense

Josh's argument that he gets good grades and is not on drugs is a common ploy among teenagers. The trouble with this argument is that it so often works with parents who are confused about their role and responsibilities in raising kids. But it's not enough to just raise a kid who gets good grades and doesn't drink or do drugs. The parenting job also includes raising kids who are honest, considerate, respectful, responsible, and of good character.

Josh, like many lawyers, had created a defense for breaking the rules and lying. How would it sound if he presented this defense in court?

> Your Honor, my client is a good boy. Look at his good report cards. That alone should prove it. But you also need to know that he is not a drunk, druggy, or a low-life punk.
>
> Now, as to this minor issue about breaking his contract and lying about it, the court has no business even considering sanctions against my client when there are other teenagers who do much worse things. The court should simply appreciate the opportunity to work with such an outstanding young person.
>
> And, Your Honor, the plaintiff did not see her son break the contract. The only way this contract could possibly be valid is if the plaintiff actually sees, with her own eyes, the rules of the agreement being violated. The eyewitness accounts of this violation do not apply in this case.
>
> And there is an additional reason to find my client not guilty. He had to agree to his mother's lame rules in order to be allowed to buy the car in the first place. Most kids don't have to do this. Their parents even buy their cars for them.
>
> In other words, my client was coerced into agreeing to a contract that should, in fact, be null and void by the nature of its unreasonable demands. My poor client had to sign the agreement under duress, and therefore, should be excused and found not guilty.
>
> And, as if that is not enough, my client paid for the car with his own money. It is now his property to do with as he pleases. The plaintiff in this matter has absolutely no rights to tell him how to use his own property. The court has no other choice than to find my client not guilty. Thank you.

We know that a judge would laugh this case right out of court. The defense that only bad people should be held accountable for their actions doesn't stand up in our justice system. And it should never stand up in a family.

The Personal Property Issue

There can be no argument that the car was, in fact, Josh's property. Jan agreed that he could own a car. However, as it was with all of the other possessions Josh owned, his mother still had a responsibility to place limits on their use. The fact that Josh owned a bow-and-arrow set did not mean that he could use it to shoot at passing bicyclists. Jan, not Josh, would ultimately be held financially responsible for any damage he did to property or life and limb. Josh's ownership of a computer did not give him total control over its use. The same was true of the car.

Mom Takes Action

Based on all of this, Jan took action, but not until later. She did not take the car away. Remember that Josh told her that the car was his and his mother could not take it away. So this wise mom did the next best thing. She purchased a club for the steering wheel and locked it into place. Josh discovered the locked steering wheel and was furious. "Mom! This is so stupid! You have no right! You get that off my steering wheel right now! I don't have to put up with this! This is my car!"

"Yes, sweetie. It is your car, and I won't take it away from you. You have the right to own it. I'm your parent and I have the responsibility to decide when you drive it. I'll take that off your steering wheel the day I no longer worry about how you use the car. I'm living up to my end of the bargain that we both made."

Needless to say, there was a major teen temper tantrum followed by much pouting and grumbling, but Jan stuck to her guns, and two weeks later the two of them created a new agreement.

Love and Logic Principle: Building a Lifelong Relationship

Our stories about Phil and Tiffany and Jan and Josh illustrate the poignant pains and joys of growing up. They also provide a portrait of Love and Logic parents in action: parents who respect their children and guide them to live with the consequences of their actions.

The teens are still their children; the parents are still in authority. That relationship would exist whether the parents chose to be helicopters, drill sergeants, or consultants, but consultant Love and Logic parents are able to help their children learn how the real world operates. (Laissez-faire parents give up their authority through neglect and thus sabotage their relationship with their kids.)

Teens gain confidence in themselves by making decisions and charting the course for their own lives. You will notice that as they settle into their mid-twenties, their conversations turn to adult topics and their maturity level catches up with their physical size.

Love and Logic parenting techniques aren't just to help you get through the rough spots of raising teenagers. They're tools to help you achieve the goal of guiding your youngster to live a responsible, productive, and happy life. By allowing your teen to achieve independence, you watch an adult blossom. And that adult, who happens to be your child, becomes your friend.

Living on the Edge

We hope we've encouraged you so far. But we don't want to give you the impression that parenting teenagers can be reduced to following a few easy steps. The steps are part of an overall process.

This process is primarily one of *change*. First, you're going through changes. After all, you've never parented teenagers before. Second, your teens are experiencing changes—both internally and externally—that you never could have imagined.

We'll be exploring those changes in part 2. They're a big part of what keeps parents of teenagers living on the edge. But with the basics of self-esteem, responsibility, sharing control, and expressing empathy while allowing consequences to do their work, you can confidently guide your son or daughter along the wild ride of adolescence. It doesn't have to be a white-knuckle trip—not all the time anyway. Take heart and have fun.

Part 2

Living on the Edge

*The Wild and Wonderful Challenges
of Parenting Teenagers*

5

Fasten Your Seat Belt
and Enjoy the Ride

One of the most beneficial things Jim learned to say to his daughter Susie was, "Well, I've never been a parent of a fourteen-year-old before, so I'm probably going to make a lot of mistakes this year with you. I hope you'll help me through it. I'll try to help you through it."

Guess what he said when she was fifteen? "Well, Susie, I've never been a parent of a fifteen-year-old before. This is tough, isn't it? We have to go through it every year." She got to the point where she would empathize with Jim and say, "Dad, you're not doing that bad." That kind of reassurance helped him ride out the storms of his children's adolescence.

Perhaps you're riding out the storms yourself. A hurricane of questions, doubts, and fears swirls around parents as their children approach adolescence. For parents whose children are already teens, it may feel that the hurricane has already hit your coastline and looks to do about as much damage as Katrina did to New Orleans.

These questions and feelings are natural. And although it sounds like odd advice for weathering a hurricane, the best thing you can do is to get calm and relax.

As we stated earlier, it's important for you to take good care of yourself. The feelings you have are real; the questions you have about your children are important. But stay calm.

How do you find calm in a storm? The first order of business is to organize your thoughts. We'll start with what's happening to you, and then we'll deal with what kind of teen you have.

Why Parents Should Relax

We're raising children, and we wonder how we're doing. For a lot of things we do in life, we receive some form of tangible recognition. In school, we get report cards. At work, we get performance evaluations or paychecks. But nobody gives us a report card or paycheck for parenting. How our teens develop is really our only performance evaluation.

But that's a dicey proposition. One day it might tell us we're doing okay; the next day it might indicate we'd better hurry up and get some job training.

We wrestle internally with how our daughters and sons will turn out. What if they don't become model citizens? What does that say about us as parents? Guilt creeps in.

Maybe that's what makes us typical parents. We often feel guilty.

Have you spent time wondering how other people think of you because of the way your children behave? Your teen is out doing such-and-such and you don't have control. You feel guilty.

Guilt springs up from all sorts of nooks and crannies:

- Our teens have mood swings.
- Our teens don't talk to us as much as they used to.
- Our teens would rather be with their friends than home with us.
- Our teens tend to question or even reject our values.

Are we justified in feeling guilty about these things? No. These attitudes and behaviors are common for teenagers. That nagging thought *If I were a better parent, my teen wouldn't be this way* is normal. Other parents are feeling the same way. That doesn't mean it's true.

Guilt isn't the only thing going on when we're parents of teenagers. We also have a sense of failure. And our offspring obligingly assist us in that. They keep a tally on where they think we're falling short: "My friend's dad owns a BMW," they'll say, with the not-too-subtle hint of "so when are you going to get with it?" They're quick to point out that all the other parents are doing a better job than we are.

But remember, all of this shall pass, and they shall be teenagers no longer. And you'll notice that their attitudes will change, and your guilt will fade. Mark Twain is quoted as having said, "When I was a boy of fourteen, my father was so ignorant I could hardly stand to have the old man around. But when I got to be twenty-one, I was astonished at how much the old man had learned in seven years."

Why Worry?

A lot of people spend a lot of time worrying about what could go wrong. Remember, worry is the price you pay in advance for most of the things in life that never happen.

You only have so much time with your children, and you have two basic ways of looking at it. You can choose to spend that time thinking about all the things that could go wrong. Yup, plenty of opportunity there. Or you can put that energy into thinking about how you can build a more positive relationship with your children. It's up to you.

Personally, we'd rather you made the second choice. And one place to start is learning to work with your children without criticizing or interrogating them.

Many parents overanalyze their parenting until they're afraid to open their mouths because they might say the wrong thing to their teens. And sure, they often do say the wrong thing. So what? That's not going to hurt the teenagers. That can get repaired along the way. It's a whole lot better to communicate something than to clam up because you're afraid it's going to come out wrong.

Relax. Don't let worry make you tongue-tied.

Listen and Learn

Getting close to your teen requires your effort to understand what he or she is experiencing. You can learn by listening to what your teen is telling you, but don't expect polite explanations.

Just as salmon are driven to swim upstream to spawn, so teenagers are driven to meet the awakening needs of independence and adulthood. But it's highly unlikely that a teen is going to sit you down to explain his or her needs: "Mom, Dad, let's talk about us. I'll be going through some pretty needy times during the next few years. You just have to understand that I'll need *this*, and I'll probably act like . . . " This conversation will not take place. Your teen will show you what he or she needs by acting it out. And you can listen and learn.

Teens may try to meet their needs through foolish or even danger-ous actions. As a result, parents feel threatened. We feel as if we're doing a bad job. We feel guilty. We're failing—we'd better tighten control. We worry some more.

What do our teens feel when we clamp down on their actions? A stronger desire to show us how important those needs are. So they act out to communicate to us, "You will not control me. I will get my way." The teenager also feels a loss of love: "My needs are not being met, and Mom and Dad are doing everything they can to control me."

Then we feel a loss of control, and we too feel a loss of love. The relationships start to go downhill. It's a deteriorating cycle.

What should you do when your teen is acting out? Relax. Listen and learn. Don't worry. We often dig a grave that's pretty hard to get out of during these teenage years. Instead, maybe we can just back off a little, acknowledge those needs, and say to our teen, "Yes, this is important. Let me help you grow through this. How can I help you accomplish things that are important to you?"

We're not talking about material things here. We're talking about giving our teen the chance to feel independent. We can say, "How can I help you do that so that you still take good care of yourself and I don't have to feel scared? Let's talk about that."

If we can get our teens to talk with us by saying to them, "Yes, I want you to get your needs met," do you think they might help us get *our* needs met? Maybe you could say, "You know, as a parent, I have needs too. I need to feel like I'm doing a good job. I need to feel like I'm getting you ready for the real world. I need to feel like I've been doing the job in such a way that you'll take good care of yourself and will continue to be a happy person as you go through life."

Parents and teens need to talk to each other about their needs. It's okay for us to say, "Here's what I'm trying to do. Am I doing something that's getting in your way? Am I hurting you in some way? Tell me about it. What's the pouting all about? Can you put it into words? What are these tears telling me? What is the anger and the stomping around really trying to tell me?"

In other words, we're taking our teen's actions seriously as often as possible and saying, "Can you put that in words for me so I'll really understand it and I won't misread it?" With this style of communication, you'll find that many of your parenting worries simply melt away. Once your teen does put feelings into words, never try to straighten out his or her thoughts. You will get much better results by saying, "Thanks for sharing that!"

Some Things Parents Need to Understand

Parents who have learned to ask their teens questions and get them to think have faced the issue of what lies ahead: "My thirteen-year-old is going to be out in the world in five years, assuming that she doesn't run away from home first. How can I start operating this home the way the real world operates?"

These parents have also come to grips with what happens to their children during the teenage years:

Changing thoughts: When children are elementary-school age, they usually want to tell us everything—who did what, who said what to whom, what they think about all of it. Often you can't get them to stop blabbering about their day.

Then when children move into adolescence, they start having a lot of thoughts like, *Gee, I wonder if my mother can handle what I'm thinking—maybe I shouldn't tell her.* They also have a lot of thoughts they can't articulate.

Changing values: There are many things adolescents would rather not share with us because it might be different from our value system. They are also "trying on" a lot of new thoughts and systems of thought. What they are talking about today is often gone tomorrow.

Changing sexuality: Teens aren't going to whip hummers on their parents like, "Hey, Mom, let me tell you why my showers are so long." Their bodies develop, their hormones kick into gear, and they find themselves experiencing sexuality for the first time—and none of those changes is conducive to open discussion with Mom or Dad.

Changing appearance: Youngsters get extremely sensitive in early adolescence—ages twelve to thirteen—because they're not quite sure what's right or what's wrong in appearance, what to do with their fantasies about sex, and whether or not that zit is the only thing that shows on their face.

Parents who can interact well with their teens also know that birth order typically affects how their children will behave and act on their needs.

1. The firstborn is basically Einstein — the thinker, the doer, the doctor, the lawyer.
2. The middle children tend to be Picassos, because they look in on themselves and become sensitive.
3. The youngest child is the talk-show host. By the time that last one comes along, we're pretty relaxed as parents. We allow natural consequences to fall, and we give the child a lot of love. We're not quite as uptight, so he or she has the freedom to say, "Hey, world, here I am!"

All teenagers possess these common traits. But the common traits will work themselves out in different ways, depending on what kind of teen you have.

Three Types of Teens

Five-year-olds may have tremendous similarities in their parenting needs. But as they get older, their paths diverge. We've observed the following three types of adolescents:

1. Early bloomers: The first type describes those children who get along well in the first and second years of life. By the time they reach the sixth grade, they're good kids. They turn out well, regardless of how rebellious they may have seemed during adolescence.

These children will move along smoothly for several reasons. First, their mothers didn't abuse drugs during pregnancy. Second, their parents provided love and nurture for them during the first twelve months. Third, their parents applied wise and loving discipline in the second year of life, saying no and meaning it when the child's behavior was inappropriate.

2. Late bloomers: The second type of teenagers have problems in their first and second years, but by age eleven they have their acts together and make it all right through adolescence—and probably through life.

3. Troubled teens: This third type describes children who have problems originating in their first and second years that continue through age eleven and beyond. They don't get along well with parents or peers. They play the role of victim all the time, charming and conning people easily, hoarding or gorging on food. These children often become delinquents.

The foundations of personality are laid in the first two years of life. Children are predisposed to difficulties during adolescence when, in their early years, they have

- pain that the parents can't relieve
- genetic predispositions that the parents can't alleviate
- early abuse and neglect
- the use of drugs and/or alcohol by their parents

These predispositions are more pronounced in some children than in others. Their genetic makeup can determine how well they will be able to handle environmental factors such as neglect or abuse. And the way they cope with adolescence can also depend on the ability of their parents to discover proper parenting techniques.

Some of those predispositions will not easily be relieved by the techniques outlined in this book. If a child has fetal alcohol syndrome, for example, no amount of parenting will bring about an easy adolescence. Nor will parenting techniques erase problems such as developmental defects and abnormalities resulting from certain congenital illnesses. The child will inevitably "feel different" from other kids during the latency years between three and eleven. If you suspect your child has experienced such predispositions, we strongly urge you to seek competent professional help.

Because personality is shaped so early in life, parenting is a lot easier when the foundation is correctly laid. Many parents of nineteen-year-olds will ask, "What can I do for this kid?" Not a whole lot, really, except give them something to read on personal development. At nineteen, children are now in the adult world. The patterns they developed through their adolescence are firmly set, and they've achieved independence—for better or for worse—from their parents.

But parents can and still do have an influence on their fifteen-year-olds. They can use their influence in the home to help their youngsters learn how to make choices and live with the consequences.

Now let's take a closer look at the three types of adolescents we identified above.

Early Bloomers
The majority of teens fall into the first category of those who were well-adjusted from birth through age eleven: the early bloomers. If parents got along well with their children through sixth grade or age eleven, it doesn't matter how bad adolescence goes. Everything will tend to work out all right in the long run.

Of course, tragic behavior such as heavy drug use or promiscuity can threaten adolescent development and parents' relationships with their teens. But barring those extreme conditions, if parents have enjoyed good relations with their children through age eleven, they can relax.

Sure, there are teens who don't want to talk about things because they're too ashamed and too uncertain and too thrown off balance. Others are very lucky teens. They have a very good self-image and have had very good communication with their parents all along. They will go through periods of withdrawal and questioning because body, mind, and emotions are changing faster in adolescence than at any other time in life, but these are normal issues, and these teens will turn out fine.

For example, even normal, well-adjusted children verbally snipe at their parents. It's common for eleven-year-old boys to be angry and for thirteen-year-old girls to get irritated and make nasty comments. That's part of the natural processes of growing up. Part of it is hormonal and developmental. Part of it is the teen's apprehension when realizing that in a few years he or she may have a job or a new name. These are profound changes, and often teens' only response to such anxiety is to lash out verbally at their parents. Under such stressful conditions, adults do the same thing.

In response to this behavior, parents can say to their teens, "I know you're angry—that happens to kids and adults too. But it's an irritation to be around you, so why don't you have dinner in your room?"

Late Bloomers

Then there are teens who had difficulties in the first and second years of life such as undiagnosed health problems, but otherwise experienced a relatively well-adjusted childhood. These late bloomers likely will have few problems during adolescence. Early problems can crop up again in several ways.

Those problems often revolve around early developmental issues over health, appearance, and social adjustment. But they're overcome by understanding the causes of the problems, not by excusing wrong behavior.

Fred was an ugly kid. Not only was he gawky like a lot of youngsters, he also was severely nearsighted from birth. He couldn't play catch because he never developed eye-hand coordination, and he had trouble with his schoolwork because he couldn't see the chalkboard. His teachers and parents gradually found out about his vision difficulties and were able to correct most of it with glasses.

Now Fred is thirteen. He's learned to apply himself to his studies, but he sometimes exhibits antisocial behavior from the years of taunts of "four-eyes" and other insults.

Fred's parents waited until they were in a good mood to talk about his difficulties with him.

"We know you're mad a lot," they opened.

"Yeah," Fred responded, and looked down at the floor.

"How much of the time do you think others have it better?" they gently asked.

"Other kids *always* have it better," Fred hissed. "They can see without any stupid glasses."

"Well, to tell the truth, Fred, when you were little, other children *did* have it better," they agreed. "When other kids were playing catch, you couldn't see the ball; when others were making friends, you couldn't see them from across the classroom. Pal, we really understand that. If we grew up with those problems, we'd probably be feeling that too."

"Yeah, well, I don't know what to say," Fred went on. "It's all so unfair."

Then Fred's parents turned the conversation to a new angle. "However, those who have an early handicap are given an equally large opportunity: when they get over that handicap, they become more thoughtful, more understanding, and more aware than the people who never had that problem. Some of our greatest leaders were those who had to overcome difficult times."

"Yeah, but it's still not easy," Fred replied.

"We understand, and we do love you very much and want you to succeed."

Parents of late bloomers should level with their teens and tell them why they may be having problems in the family or society. But past or even lingering problems such as these are not excuses for antisocial behavior. Parents should offer explanations as ways of *understanding* the behavior without *excusing* the behavior. Teens need to grasp this reality: "My background means I have to work especially hard."

Teens with early-childhood struggles should be given the expectation that they can overcome those early things and that their parents really appreciate their efforts. For example, when a child with early coordination problems makes the soccer team, it means they did extra work. Parents can also encourage their teens to make friends despite their earlier problems.

With this kind of parenting, late bloomers learn to own their own triumphs and failures. Parents should neither overprotect teens nor aggravate their problems by excusing outbursts of anger or other manifestations of earlier developmental problems.

The same techniques can be applied to troubled teens. For example, parents can say, "Sweetheart, you were abused by your grandfather when you were a child. That was awful, we know. That's why you're angry. So you're going to have to work on it." The background is a reason without being an excuse. It is understood, not excused, on the basis of the background or the problem.

This brings up another parenting approach for teens struggling to overcome early difficulties: *toleration without permission*. Don't ever say, "Oh, now that I understand it, I excuse it." Give your child a background for understanding why he or she may be having difficulties. But regardless of cause, do not tolerate antisocial and especially criminal activity. Teens often imply by their words and actions, "You are going to tolerate this," while using their past to justify it.

Let your teen know you're empathetic with his or her difficulties. But make it clear from the outset that you won't tolerate inappropriate behavior. And then act on your convictions. If you warn your teen not to throw rocks at houses, don't excuse the deed when the neighbors call up to complain about broken windows.

For a geopolitical analogy, European leaders constantly warned Adolf Hitler in the 1930s to curb his expansionist policies. But after Hitler seized Czechoslovakia, they said, "Well, all right, but don't do it again."

Sometimes a teen's early developmental problems were unintentionally caused by the parents themselves.

Lisa, for example, was allergic to milk. But her parents didn't know it, and they constantly scolded her for crying, especially after feeding her. Lisa and her parents didn't find out that she had this allergy until she was fourteen.

How should her parents respond now? "We're sorry that it happened, and at the time we were doing the best we knew how." Parents don't need to ask for forgiveness for their earlier well-intentioned actions. They should just state the facts of what happened and express their genuine regret. Teens can use a request for forgiveness to validate their resentment. It also opens them to the idea that they just might *not* forgive it.

If your teen seems to resent you, don't say, "Boy, this resentment hurts me." If you do, the young teen is going to respond, "Good, Mom and Dad deserve to hurt."

The better response and the one that will help build trust is, "If you go through life resenting me, it's going to eat you from the inside out. I hope you won't hang on to resentment, because it's going to hurt you."

For teens who had problems in the first year of life, a little bit of trust can go a long way. Over time that trust will build, just the way a pearl forms over a grain of sand.

One way to build on that trust is to ask for more eye contact. Say, "It looks like you're having trouble with eye contact. I hope you get over it." Or "I'd appreciate it if you looked me in the eye," or "I'd appreciate it if you'd lower your voice."

Again, the point here is that parents are telling their children what they want instead of telling their children what to do. We're almost always on shaky ground when we try to order our children, saying, for instance, "Look at me when I'm talking to you." When we try to force our children to maintain eye contact with us, their eyes will focus on an object behind us; they are therefore ignoring us but still appearing to be looking at us.

But there are some disturbed teens who don't have even a grain of trust to build on. This happens if your teen had first-year-of-life difficulties and never developed basic trust. Such children grow through toddlerhood with extreme control problems that continue through elementary school. Those kids are control problems for everyone in the environment—parents and teachers.

To be reached, such children generally need a highly structured situation that forces them to conform. This leads the teen to explode in anger and rage. The rage and anger are accepted by the authority figures, and this acceptance leads to trust. Thus, seemingly harsh environments can build a great deal of trust, especially when the process is completed. This is the reason that some states work with delinquent teenagers in boot-camp settings.

Troubled Teens

Almost all children who suffer chronic problems from birth through age eleven are going to have significant problems in adolescence, and parents are going to be caught in the storm. Perhaps the parents didn't cause the problems, but they will certainly have to live with them. These troubled teens are still a minority group, but their numbers are rising.

Disturbed teenagers have blocked in a great deal of rage, which smolders in some of the following manifestations:

- They don't like to be touched.
- They avoid eye contact.
- They don't want people to give them relief.
- They have no trust.
- They have learning and food problems.

These teens probably will need professional help, and parents should not be embarrassed to seek it. Here are three ways parents can find out whether they have a troubled teen:

First, the best way is to *get a professional opinion* from a child psychologist or child psychiatrist. Be sure to find somebody who's very busy. That way, you screen out professionals who may simply be trying to hustle more clients to support themselves. Remember that credentials are no guarantee of a high-quality professional opinion.

Second, *ask for an outside perspective* from someone with good teens. Don't compare notes with someone who has similar problems. Church and school parenting groups can be helpful here. Parents can find out through friends or parenting groups whether or not their problem is a normal part of adolescence or a serious situation requiring professional resources.

The third and least reliable way is to *rely on your own intuition.*

Don't assume your teen is disturbed just because he or she does things you don't like. That's a meaningless indicator. All children do things we don't like. The key question is this: Are the things my teen is doing likely to be destructive to his or her life?

Destructive does not always mean something that will eventually be harmful. Self-destructive behavior may result in a learning opportunity. Just because teens get hurt doesn't mean all aspects of wrong behavior are ultimately bad. For example, running away from home could in part be beneficial, because the teen could learn some valuable lessons about life, even though we all prefer he or she had stayed at home.

Destructive generally does mean something that teens do that will not teach them a lesson and enable them to benefit from the hurt. It also can mean that the lifelong lesson of the pain of an action will outweigh the value of the learning experience. For example, if your son gets a girl pregnant and chooses not to marry her, the pain of child-support payments will last at least eighteen years, overriding any lessons he would learn from the consequences of irresponsible sexual behavior.

But parents should not protect their teens from reality. In a few years, they will be unable to of protect their teens. The adult world is more harshly consequential than what most parents lay down to their teenagers. And parents provide a loving context: "I'll let you experience the consequences of this because I love you." The adult world is either antagonistic or indifferent.

Parents of troubled teens can respond best by realizing that they must first take care of themselves and protect the rest of the family. A wise parent will say, "I can expect that Joe is going to have problems. I've got to make sure the family and other kids are safe. I can't burden myself with guilt, and I can't burden my family with continued hardship. I can't burden the family with bills, because we could liquidate our estate with psychiatric or legal bills."

These parents can also reasonably lower their expectations because that's the reality of the situation. Reasonable expectations can reduce hurt and avoid paralysis from shock or surprise when something happens. Parents who stay away from hand wringing are freed to be more effective in their responses.

What youngsters in this situation need most desperately before they finally leave the home is to be around a role model who can show them how to live a healthy, balanced life once they're on their own.

Often, however, parents rant and rave and threaten and accuse, which is just the opposite of taking care of themselves. When teens leave home and turn their backs on ranting parents, they've lost their last chance to learn how to take care of themselves. Once they get out in the world, the odds are that they will take the lead of the modeling they saw in their parents. They'll go through life accusing and blaming everybody else and trying to control other people, instead of first taking care of themselves.

In most cases, parents who do a great job of taking care of themselves feel horrible and guilty and selfish when in fact they're doing the best thing possible. Paradoxically, taking care of ourselves first is what gives teens the possibility of getting better themselves.

If the family members allow themselves to suffer from Joe's behavior in order to make it easier on Joe, they become enablers for Joe's destructive behavior. Joe will think, "If I'm hard on my brothers and sisters, my parents will take care of me. If I'm in trouble with the law, my parents will bail me out."

In this context, helping becomes hurting. Helping becomes excusing. If you want to see people ravaged by such "helping," look at those who are dependent on long-term government subsidies. Look at those whose parents "helped" their children well into adulthood. When people are given a free ride, they never learn to start their engines. As a result, they become emotionally crippled, except under extraordinary circumstances.

When teens don't respond to the natural consequences of their wrong behavior, they might need to enter a day treatment program or move in with a relative. However, when parents send a teen to live with relatives or in a detention home, they have to compare the resentment of a forced change of residence with the positive benefits that might occur. The teen will probably resent it. The more a teen can buy into such a decision by having a say-so in it ahead of time, the better.

But there can come a time when a parent might simply say, "Kid, you have to go." This may occur when parents feel that the situation is intolerable for themselves and the rest of the family. At this point, they need an outside opinion on the legality of such a decision.

Incorrigible fifteen-year-olds will be incorrigible at home or on the street. They might as well be incorrigible on the street so they can be locked up in a structured environment. It sounds extremely harsh, but if the rest of the family is at risk it's a tough but necessary decision.

Again, Relax

Sometimes we forget that *we* went through periods in which we didn't communicate with our parents. When our teen starts to withdraw or experience difficulties, we may automatically assume that we've done something wrong. Or we may think back to what we were like at their age, and then jump all over them in fear of what they're up to.

Because parents don't get report cards or other feedback, it's typical for us to worry that things are going wrong. "The kid isn't talking to me: I've got to do something better!" But most times it's just a normal phase our teen is going through.

Some phases are tougher than others, especially if a teen's behavior threatens the safety of the rest of the family. But most times, we stand a good chance that things will work out all right if we remember that we are the parents, that we're in charge, that we must take good care of ourselves first, and that our goal is to help our children grow up to be responsible adults.

We'll make it; they'll make it. We could call these years of raising teenagers "Goof and Grow." We learn the hard way, don't we? We make a lot of mistakes. But the end result, a responsible teenager about to become a responsible adult, is worth it.

6

Understanding Teens from the Inside Out: Internal Changes in Adolescence

ourteen-year-old Joni came into Foster's office, sobbing. "When I was a little girl, Dr. Cline, my parents didn't have to know where I was every minute. They didn't have to know who my friends were or why I was late for dinner," she told him. "But now I'm fourteen. I grew up and they pick on me because I'm not a little girl anymore and I look like a woman. It's not my fault that I grew boobs."

It's normal—and regrettable—that when the girl curves out, the parents clamp down. Boys, too, experience similar clamp-downs from their parents.

The rapid physical, cognitive, and psychological changes that adolescents undergo can frighten parents who have forgotten that they survived those very same changes. These children are literally and physically becoming adults. Yet as parents grow out of parenting children into parenting teenagers, they often react like Joni's mom and dad did: they unwittingly impose more rules when their kids don't look like children anymore. Teens are not children, and the way they're treated should change accordingly.

We must not minimize what happens in our youngsters' bodies and minds nor should we dismiss those changes by telling our kids they're "just going through a phase" or "just looking for an excuse to rebel." Teens themselves don't know what's happening and often can't explain what it feels like. They're like big fish outgrowing a small aquarium.

In a sense, adolescence is the toddler stage of adulthood. Toddlers can go through ups and downs as they experience rapid changes in their physical and verbal dexterity. For the first time in their lives, toddlers are learning that they can be independent in their own little ways, and they will ride their new freedom for all it's worth until Mom or Dad says no in order to protect them.

In adolescence, children go through another phase of growth and independence. But now the consequences of children's independence are a lot more intense. How parents deal with their children's adolescence depends in part on the way they handled their children's earlier years. If teenagers didn't establish their identities in healthy ways when they were younger, they may push their needs for independence that much further. In other words, they have to take more risks, be more bizarre, and act out in ways that communicate, in essence, "I am not my parent." Those actions are often perceived as rebellion.

If parents have brought up their children to see themselves as individual persons—not just "so-and-so's child"—most likely the adolescent identity crisis will not be as intense or the rebellion as deep.

Most of what we call rebellion is a natural outgrowth of a series of profound changes in a teen. Those changes—the greatest changes a person experiences in his or her life—include radical shifts in mind, body, and values. They are wonderful and weird all at once. The more you understand them, the better a parent—and friend—you can be to your teen.

That's why we're going to devote this chapter to understanding teens from the inside out. We'll look at the primary internal changes in the areas of cognitive thinking, physical development and sexuality, psychological development and values formation, and self-expression (adolescent rebellion).

Changes in Thinking

Don't be surprised if your thirteen-year-old replaces her play-by-play descriptions of her day with sudden, angry outbursts. What's happening is a gradual, almost magical shift in the way she thinks.

Until the early teens, a child thinks immaturely with little ability to conceptualize. Psychologist Jean Piaget closely studied the development of thinking in children. He referred to the thinking of elementary and early junior high children as "concrete operations" and named mature thinking "formal operations." Piaget found that mature thinking arises out of the natural transitional stages in growing up and can be neither hurried nor delayed by parents or educational structures.

Preadolescent children are very "concrete" in their thinking. They follow the rules. They do what their parents say. They think in terms of the specific, or concrete, objects in their world. Later, when they reach the developmental stage in which they can think abstractly, they can make judgments such as, "Well, in this situation, this makes sense."

For instance, let's say seventeen-year-old Frank is required by his parents to be home by 10:00 p.m. But at 9:50, Frank is thinking, "It's getting late, but Jordan's out of gas and needs a lift home. It'll take me a half-hour. I'll be home late, but circumstances require it." A fifth-grader, however, would cling to "My parents said be home by five. No matter what, I have to get home by five."

During the first eleven years of life, the mind is in a very concrete mode, which is necessary for our very survival. We learn to follow Mom around and do what Mom tells us. Why? Because human beings are born nine months premature. They can't get up and move around right away when they're born. All other mammal babies start swimming or walking shortly after birth. But not human babies: in their first nine months, their heads and brains are still developing. They're not doing much to take care of themselves. They're heavily reliant on their parents to do their thinking for them.

When our kids haven't yet reached their twelfth year, it's very easy for us to tell the child in the drill sergeant way, "Do *this*, do *that*. Do it my way." Or we might take the helicopter approach: "Oh, honey, don't worry. We'll take care of you."

Children change as their modes of thinking change. About the time Alex reaches twelve or thirteen, his brain switches over to abstract thinking. Now he can start making conceptual connections that he couldn't make earlier. For example, think of how strange and funny little children's jokes are. The things they laugh at—bald slapstick is a knee-slapper every time—are very concrete. They miss our humor when we try to joke with them. But when they become teenagers, they can be a lot of fun: they can participate in our jokes.

But it isn't much fun when little Alex turns into big Alex with a shaved head, a pierced ear, and a snarl on his lips. He may not want to participate in the family, never mind our jokes. But Alex has no control over these changes, just as he has no control over his developing fertility and the level of testosterone in his body, the hormone that will give him his secondary sexual characteristics. Alex's sister Anna isn't much different. She too will go through changes in thinking and behavior leading up to her body's release of the hormone estrogen, producing her secondary sexual characteristics.

Your Teen's Brain

Looking at your adolescent, you might think that the changes you see are the most important changes. Your little boy becomes a hairy gorilla with acne; your little princess goes from pretty to curvy to downright gorgeous. But it's the physical changes that you don't see, under that mop of stunning hair and behind those attractive eyes, that are probably the most important.

The adolescent's brain is both sorting out what's important and losing masses of unused neurons. At the same time, those neurons that are used develop tighter cohesion to have greater impact on personality: neurons that fire together wire together. Actually, it's the physical changes in the brain that account for most adolescent behavior. Cortical changes in neurons lead to the apparently crazy behavior on skateboards and other reckless acts. It's those brain changes that can lead the compliant to become defiant, the modest to become revealing.

It is sufficient to say here simply that your teen's brain is undergoing massive changes in structure and chemistry. The hypothalamus, which deals with impulses, is being impacted by very provocative hormones. Oxytocin, the neurochemical elixir of love, tries to wiggle in the door of hypothalamic synapses while the prefrontal areas of the cortex, the thinking and reasoning area of the brain, rush to make changes as if hoping to keep the hypothalamus in check with just a bit of rationality.

Alcohol and drugs can substantially impact the developing prefrontal cortex, making substance abuse in the teen years particularly damaging. Even the parietal lobes, which are involved in processing sensory information and evaluating spatial relationships, and the occipital lobes, dedicated to processing visual information, get into the act with changes of their own.[8]

External environment shapes your teen's brain growth just as in toddlerhood. Current findings confirm that the adolescent brain is indeed plastic and changing. For parents who are interested in the chemistry of the changes in both structure and chemistry, there is a wealth of information easily accessible on the web and at libraries.[9]

What can you as a parent do with your knowledge of these changes?

First, encourage your teens to explore the important changes too. Most teens are very self-centered and love to find out information about themselves.

Second, with Love and Logic tools and techniques, help your teen understand how important it is *not* to take the chance of hurting his or her developing brain with drugs, alcohol, or other addictions.

Third, understand that your teen's developing and still partially immature prefrontal cortex may need a bit of encouragement from you in helping to keep that darn hypothalamus and all of its impulses in check. You best do this by encouraging it to operate by asking the questions and loving your child—two things the frontal lobes always find so appealing and stimulating to their growth.

New Ways of Relating

As children transition into formal operational thinking after age eleven and begin to question their parents' behavior, they often display their new thinking style through anger, outbursts, and stinging retorts.

For the first time, they can truly judge their own ability to handle difficult situations, and for the first time, their judgment on issues affecting their lives may be better than that of their parents. This new ability to think is at the heart of many parent-child misunderstandings.

Here are some of the changes you may notice as a result of your teen's newly mature thinking:

- You will be less likely to hear long and detail-packed stories of movies, friends, school, or other activities.

- For the first time, your child understands the meaning of parables and sayings such as, "People who live in glass houses shouldn't throw stones."
- Your teen will begin to appreciate political cartoons for more than just a character's big nose or funny appearance.
- You will no longer hear questions that seem to have such obvious answers. The phrase "I don't get it, Mom" will fade away.
- Your youngster will begin to question, for the first time, whether or not the end justifies the means.
- Your children will no longer buy into your value system automatically just because they love you.
- Your teen will begin to question and comment on parental behavior from a more objective perspective.

Let Them Take Flight

Although parents may find some of these changes confusing, and at times disruptive, it helps to understand that changes are a natural and important part of a child's development. You can expect this shift toward conceptual adult thinking to take place over a period of about six months, for most children during ages eleven to twelve.

Parents who have raised responsible children can welcome these changes as a major step in their child's development into adulthood. They can also recognize it as a time to back off, let their children unfold their newly found cerebral wings, and take flight. They'll be equipped to leave the nest when it's time.

Another amazing thing is that just about the time the brain switches over to abstract thinking, children are also given the power to reproduce. In other words, the Creator—with utmost wisdom—created humans so that they would not be able to procreate before they could think maturely.

Physical Changes

Scientists still don't know yet exactly what causes these changes in thinking and in the body during adolescence. The changes might be triggered by a cause-and-effect relationship of brain on body or vice versa. They may be a part of the natural unfolding of DNA, the genetic material supplying the building blocks of life.

We know that physical changes can affect emotions and thinking. As soon as hormones fluctuate, so do thoughts and emotions. For example, women experience postpartum depression; men often experience anger and depression after a coronary attack.

Changes in teens' ability to think may relate to these physical and emotional shifts. As children develop physically, they can step out of their environment and look at it in a more conceptual and rational way. They can put words on it: "My mom worries too much," or "My dad is overprotective." A younger child couldn't articulate that except in a vague way.

Many physical changes are common to both girls and boys. These range from growing bigger in size to changing preferences for a variety of foods. It's also normal for teens to like loud music with a pronounced beat. Their brains, which are busy changing, pruning, and developing, don't produce the same pleasures from the same inputs for a time, so everything needs to be louder, brighter, and more intense to create the same "entertainment value." This doesn't mean we have to tolerate airplane-landing-decibel music, but it does mean that our teens are not consciously turning it up loud just to get to us.

The changes that make parents the most nervous, however, are clustered around issues of sexuality and gender identity.

Changes in Girls

Joni, the girl we mentioned earlier who resented her parents clamping down as she matured physically, found out firsthand that girls develop earlier than boys. Parents naturally get concerned about girls earlier than about boys.

Many girls start menstruating as early as age nine or ten. Parents can take development in stride as they discuss it with their daughters. The best way to handle it is by asking questions: "Brenna, how much do you know about menstruation? What do you know about your first period?"

Questions are far better than lectures. Otherwise, your daughter —who probably has learned an immense amount about sex on the street—goes to her friends, rolls her eyes, and tells them, "Can you believe it? My mom told me about the birds and the bees!"

If Mom isn't around, Dad can discuss it with the daughter. It's best, though, to have a female confidante.

Girls start wearing bras at about age nine or ten. They should be allowed to decide what kind of bras they want. Their mothers, in turn, should be excited for them and shop with their daughters. It's best to take the attitude "Isn't this neat?" instead of approaching bra shopping with apprehension.

Even though the girl is filling out, she still needs hugs from Dad and Mom. She still needs the touching, tickling, and roughhousing that the family has done in the past. The interpersonal relationships between daughter and parents should continue to develop as she develops physically.

Regrettably, fathers sometimes feel nervous and quit touching their daughters. Girls may interpret this hesitancy as rejection, reacting in ways their fathers don't know how to handle. A cycle ensues as the daughter's apprehension fuels her father's apprehension, and so on.

Changes in Boys

Boys don't develop as early as girls. Male hormones kick in a little later than female hormones.

Parents should be able to discuss sexuality with their sons matter-of-factly, just as with their daughters. And again, using a line of questioning is the most effective approach. Adolescent boys, in most cases more so than adolescent girls, have picked up a library of knowledge about sex on the street. Parents shouldn't assume that their teens know it all or know it correctly. So instead of telling them about erections, Mom and Dad should ask them what they know about them.

Parents should be matter of fact and pleased to help their sons pick out jock straps. As with their daughters, they should convey to their sons, "Isn't this neat?" when shopping for such personal items. Teens are sensitive, so be careful with the quips. Families handle such issues differently from one another. Some can joke, while some parents or kids would take offense.

As boys develop physically, the fathers may subconsciously feel threatened: There's another buck in the herd. They might be resentful of Mom hugging the boy. It's usually a low-grade, back-of-the-mind kind of irritation. So Dad responds by being more distant or more controlling. And the boy reacts by rebelling and being more demanding in return.

The other problem is that Dad may not give the boy the hugs, the arm around the shoulder, the fun stuff that went on when the son was eight. But even at thirteen, the son is still a little boy inside. His need for affection from both parents hasn't let up.

Teaching Youths About Sex

There's more than one "right way" to teach your teens about sex and growing up, as long as they feel listened to and taken seriously.

As a parent it is important for you to clearly express your own religious and moral values on sexuality. To stay silent is to rob your child of the wisdom you have accumulated.

For example, the instruction related to sexual behavior in the Bible has stood the test of time. In a day when an increasing number of young teens are reaping the serious emotional consequences of premature sexual activity, out of wedlock pregnancies, and AIDS and other sexually transmitted diseases, the Scriptures' advice to save sex for marriage (which is a commitment to lifetime monogamy as much as possible) is extremely relevant, the only "safe sex," and effective.

There is a debate going on in our high schools over "safe sex" programs supporting condom distribution (often called "comprehensive sexuality education") and "abstinence until marriage" programs. We don't pretend to be experts on these issues; however, we can say that sex outside a lifelong monogamous relationship (of which marriage is the best example) is considered by the vast majority of health professionals as a health risk and that the longer sexual activity is put off by our kids the better.

Currently, the most effective program in addressing the AIDS epidemic in the hardest hit sections of Africa is what is called the ABC method, which stands for abstinence, be faithful, and condoms. However, this program works best when the emphasis is primarily on the A and B.

Because of the intense emotions surrounding the hot-button questions of human sexuality, our kids can be left confused and uncertain. A sixteen-year-old with hormones firing at 10:47 on a Saturday night isn't in the best frame of mind to make the right decision about where to draw the line in his or her sexual experimentation, especially if alcohol or drugs are involved.

Parents need to emphasize to their children the seriousness of sex in its nature and consequences. Our language reflects how we take this beautiful, loving gift and turn it upside down: "making love" turns into language reflecting being hurt such as "getting screwed."

You can joke about sex as long as it's clear that you're taking the subject and your teens seriously. It's okay because humor can relieve tension. We also joke about nuclear war sometimes, but we know it's serious.

Most important is maintaining open communication, so our teens don't withdraw from talking about things that are troubling them. If you don't know the answer to a question, tell your children you'll find the answer and get back to them. If they shock you with their comments or questions, remember that they are still "trying on" new ways of thinking and believing. Remain even-tempered, listen, ask questions, and offer alternatives. Ending with a statement such as, "Well, that sure doesn't sound like the healthiest way to see that to me, but I can understand how a teen might see it that way," is acceptable, even though the conversation might have hit every one of your emotional hot buttons.

Part of the difficulty in teaching teens about sex occurs when parents project their own thoughts and values onto their children. Some adults think to themselves, *If I were young again and knew then what I know now, I might have sex.* Then they unfairly assume that their children are out looking for opportunities.

Give teens some room to grow on their own while letting them know that you expect them to be responsible. Instead of giving them the impression that you think they're on the prowl for sex, communicate to them the assumption that they are morally responsible and will live up to your expectations.

Despite what you might think from pop culture, many teens don't rush out and have sex. Responsible teens are still reticent to have sex early. It is good for them to know that this is still healthy and normal. At the time of this writing, the median age of first intercourse is 16.5 years, and by the end of high school, half the teens have not had sex.[10]

Have you ever wondered how much of the considerable sexual activity among high school students is fueled through subtle encouragement from adults? Teen sex appears to have become a self-fulfilling prophecy. Society assumes that teens have sex, so they do have sex—and then society says, "Oh no."

Many teens feel resentful about all the talk about sex, saying, "Why are they talking to me about contraceptives? I don't want to have sex." This kind of emphasis tends to shove teens into it rather than present them with healthy alternatives. The messages we send on this topic must not only be sensitive but clear: "Despite pressures in the opposite direction, saving sex for later in life is a great and responsible decision."

Sex and Teenage Rebellion

Some teens who harbor chronic resentment toward their parents will use sex as a means of rebellion. As their resentment becomes self-destructive, they may think they can vent that resentment through inappropriate sexual activity, tacky friends, and delinquent behavior. Some daughters try to get back at their mothers by getting pregnant, especially if they have been raised in extremely rigid, religious homes. They may go out of their way to find boys who grew up in homes with a different value system. When something like that happens, it's often rebellion.

To thwart rebellious sexual behavior, parents can make it clear to their teens that they mess *themselves* up when they engage in such activity.

Dads should have a discussion with their sons (without implying that their teens are going to have sex) that is sensitive and to the point. In addition to addressing the rights and wrongs of premarital sexual behavior, Dad should make clear that in this day and age it's legally dangerous for a boy to have sex with a girl. If the girl gets pregnant, wants to keep the baby, and marriage for whatever reason is not an option, the legal cards are stacked against the boy (no matter what assurances the girl might have given him about what birth control she was using). He's legally and financially responsible for his child through college. If the girl ends up feeling rejected or is controlling or angry, she can make the boy's life miserable for the next seventeen years.

Another major risk of promiscuous behavior comes from sexually transmitted infections (STIs). There is an astronomical multiplication factor in the infection risk for people who engage in promiscuous sex. When individuals have sex with another person, they virtually have sex with every person that partner had sex with in his or her lifetimes and with all the people *those* partners had sex with, and on and on. A recent study at a Midwestern high school showed that by having sex with one person you were also indirectly having sex with 286 others at the same time. Interesting as well was that the same study "also showed that despite reputations and popularity, most teens in their study did not engage in promiscuous behavior with many others."[11] The risks for diseases such as HIV/AIDS, gonorrhea, syphilis, herpes, hepatitis B, human papillomavirus (HPV), trichomoniasis, and chlamydia multiply with frequent sexual behavior, and the most popular contraceptive, condoms, does not prevent against all of these. STIs have a history of decimating entire cultures.

Male/Female Differences in How Teens View Sex

Guys and girls look at sex in different ways. A girl usually regards sex as being closely related to reproduction. A guy usually considers sex a physical and emotional release.

Both guys and girls should understand that they'll probably feel guilty when they have sex, although girls tend to experience the consequences more intensely than boys.[12] Recent studies indicate that roughly two-thirds or more teens that had sex regret it. One of those studies said that parents are the greatest influence in their children's decisions to have sex or not, greater than either friends or the media. The emotional consequences include not only the risk of getting dumped by the other person but also the possibility that early sexual activity can dull the pleasure and bonding sex adds to marriage. Premature sexual activity is also linked to higher rates of depression and suicide.

Sexual Orientation

Parents are increasingly having to face the issue of sexual orientation, and sweeping it under the rug is not helpful. This book is about open communication. Not bringing it up means that we aren't open and we're being hypocritical. Our impression is that when teens move toward a homosexual orientation, it should not be considered rebellion and is best addressed openly and nonjudgmentally.

Obviously, it's okay to express the desire and hope to our children that they will live a heterosexual life. But if they have a homosexual orientation, we must love them just as much. Christ's message in the New Testament is very clear: God's children are all and equally loved. And just because we accept the lifestyle of our children doesn't necessarily mean we approve of it.

Regardless of your concerns surrounding your child's orientation, it is important to continue the physical contact you extended when the child was younger. Touch is one key to kids feeling loved. Dads should be physically loving toward sons, just as moms should be physically loving toward daughters. If your teen has a homosexual orientation, it doesn't mean you have done anything wrong. Some parents think it's a negative reflection on them. These parents face a growth experience. They have to sort through their feelings to figure out how much is guilt, sorrow, fear, and anger.

There is disagreement on the etiology of homosexuality. Some authorities feel strongly that the orientation is biological. Others feel it has to do with family structure. Still others feel it is a choice. Really, the reason for a person's homosexuality may be less important in the long run than how parents and children openly communicate about the situation and their feelings. Homosexuality may be the ultimate test for many parents of whether they can separate acceptance of their children from approval of their behavior and lifestyle. We can accept a troubling reality and still wish it were different. It is essential for our children to know that we love them no less no matter what.

Discussing Premature Sex and Other Self-Destructive Behaviors

When talking with children about many issues—from sex to a death in the family, from substance abuse to pornography—parents tend to wonder, *What should I say?* Or *What should I tell them?*

Love and Logic parents have a much easier time; we revel in being consultant parents. It's more freeing to simply wonder, *What should I ask?* Thus we allow our children to talk to themselves, often winding up with the children giving themselves advice, and even a lecture.

Again, questions need to be asked with kindness and interest, not with the manner of a lawyer questioning a witness. Consulting parents know that discussing beliefs or attitudes with their teens does not signify approval of those beliefs and attitudes. They know they can show acceptance without approval.

After giving the teen a choice of when they might talk and making sure both are in a good mood, a mother might ask:

- "What are your thoughts on touching and loving a boy you cared about, short of actual intercourse?"
- "What, if anything, do you think might be a problem with going 'all the way' if you love a boy dearly?"
- "How do girls make a decision about how far to go these days?"
- "What are your thoughts about checking for disease and health before ever deciding to go all the way?"

After listening to her adolescent's thoughts, a mother could follow up her ideas by asking, "Can I share some of my thoughts on this with you?" Or "I have some ideas. Would you feel okay about hearing them?" Wise parents know there is an essential difference between an adolescent listening to a parent and an adolescent really attending to parental ideas. If we want others, especially teens, to really pay attention to us, we must make sure they are willing to hear us in the first place.

Let's listen to an actual consultation that a Love and Logic mom had with her fifteen-year-old daughter:

MOM: Honey, I appreciate your point of view. Thanks for sharing it. I have some thoughts. Can I share them with you?

JENNY: Sure, Mom.

MOM: Well, you know those petri dishes in your biology class?

JENNY: Yeah.

MOM: I've always been impressed with how clean, bright, and shiny they look on the outside. They really sparkle on the outside. But wow, the ick that grows on the inside! The scum, the scuz! When I look at folks, I realize that no matter how spiffy they look on the outside, there are a lot of folks who are walking petri dishes. It's just really hard to tell. Those darn venereal diseases have wiped out whole cultures of people. Whole populations. Shoot, the Black Death in the Middle Ages only killed half the people. So many of those sexually transmitted bugs really mean business.

Oh, that reminds me; do you know how the age at which women first have sex affects reproduction?

JENNY: Uh . . . no.

MOM: Well, when young girls have sex early, the darn bugs have a lot more time to gnaw away at the cervix of the uterus; they can make it pretty ragged, you know. Even up inside further. And then, when the woman wants to have a baby later on, what do you think is the problem?

JENNY: The sperm . . . ?

MOM: Yeah, the sperm have a real challenge. When things get a little ragged in there, the sperm have a hard time getting in the door and up the escalator of the fallopian tubes. It gets too crowded with bugs and scar tissue. So fertility clinics are pretty busy helping woman have babies in all sorts of ways because it is so difficult the old-fashioned way.

JENNY: Um . . . (Jenny is definitely paying attention.)

MOM: That reminds me. If you ever did decide to have sex with a boy, do you think you'd have him checked out first? I mean, just to find our what is growing inside him, or do you think you probably wouldn't?

JENNY: I probably wouldn't, Mom.

MOM: I understand. That's the way most people handle it. Why is that, honey?

JENNY: I'd be embarrassed, Mom. What would he think? And I might not even know if I was going to do it when I did it.

MOM: Oh, I understand. You think you would probably do it without thinking about it ahead of time. I do understand.

JENNY: Well, Mom, I'd think about it — probably.

MOM: Great! I was kind of hoping that a person as smart as you wouldn't do something like that on pure impulse. If you and a boy talked it over ahead of time and he wanted you to be checked out first, would you think you'd be mad, or think he was weird, or would you think, *What a wise person. He doesn't want to risk some disease?*

JENNY: I'm not sure. I'd probably think he cared. . . . I guess.

MOM: Well, it's something to think about, dear. Maybe some boy might think you're pretty smart wanting to check him out too. 'Course boys are different. I guess that if I wanted some guy to be checked and he got all bent out of shape about it or wouldn't do it, I'd probably give real thought to how far I wanted to go with the guy. But that's just me.

    I guess most people do have sex these days before they get married. Probably not too many wait, but I'll tell you one thing for sure, darling. It is so very special if, after your wedding you snuggle in with a boy that you know is loving you so special like that for the first time in his life, and he knows that he is first with you. It's just something so special that not many can achieve it. But whatever you do, who is able to figure it all out?

JENNY: Me.

MOM: Right, whatever you decide, I know it will probably work out. And the thing I love about you is that we can talk like this and share thoughts. Thanks, honey.

Some years later, these parents received the following note from an obstetric physician employed at a student health clinic where their daughter had gone for a routine examination:

Dear Dr. and Mrs. _____:

    I have had the opportunity to examine and speak with hundreds of co-eds here at UNC. And you have a remarkable and lovely daughter. I simply have never seen another upper-class girl going with her betrothed for over a year, planning to get married, and yet, never having sex, committed for her marriage night. Your daughter is a lovely, unique person, and I just had to write. Congratulations![13]

Psychological Changes (Changes in Values)

Teens say the darndest things. Sometimes they say *outrageous* things such as, "I don't want to go to your church anymore because I've decided to become a satanist."

Why do they do that? Here are four big reasons:

1. They want to hear what's right. They want their parents to respond and give them the right perspective, and so they try to provoke the correct information.

2. They want interaction and attention. If teens are hungering for some emotion and reasonable comments don't elicit a response, they'll try a different tack. When parents don't express joy and excitement over the right things, teens will seek negative reaction over the wrong things. An apathetic reaction is as bad as an inflexible reaction.

3. They want to make the parent become upset and feel pain because the parent-child relationship isn't good. When teens are in pain, they want their parents to recognize it and feel it too. An outrageous comment can give them the momentary satisfaction they're looking for: "Yes, I got a response; I got my parent to hurt."

4. They're using the conversation to get control. Shocking declarations get parents' attention — reluctantly. Suddenly, the teen is initiating and the parent is reacting. In that moment, the teen is in control; the parent isn't. This gives the teen a feeling of power.

These encounters are evidence of the psychological ferment in the adolescent psyche. As children turn into teenagers, their mental tumblers are falling into place. They can make observations about parents that reveal sharpening psychological insight such as, "Dad, it's hard for you to let go of little things."

Teens are increasingly able to articulate these observations, but not diplomatically. They might make an insightful remark to parents but in a harsh manner.

Parents defeat themselves when they try to thwart their teen's psychological development by saying, "Don't ever say that again." Every time "shut up" is expressed, it's a shutdown of communication, which undermines parental authority.

Basically, teens' psychological development is what happens when their new brainpower interacts with their old values. Coping with this clash of realities takes time and patience on everybody's part. Good communication skills don't unfold in the DNA, but they can be learned. We're always on safe ground when we present our thoughts in a non-threatening manner. Generally, we're on dangerous ground whenever we tell others how to think, how to feel, or what to do.

Let's say Heather comes home from school and tells Mom, "I want to be like the Buddhists, so I'm not going to eat meat anymore."

A typical drill sergeant response to such a comment would be, "Nonsense! I don't want you hanging around those weirdoes at school. Now sit down and eat your dinner." And a typical helicopter response would be, "Oh, honey! Isn't our religion good enough for you?"

In this case, Mom just spent two hours on a mouthwatering prime rib dinner. She should concentrate on her own tastes and desires and say, "Well, that's more beef for Dad and me. I hope it works out for you and us." (After all, Heather could be absolutely right about the vegetarian diet.)

Once again, parental acceptance does not mean approval. The family does not have to make the change with Heather. Mom doesn't go out of her way to cook tofu and soybeans, nor does the rest of the family avoid meat. That would put Heather in negative control of the family. If, in a case like this, you can make everybody happy and cook vegetarian, then great.

When Values Become Self-Destructive

Not all teen psychological development issues involve outrageous comments or flirtations with values that are in one week and out the next. Some choices in values are destructive and can threaten a teen's personality or slow down his or her development for a number of years.

For example, Todd wanted to join a rigid, authoritarian religious sect. The sect was known for financially fleecing its members and splitting young people from their families. Todd's parents sent him to live with his grandparents for a while. Todd was a fairly healthy child who wanted to do something unhealthy, so his parents got him out of the environment.

If we feel our teens are going to do something that will mess up their life for a long time to come, it's our responsibility to protect them.

But that responsibility carries an inherent danger: If we aren't careful, our fears could override our judgment in making this sort of decision.

Parents must weigh the possible benefits of forced protection against the rebellion that it inevitably engenders. Thus, forced protection is always a judgment call, and as with all judgment calls, the wisdom of the decision can be seen only in retrospect.

Whether or not forcing a teen into a treatment environment is wise often depends on the expertise of the staff at the treatment center. Whether or not forcing a teen to live with grandparents is wise often depends on the grandparents' wisdom in handling the child and balancing that against their own needs.

In an analogous example, when a spouse forces a spouse into an alcoholic treatment center, the result is either beneficial due to treatment center expertise or backfires with increased spouse resentment if the treatment is unsuccessful. There are no cut-and-dried answers in such situations.

Dealing with Rebellion

The physical, cognitive, and psychological changes ripping through Alex and Heather and all the other kids in the neighborhood converge to produce what is known as adolescent rebellion. As we've pointed out, rebellion is one way teens announce to themselves and others, "I am not my parent."

If teens have been given choices and a reasonable amount of control from years one through eleven, they have already established a healthy base of an identity independent of their parents. Kids raised this way often don't go through a rebellious phase at all.

The poor teens who have been raised in a drill sergeant environment—where Dad barked orders and kids obeyed—know only how to listen to an outside voice. They've never learned anything else. Children of helicopter parents aren't much better off, because their parents have protected them out of a warped understanding of love.

If the drill sergeant pattern has been predominant, Mom and Dad had better watch out when Joey gets into the eighth grade. As soon as he starts thinking abstractly, he switches from listening to his parents to listening to his peer group. Joey hasn't changed; he's still listening to a voice outside his head. But now somebody else is handing out instructions, and Joey's not thinking for himself.

But here's some good news for the drill sergeant and helicopter parents, which many of us tend to be because we were raised that way. Actually, there's good news and bad news. The good news is that if you got along well with your child from birth through age eleven, you have pretty good grounds for telling yourself, "It'll all work out all right in the long run." Even if your child turns hard-core rebellious, if life was basically fine through age eleven you can take heart that things will turn out all right.

The bad news is that the long run may be a *very* long run. Some of these teens don't get through those rebellious years until they're around thirty.

Rebellion — Harmless or Destructive?

Consultant parents already know — and drill sergeant parents can learn — that a lot of adolescent "rebellion" is not self-destructive. Expressions such as haircuts or clothing styles and tattoos are really quite safe, however weird or threatening they may seem to parents. In recent years, teens have taken to having their ears, tongues, noses, and other parts of their bodies pierced, and parents have once again been forced to learn how to cope with a new fashion.

Let's say college freshman Matt comes home and surprises his parents with an earring stuck in his left ear. His mom has a range of responses to choose from:

- "YOU GET THAT THING OUT OF YOUR EAR RIGHT NOW BEFORE YOUR FATHER COMES HOME! WE DIDN'T RAISE OUR SON TO BE A HOMOSEXUAL!"
- "Matt, why did you do this to us? Don't you love us?"
- "Well, son, I'm sure it didn't cost as much as when you got that pink Mohawk."
- "What a lovely thing; maybe I ought to get one for myself."
- "My male friends aren't into earrings, but I'm sure you know what's best for you."

Love and Logic parents realize that although Matt may be trying to impress or shock his parents, more than likely he's just doing what his frat brothers are doing. These parents realize that most teens who do apparently "rebellious" things don't try to push them on others. Matt is not about to suggest, "Let's get Grandpa to pierce his ear."

When teens rebel in an isolated area but are generally responsible in other areas of their life, then it's okay for parents to acknowledge the behavior while not approving it. They can say to their teen, "This is my thought on it."

If rebellious activity is self-destructive, however, then it's not okay simply to accept the behavior. For example, if teens are abusing drugs or hanging out with a friend who's been ripping off cars, then a parent should *neither approve nor accept* such activity. Parents can't control their teens in these activities, but they can say, "I don't want to see you with that friend around me," or "I don't want to see that cigarette dangling from your mouth."

Resist the Urge to Control
When your teen's rebellion gets in your face, resist the urge to control; switch to what *you're* going to do. If your teen wears an earring to get your goat, you can say calmly "not around me." In this way, you throw the consequence back on your teen while you take care of yourself.

If we come across as trying to control our children, it can injure our relationship with them. It's important that we recognize the potential resentment we may provoke with demands such as, "You're not going to do that around me!" Such comments put stress on the relationship, often with negative results. As we decide whether to overlook or actively oppose rebellious behavior, we must weigh the potential destructiveness of that behavior against the damage we might do to our relationship with our teen by opposing it.

Let Them Go and Let Them Grow

We can help ourselves and our teens by understanding them from the inside out, recognizing and responding appropriately to the internal changes they all go through.

In general, despite the bewildering barrage of adolescent cognitive, physical, and psychological changes, and the rebellion that goes along with them, things are going to turn out okay. Children on the road to independence still want acceptance, even if they don't get approval. Teens generally don't ask for across-the-board approval, but they do need the deep assurance of being accepted for who they are, regardless of what they wear, what they do and who they do it with, or what they believe.

Parents who lean toward the drill sergeant mode in their need to control might be able to keep their teens from bolting out of the family's value system. But sadly, this can bear bitter fruit in later years as their children's marriages, families, and jobs disintegrate under pressure from a mid-life crisis because they never learned to evaluate their values critically when they were younger.

If there's going to be a hard and critical look at values, better to have it occur now in adolescence than midway through life. Later it will often mean a change of job, a change of spouse, and a rejection of the parenting role. As we're fond of saying, "It's always cheapest to pay for a mistake today; tomorrow the cost goes up."

Parents, take a deep breath and trust that you have given your children what they needed in the first eleven years. Let go of your attempt to hold on to control (which you can't really keep anyway) and say to yourself, "My children are going to do things I don't approve of, but I accept them. I'm going to love my children on the faith that they know what they're doing. I may not like it, but I know that my children will have to live their own life."

(Teens themselves can help foster communication when they ask their parents what life was like for *them* as adolescents. This kind of exchange can have healthy results in greater understanding and respect between children and parents. And they just might learn something from each other too.)

Keep in mind that your adolescent is going through a phase. But so are you; being a parent of an adolescent is also a transitional period. You're not the only one so worried about your teen, although it may feel that way sometimes. Relax and ride the changes through. Sure, it may be a wild ride, but it can be a wonderful one too.

7

Understanding Teens from the Outside In: External Changes in Adolescence

Kids grow up. They become parents. Their kids grow up and *they* become parents. On it goes.

So parenting should be simple, right? Just do what your folks did. Well, that would work great if we still lived in the same era our parents lived in.

When Craig was growing up, the most complex piece of electronics his family owned was a television. He saw his father snap pencils in half as he struggled to fill out IRS forms. And Craig was forever wishing his mother would put all her recipes in one place instead of frantically rummaging through the kitchen for a missing index card when she was halfway through cooking dinner.

Craig pursued a career and started a family of his own. His wife, Cindy, had a full-time job. But the more they tried to get ahead, the more they seemed to slip behind.

So Craig bought a computer with programs for filing recipes, tracking automobile repairs, and completing tax forms. The more he found it could do, the more he did. Paradoxically, the computer made family life busier at the same time that it made family life easier.

The kids, fifteen-year-old Krystal and thirteen-year-old Seth, found that the family computer could make their lives easier too. It sped up their homework. And it offered all kinds of games they could play, which started becoming an obsession each time they turned on the machine.

They also discovered the Internet, which was again both a help and a drain.

Times of study and recreation quickly degenerated into screaming matches between Krystal and Seth. During one heated argument, Seth knocked over a glass and spilled soft drink into the hard drive. They lost not only the game, but everything else stored on the hard drive as well.

Craig—who was staring at the April 15 tax deadline—lost it too. "We didn't have computer games when I was your age!" he yelled at Krystal and Seth. "Now look what you've done!" Craig didn't understand that the same tool that made life easier could also make life more complicated.

That's how many of us approach technology. We appreciate what it can do for us, but we're not aware of its liabilities. We know it's changing our world, but we're not sure how and where it's taking us.

This uncertainty in facing the unknown illustrates well the challenge of parenting in today's turbulent world. We can't just reach into the past and grab the tools we need for the present. In many ways, it's a brand-new world out there.

Understanding our teens from the inside out gives us a foundation of knowing their special needs. But in order to identify how to wield appropriate parenting tools to meet those needs, we must understand our teens from the *outside in*.

The Pressure of Social Change

The technological revolution isn't the only social force pressuring us to forge a new set of tools for parenting teenagers. We've also experienced a revolution in human rights. Our collective social conscience now acknowledges that it's wrong to discriminate against people based on their age, race, religion, nationality, sexual orientation, or gender. Groups have sprung up to champion children's rights, many of which are very important. There's no going back to the "good old days," which often weren't really all that good anyway.

We've felt the pressure of social change—if not revolution—in other areas as well:

- *Relationships.* We no longer know our teens' friends the way our parents knew ours. Yet those friends have more influence on our children than our friends did on us a generation ago. Our teens need more ways to evaluate critically what others are telling them.
- *Media.* The "tube" was a fascinating curiosity for our parents' or grandparents' generation. Now it's a permanent fixture in daily life. Teens spend more time glued to the screen than they spend in the classroom, not to mention doing schoolwork. And video games—television's faithful sidekick—can quickly turn from a hobby into an obsession.
- *Trends.* Trends are even trendier now than when we were scrambling to keep up. Many fads are harmless, such as clothing or hairstyles that, oddly enough, are the same styles many of us had in high school (well, at least leisure suits didn't come back). Other trends, such as technological advances, occur with such dizzying frequency that they're disorienting. Still other trends, such as the sexual revolution, have had widespread and harmful effects.
- *Consumerism.* Peer pressure can terrify teens into demanding that their parents buy them high-priced sneakers, 250-dollar handheld electronics, and game systems with games at outrageous prices, or at least give them enough allowance so they can buy them on their own. Advertising teases kids with the myth that personal satisfaction is just a purchase away.
- *Divorce.* One out of two marriages ends in divorce. Guess who gets caught in the middle?
- *Rising violence.* As our society becomes increasingly violent, that violence is reflected in and acted out in our homes and schools. Children carry those scars for a lifetime and are dangerously prone to inflicting their pain on their children.

These and other changes have forced us into reevaluating what effective parenting is all about. We've been shocked into the awareness that we need new styles for teaching teens how to think and prepare for the future.

couple of generations ago, a young person could expect to spend a lifetime in one career, if not in one job. Gender usually determined vocation: he dug the coal, smelted the ore, designed the bridges. She taught the classes, styled the (women's) hair, did the homemaking. But the world is changing so fast that we can't prepare teens for lifelong occupations. Our kids will need to retrain themselves over and over as new developments force some occupations into obsolescence and bring new ones into existence.

We can prepare teens for the future by teaching them how to think, how to respond to the stressful influences they face, and how to make their own decisions and live with the consequences.

Different Circumstances, Same Needs

Although circumstances change, teens' needs stay remarkably constant from generation to generation. Before we take a closer look at the pressures from social forces, let's examine teens' fundamental needs in relation to the external changes they experience. Teens today, just like teens a generation or a century ago, have the same three basic needs for *control*, *affection*, and *inclusion*.

The Need to Feel in Control
All of us have a strong need to know we're in control of our lives. Without that assurance, we get anxious. So we will naturally do what it takes to restore the comfort of having a sense of power over our circumstances. Until we obtain that sense of control, we will remain in some kind of a battle to get it. Teens are no different from corporate vice presidents in this.

Recall that in chapter 4 we described the Love and Logic approach to parental control: "Don't be greedy. Never take any more control than you absolutely need to have." The most effective parents surrender control thoughtfully by offering choices.

Car dealers have this down to a science. They know that a car dealership selling only cars soon will go out of business. Dealers who stay in business also sell *control* to their customers. They ask, "Do you want automatic or standard? Do you want a four-door or a hatchback? Do you want two- or four-wheel drive? Do you want that with a CD player, a DVD entertainment system, or GPS tracking and hands-free calling?" With every question, with every response, the dealer is sharing control with the buyer. This gives the buyer a feeling of power, so the buyer doesn't feel shut out of the deal. Car dealers know how to meet this need on their own terms.

Parents, however, often behave just the opposite of car dealers. They refuse to share control and power with their teens, especially in battles they can't win anyway. The more control they retain, the more frustrated they get. Their teens, who have no control, are even more frustrated, and that's when they get revenge.

For example, it's disastrous to have a power struggle over an issue like grades. Teens' basic need for control will kick in all too easily. They can't win when their parents are crabbing about that D and vaguely threatening them to shape up "or else." They feel powerless. Therefore, just to show that they have power, they'll get bad grades to win the struggle.

Wise parents don't get mad and spark control battles. Instead they shower teens with sadness over a bad grade. Teens will then seek control through other channels, rather than through fighting with parents. Instead of "I'll show them," it becomes, "What am I going to do about this grade?" This way, they must take control over their own studying.

The Need for Affection

We all need the assurance that other people care for us. When we don't get it, we may act in strange ways. Any office manager can tell you stories about what happens when a new guy comes in and gets more attention from management than the supervisor who's been there five years. The old hand acts hostile and throws petty barbs. He complains about a lot of little things. Lines are drawn between old and new, and "office politics" take over.

Teens are no different from supervisors. In the classroom or on the team, teens who are assured of the teacher's or coach's care will take risks they would never endure for anyone else. On the other hand, teens who do not feel they're receiving affection will not do their work and will probably engage in antisocial behavior.

The Need to Feel Included

None of us wants to feel like an outsider. This is especially true of teens. They want to know they're an important part of the family, the committee, the peer group. When they feel they're not accepted they will respond, "I want to go where I'm appreciated, where I'm included, where I'm an important member, where I have some control in what goes on."

But there's a paradox for teenagers in their quest for inclusion. On one hand, they want to be included as part of the family. On the other, they want to be independent, which means they do things that seem strange, if not hostile, to the family.

Simultaneous with their need for inclusion, teens will invariably do things to declare independence:

- get a radical haircut, tattoo, or body piercing
- announce, "I'm not having Thanksgiving here; I'm having it at my girlfriend's house"
- hang out at the mall with friends
- abuse sex or drugs

In turn, the parents react, which to the teen feels like rejection, whether it actually is rejection or not. At that moment, the teen feels loss of control, withdrawal of affection, and exclusion instead of inclusion.

To make matters worse, when the teen displays his or her unhappiness and bitterness because these needs are threatened, the *parents* feel that they're losing control, affection, and inclusion. Now we're into a destructive cycle.

What's Different Today

If these needs have remained constant through generations, then what's different about today?

One of the biggest shifts took place with the advent of the teen culture of the 1950s. Ever since, teenagers have had an expanding array of options for declaring independence. All those options, to a lesser or greater degree, appear scary to the adults, who may react in a rejecting way.

In the high school Jim attended in the 1950s, there were three thousand students. In those three years of high school, he saw only two kids drunk. Everyone who saw those two was repulsed and embarrassed. These days, many teens drink just to get drunk. Times have changed.

Teens express their independence today in ways that are very different from those their parents used. Each generation of parents must wrestle afresh with a whole new set of behaviors, values, and temptations teens throw at them in their pursuit of independence. No doubt these trends and fads will continue to have shock value. The trick is how parents deal with things they least expect.

Pressures from Outside the Home

We won't dwell on relatively harmless trends in pop culture, because they come and go so quickly. Instead we'll explore the more significant external influences that can have profound impacts on how parents guide their children through adolescence. Following are a few that parents especially need to be aware of.

Changing Relationships

Parents often say, "My teen has changed so much. He used to listen to me, but he doesn't anymore. He only listens to his friends now."

That teen hasn't grown into a different person. He's still the same child he always was. But he's just gone through eleven or twelve years of listening to his parents. Now he's trying to figure out who he is. It seems to him that he's not going to solve that struggle unless he quits listening to the parental voice. The handiest substitute is the voice of his peers.

As we discussed in chapter 6, kids switch from concrete to abstract thinking at the time they enter adolescence. When that shift occurs, the budding teenager realizes, "I can think for myself."

How do we teach teens to think for themselves instead of listening to their peers? Starting as early in life as possible, by saying to them, "You have to decide." In other words, we train them to listen to a quiet voice inside their heads, saying, "I have to decide that. If I make a good decision, it's going to feel good; if I make a bad decision, it's going to feel rotten."

So when your teen comes in and says, "Well, my friend thinks this, this, and this," you can say, "Thanks for sharing. That's an interesting way to look at it. I wonder where she picked that up. What do you think?"

But too often we tend to react in the opposite way: "Gee, where does she get off thinking like that? That's crazy. What's the matter with her?" And that's scary to our own teens because they think, "Wow, if my parents criticize my friend, what'll they do to me?" Pretty soon they won't want to talk to you.

The Consumerism Crunch

"Mom, can I have . . . ?" How many times have you heard that? Too many, right?

And of course, if you buy it for your teen, it's never quite good enough. His or her friends always seem to have a better model, a flashier color, a more recent edition.

If you feel that you just can't win when you cave in to your teen's demands for more stuff, you're on to something: you *can't* win. The "best" is always about two feet—or twenty dollars, or two hundred dollars—out of reach. Out of *your* reach.

Instead of indulging their teens' whims for more and better, Love and Logic parents do what they do in so many other areas of life: throw the issue back to the teen, the way real life always does.

Teenage consumers always seem to want the best. How can parents sidestep the consumerism crunch and let their teens handle the pressure instead? We suggest this rule: *No matter how affluent they may be, parents should never get their kids the best of anything.* Parents should let their teens know that they deserve the best, but they should always require their teens to pay the difference between" average" and "best," just as in real life.

When your teen tells you he wants an expensive item, say to him, "Buy it." And your teen, of course, will answer, "But I can't afford it." And then you say, "Well, you're resourceful. If you want it I'm sure you can find a way to afford it."

Simultaneous with this kind of response we should be teaching our children that the real values in life center on love for people, not the acquisition of things. That love must be extended to all, regardless of social or economic status. And that love must override pressures — from peers or advertising — to consume more things.

However, parents sometimes send decidedly mixed messages on this when they don't walk their talk. If they're driving a car that costs a lot more than a college education, they're wasting their time telling teens to resist peer pressure.

But even if your values are in place, it won't soften the vicious sting of peer pressure your children may feel when they aren't wearing the newest and hippest clothes. Regrettably, in some of our upscale communities all the teenagers have the very best. And for all the alleged refinement of those communities, teens can be mean and shove their affluence down the throats of their peers.

Some of that arrogant affluence gets downright ridiculous. The most outrageous example of conspicuous consumption we've come across lately is teens who leave price tags hanging out of their clothes so other kids can see how much they're worth.

We need to be careful in how we teach our teens proper values and a sober attitude toward possessions. We can set our kids up for problems if we buy them unfashionable clothes that make them look "weird" in the eyes of their peers. But that doesn't mean we have to go out and buy the best of the best. Let's use common sense.

Here's a sample conversation showing how a Love and Logic parent might handle a discussion about possessions:

"Mom," says Randy, "all the kids now are wearing Super Hi-Flight Pump-Up Get-Down sneakers."

Mom low-keys it. "That's nice, dear."

"So when are you going to get me a pair? Can we go now? All the kids have them."

"*All* the kids, dear?"

"Well, not all — the dorks and nerds of course don't have them. But the parents of the cool kids get them the Super Hi-Flight Pump-Up Get-Down sneakers."

"And how much did they pay for those sneakers, Randy?"

"They cost a hundred and thirty dollars. For five bucks more you can get the day-glow laces too."

Mom, of course, freezes inwardly in her financial tracks. But she keeps her cool. "Well, dear, you know that we want the best for you, but we can't afford them. We believe that you're smart and can work hard enough so if we give you the money for the sneakers we usually buy, you can earn the difference. Then you'll have the sneakers you want."

Randy, of course, is highly displeased with this answer. So he pushes the ultimate parent guilt button: "Mom, don't you love me?"

Mom doesn't fall for it. "Of course I do, dear. That's why we buy you average good sneakers and allow you to earn the money to get better ones if you wish." Mom doesn't let on that she thinks the other parents are pushovers. Instead she lets Randy know what her value system is without putting others down.

"But Mom," Randy tries one last time, "what am I going to tell the other kids if I can't get the sneakers?"

Mom closes with an alternative: "Well, honey, you could tell them that you'd rather use the extra money for something else."

The more responsible our teens are, the more say-so we can allow them in what they wear. But if they want to wear outlandish clothing or a green Mohawk, it's on their nickel.

Our teens may object to our approach and protest, "Well, your value system stinks." We can reply, "Fine. That is my value system, and it's what allowed me to earn my money. So if you want to wear your green Mohawk, fine — go earn the money on *your* value system."

The Media Blitz

The media blitz is all around us — wide-angle, narrow-angle, pan right, pan left, up, down. Images flash before us: youth, sex, beauty, sex, conspicuous consumption, sex, music, sex, emotion, sex. And if that isn't fast enough we can jump channels: click, click, click.

We live in a visual-media culture — don't blink, you'll miss the next image. The changes are happening not only *around* us, but also *to* us. Some are good, some are bad, but we need to be aware of them.

Before the current electronic and information revolutions, children had to read, and their minds would work faster than what was on that page. Their minds were compelled to visualize what they were reading. The same thing happened with radio. Broadcasters and radio actors told stories and read the news. Listeners used their imagination to form mental pictures.

Television dramatically changed that. The camera does the imaging in astonishingly rapid succession. The mind doesn't have time to imagine, and it doesn't have to. The camera does all the work.

Teens in our television culture are conditioned to be passive while a machine does their mental work for them. If an activity involves thinking, perseverance, tedium, or patience, they call it "b-o-o-oring."

True, the proliferation of technological and media wizardry has brought tremendous benefit. We can see our world, literally, as never before. We can understand more of what's happening in it, and we can communicate with space-age speed and accuracy.

But these benefits have come embedded in a barrage of information and images. The blitz is not slowing down. And it's bringing with it plenty that is *not* of benefit. Battles are raging over what kids are exposed to in network and cable TV programming. It didn't used to be that network television would tell us, "Viewer discretion is advised"; everything was safe for children and families to watch. But this new trend suggests that the more discretion we have, the less we will be watching TV.

In a highly technical world, relationships are often the first things to drop out. A few very wise and gutsy parents ditch the TV entirely, but most parents are bonded to the TV from their own formative years. And even if there is no screen in the home, teens will be barraged from other sources. But we can maintain the sanity and solidity of relationships in the family. We can make it a point to create family time in which we can talk to each other without the background buzz of the screen. We can do more reading, setting an example for our teens. We can express excitement about what we're learning and how we're learning it. We can ask our teens what they see in their movies and on the Internet, and we can discuss the lyrics and music of the songs they listen to. Reading and discussion also meet the basic needs of control, affection, and inclusion.

Riding the Waves of Trends

Remember the Lambada, the hot dance craze of '88 and '89? It was sexy, it was fast, it was daring—and *it is history*.

Pop culture can be very alluring. Trends and fads tend to spice things up. Kids are especially attracted to them because they temporarily fill needs for control, affection, and inclusion. They offer a quick fix for expressing independence and winning approval and acceptance from peers.

Most of what teens do to demonstrate their independence will soon be replaced by something else. The streaking fad popular on college campuses in the early seventies died out because people quit looking at it. If you're independent, and no one is noticing, what's the point?

If nobody seems to notice your purple hair or Goth-black Matrix look, you find another way to show your independence. This quest for independence has gone on in all cultures at all times. Parents shouldn't worry about fads and trends that really are harmless.

Some trends, however, have much more serious and long-term effects, such as eighth-graders packing pistols and the rising incidence of early sexual activity. The fifties, sixties, and seventies ushered in a wave of increasing sexual activity among children in their upper teens. In the eighties and nineties, this wave reached down to children in their lower teens and below. Now we face a trend where teen pregnancy is down, but STIs continue to skyrocket. Why? Kids are experimenting with oral and anal intercourse because of what they learn in movies and through the media, and they think they are still virgins. There's a trickle-down effect as teens engage in more adult behavior at increasingly younger ages.

As our culture absorbs things that are faddish or even shocking, we tend to relax our tolerance. In the early 1960s, when people first saw the movie *Psycho*, the shower scene shocked Jim so much that he couldn't sleep well for a month. Today people hardly even think of that scene as scary; we have been so desensitized by what's happened in our culture that the horrible image of a woman getting stabbed to death in a shower doesn't really bother us much.

The magic of Love and Logic parenting is that teens raised with this parenting style express their independence through responsible decision-making. This expression satisfies their need for control, earns them respect and affection, and includes them as equal members of the family.

Love and Logic teens are normal kids. Sure, they'll probably pick up on trends as quickly as the next kid, but they're not driven to socially deviant behavior in order to demonstrate that they're individuals. (When teens do adopt such deviant behaviors, however, we should let the full weight of the law come down on them, just as the law would come down on us.)

Pressures from Inside the Home

Life After Divorce

The effects of divorce on teens have been widely chronicled, and we don't pretend to offer a deep analysis here. We will, however, give some Love and Logic tips for divorced parents.

Single parents have an especially tough time of raising children. Children tend to do better when double-teamed most of their lives. Those from single-parent homes have particular needs for love and acceptance, especially when they reach their teenage years. However, they also know that because they have one less parent to deal with, they have the opportunity to seize control of the family situation — and cause a lot of damage in the process.

We offer the following thoughts for single parents to keep in mind as they raise teenagers:

First, make time for yourself, then make time for your kids. If you burn out, you'll have nothing left to give to your children. Schedule time for yourself alone as well as with them. If it helps, think of these times as dates. Then make them a priority.

Second, don't speak negatively about the opposite sex. Just because your children are growing up in a single-parent home doesn't mean they're doomed to troubled relationships later in life. Single moms, your attitudes toward men will heavily influence what kind of man your son will be or how your daughter will regard men. The converse goes for single dads.

Third, separate what you can control from what you can't and then learn to live with both. You can work on what you can control. For what you can't, tell yourself, "I don't like it, but I can't control it."

For example, all parents — including single parents — are in control of their gifts of love, their smile, their touch, and their joy at their teens' achievements. Parents are also in control of their own reactions when their children are disrespectful or experience life's difficulties. Controlling things that go on outside the parental skin, however, is much more difficult. In the long run it is best to adjust your attitudes to put up with it rather than trying to change something that's out of your control.

Single parents who remarry have another parent in the family. Serious problems can occur when parents want to do the right thing but don't know how to resolve the tensions between their new spouse and the children. In a stepparenting situation, everyone feels caught in the middle. The tension experienced by stepchildren is so weighty that fairy tales are filled with it.

In such families, parent and stepparent must make very clear to the children that the couple's relationship is primary. When a parent remarries and the family becomes "blended," the most common problem in the reconstituted family is *triangulation*. This means that everybody feels caught in the middle. If the mother is the birth parent, she feels caught between her own children and her new spouse. Her husband feels caught between the wife he loves and her obnoxious children. And, of course, the children feel caught between their mom and the stepdad, or dad and the stepmom. They may initially feel less loved and, more significantly, less respected.

The key to the triangulated situation lies with the response of the birth parent. The birth parent must make it absolutely clear to the children that her allegiance and love lies with her new husband—the person she will be spending the rest of her life with. Unfortunately, it is sometimes true that the children, consciously or unconsciously, wish things were back the way they were before Mom remarried and may want to have their birth parent all to themselves. At this point, it is a wise birth parent who lets the children know, unequivocally, that, should family problems escalate, if anyone were to go, it would *not* be the new spouse.

A good relationship between child and stepparent is healthy and worth striving for. But when disputes arise, the birth parent must unequivocally back up the stepparent as an authority in the home. The birth parent must not take the child's side in arguments with the stepparent and validate the child's anger. The birth parent must make an important judgment before remarrying: If I think the person I'm going to marry isn't going to be a good authority figure for my children, I shouldn't marry that person. And if the birth parent is not going to play the role of his or her child's primary authority figure, the situation is doomed from the start. We have seen too many instances in which the birth parent suddenly turns the responsibility of discipline to the new spouse, only to discover that it creates a war.

Breaking the Cycle of Violence

Our society is becoming more violent, partly because more children are experiencing more violence earlier in their lives. Often we can't directly control or change many of the causes of youth violence—such as easy access to weapons—but we can control how we parent our children.

Poor early parenting often starts a cycle of neglect, rebellion, and irresponsibility in children who grow older without growing up. These children haven't learned to live with the consequences of their wrong decisions. When they in turn have children themselves, poor early parenting is repeated in succeeding generations until someone breaks the cycle.

When people have not had the opportunity to learn how to make decisions and live with the consequences, they don't know how to cope responsibly with difficult problems, especially related to child-raising. Instead of thinking clearly, they lash out in anger. Instead of reasoning with their teens, they revert to a harsh drill sergeant style of parenting. When their children make mistakes, they turn to physical abuse.

Teens who grow up in such families learn no other way to deal with their frustration—or, in the future, with their childrens' frustrations. Yet all along, these children, and especially teenagers, caught in this cycle often know in their hearts that these family dynamics are wrong.

Many parents find themselves getting angrier and more frustrated than they know they should be. For those who recognize inappropriate anger and desire to change, here are three suggestions for dealing with it:

1. Be open about your problem with other family members and with those in your community who can help. Covering up domestic violence only increases the shame parents feel, exacerbating the cycle. Many churches, community centers, and social service agencies have support groups to help parents who are caught in this cycle of violence.

Parents and teenagers caught in the web of domestic violence should not hesitate to seek help from professional counselors.

2. Get ideas, tools, and techniques from other individuals and support groups who can help you with your problem. For example, one such technique is, if you're so mad that you don't know what to say, don't say anything until you've cooled off.

If you lose control and yell at your teen, by definition you have just given control to your teen because you've lost it. That's not good for either of you. If you're angry but you stop to think it over and then decide to say something, keep your voice down. This is good for you and your teen.

Once you can control your own emotions, you're in a good position to help others control theirs.

3. Commit yourself to working toward the necessary internal change that will give you the discipline to apply techniques for controlling your anger. This inner desire is the true starting point for breaking the cycle of violence. Techniques are helpful when they're built on the inner determination and discipline to resist violent behavior.

This internal change takes place with prayerful meditation on the recognition that you do have the resources to change. Focus on the anticipation of improving, not on the defeat of repeating the pattern. Instead of saying, "Oh, Lord, grant me more patience with Jennifer," which zeros in on what you *don't* have, say, "Lord, thanks for those three seconds I had patience with Jennifer," which builds on what you *do* have. Over time, that three seconds can grow to three minutes, and then to three hours.

Save Your Emotional Energy

We've outlined only a few of the external influences on family life that affect teenagers. No book can cover them all. And even if it did, it would immediately be obsolete because of the rapid developments in technology, trends, and social ills. We don't have much control over what goes on outside our influence, but we can control and love our own corner of the world. That means we have some decisions to make about the energy we have.

Each of us has only so much emotional energy. Imagine an emotional "energy pie," the whole pie representing 100 percent of our emotional energy. If I spend 80 percent of my emotional energy focusing on what's wrong with the world and complaining that nobody's doing anything about it, I have only 20 percent of my energy left for my teenagers.

However, if I spend 10 percent of my energy observing how the world is changing and another 10 percent in legitimate efforts to change it, I can direct up to 80 percent to help mold the future of my teens.

Each of us needs to make a conscious decision about how we will divide our emotional pie. Love and Logic parents spend the majority of their energy on the family.

You and your children will outlast any hairstyles and dance crazes. You will witness profound changes in technology and politics. Devote yourself to what is of greatest and lasting importance: strengthening your most intimate contacts with spouse, parents, and children. You and your family will not only survive the pressure of external forces, but you may even have opportunity to shape those forces as well.

8

Ready, Set — Off into the Real World

S ooner than you think, your teenager will walk out of your life and into the real world. It's normal to feel that you're losing control as your teen gets older. That's the idea. You're not supposed to have that kind of control anymore, they are.

Parenting is all about raising a child who is thoughtful, capable, and loving, able to go out in the world and make it. Whatever you can give your teens to help them reach that point is what counts. The "Thank you" and "What a great parent you were" and "Oh, how I'll always love you!" are, quite frankly, frosting on the cake of life.

As a Love and Logic parent, you're cultivating relationships with your children in which there's room to negotiate. You're developing a friendship with your teen in which you can speak to him or her as a young adult: "How can we help each other through these tough times? How do we get you ready to live in that real world out there so that you've had enough practice and there are no big surprises when you get there?"

But just as you say that, another practice opportunity comes along. Your son Adam wants to borrow a hundred bucks from you.

You know that the real world doesn't hand out C-notes.

So you say, "Sure, I'll loan you a hundred dollars. No problem. What do you have for collateral?"

"Collateral?" Adam asks. "What's that?"

"Well, Adam, that's something of yours I hold on to so that if you don't pay me back by the end of the month, it's no big deal because I can sell your property."

"Why, I don't—I don't have anything like that."

"Sure you do," you reply matter-of-factly. "You have your stereo or your skis."

"You mean you'd sell *those*?" Adam asks fearfully.

"Well, not if you paid back the loan by the time we agreed on. That's the way the bank deals with me. Otherwise, sure I'd sell the stereo. Or I could donate it to charity and get a tax write-off. It's no big deal. And then you won't owe me a thing, see? And we'll both be happy."

Adam balks. "Uh, maybe I don't really need the loan after all."

Welcome to the Real World

"Welcome to the real world," you were telling Adam. That was a loving thing to do. Easy money with no strings attached is not what the real world offers to us. Love is a beautiful and lovely thing, but it can mess things up when it's wrongly applied as unrealistic protection.

To introduce our kids to the real world, we have to observe what happens there. In the real world where we all live, why do we get our chores done? Why do we do our work? Yes! Because we get paid. Why do we like getting paid? Because we like eating and having a roof over our heads.

Adam will find this out firsthand when he gets his own apartment or moves in with friends in college or after graduation. What are the rules there? Only the rules that he makes, right?

If you want Adam to be independent, does that mean you give him total run of the house? Can he go anywhere he wants to without your knowing where he is or when he's coming home? Can he freely disregard the rest of the family's rights? Of course not.

Adam, like most teens his age, has young, healthy eardrums. He likes his music loud. He likes to blast his stereo through the house so that the walls shake. It's more exciting than just wearing the earphones.

So you say, "Hey, Adam, I don't like the music this loud in the house."

Adam retorts, "Well, you know, it's my house too!"

You reply with real-world wisdom, "Check the mortgage, Adam, and look at who signed it. This is *my* house. When you grow up, you'll have your own house. Then you can listen to the music *you* want; your name will be on that mortgage, not mine. But right now, this is my house."

From this exchange, Adam learns that he has responsibilities toward other family members as long as he lives at home and will have rights of his own when he buys his own house.

Techniques for World-Wise Teens

It's never too late to start changing your parenting techniques, even if you've been a helicopter parent hovering over your teen with overprotective love, a drill sergeant parent mandating top-down authoritarianism, or a disengaged laissez-faire parent. The following practical suggestions are things you can work on together with your teens to prepare them for the final years in your house—and for the real world.

Three Rules for Teenagers
We suggest that you set out these three rules for your teenager to follow:

> *Rule 1.* Treat me with the same respect you gave me when you were in elementary school. In other words, I expect respect.
> *Rule 2.* I expect you to do your chores around the house.
> *Rule 3.* If you have average intelligence, you need to get overall average grades in school. That means that if you don't do well in chemistry and algebra, you can pull up your average to achieve the appropriate grade point by doing well in other courses that are not so difficult.

Three Messages for Teenagers
Those three rules are backed by three messages you should give your teens:

> *Message 1.* I love you.
> *Message 2.* If you have any questions, ask.
> *Message 3.* Good luck in life.

That good-luck message has tremendous power to it. It actually empowers your teens by letting them know that they have the responsibility to solve their own problems. It says, "Well, that's your problem. It's not my problem." The sweet way to say "That's your problem" is to wish the teen "Good luck with that."

Let's say Jessica has been slacking off in her eighth-grade studies, and her teachers have been talking about holding her back for a year.

You comment, "Jessica, the way you study, I've been thinking about how you're going to get pretty familiar with the eighth grade. And honey, I just want to take this opportunity to wish you luck."

"Oh," Jessica moans. She feels how scary it is for her parent to just come up and wish her luck, because now she realizes that she has to do something about it.

If parents worry and agitate about something, by definition their child doesn't have to.

Four Steps to Responsibility

One of the ironies of parenting is that the best way to influence teens to become irresponsible and fail at life is to become highly involved in making sure that they *do* make it. This is because the implied message in that involvement is, "I don't think you're going to succeed, so I'd better get in here." And the teen lives up to that.

Overly involved parents who intrude on their children's lives from kindergarten through twelfth grade will almost always raise learning-resistant children.

To help your teen, and give yourself a break in the process, follow these four steps to responsible offspring:

Step 1. Give your teen a responsibility.
Step 2. Trust that your teen will carry it out, and at the same time hope and pray that she blows it. Because that's how she'll learn the most from it. If she blows it today, there's a learning experience at the end of it.

Of course, hoping she'll blow it doesn't mean you'll be sending messages that she's worthless and can't think for herself. It's just that the cost of her mistake is cheaper today than she will ever have to pay to learn that lesson in the real world.

Step 3. When she does blow it, stand back, express your empathy, making sure you really lock it in, and allow the consequences to occur and teach the lesson.

Step 4. This is the most important one: Turn right around and give her that same responsibility all over again, because that sends the powerful implied message, "You're so smart that you can learn. People do learn from their mistakes, and you're no different. I'm sure you'll learn from yours too."

That beats the parent who criticizes by communicating, "You blew it! Now I have to do it." The powerful implied message here is, "You're so dumb you can't learn from what happened."

Encourage Your Teen

Building responsibility isn't a cold-hearted system. We need to encourage our teens by helping them draw strength from what they do well. This can help them rise to the challenge of handling difficult areas.

One mom asked our advice in dealing with her daughter, who wasn't much of a student academically but was very involved in sports. We told her to take the thing that her daughter could do the best and encourage her to do that with everything she had. We felt that would charge up her daughter's batteries so that she could feel strong enough to try some other things she felt weak in.

So her mom asked, "How can I help best? Can I help you best by nagging you, reminding you, staying out of it, helping you with your strengths?"

"Well, Mom," the daughter replied, "I like running track and I'm really good at it. It means a lot to me when you come to the meets and watch me. I'm really struggling now with English. I appreciate whatever help you can give me, but please don't nag."

Her daughter told her what kind of help she needed. Focusing on her strengths is what gave her the boost.

Never take away from teens what they *can* do well until they improve in activities they don't do well. Otherwise they will suffer the discouragement of not being able to point to anything they can do well.

Getting to "No"

We have the right to expect our children to live the way we want them to live, and sometimes that means saying no. The three basic rules for saying no, which cut down on adolescent rebellion later, are:

1. *Say no as seldom as possible.* Don't use the word if you don't need to.
2. *Say no as much as necessary.* Use the word if you must.
3. *Mean business when you say no.*

A lot of teens have trouble with *no*. But if we use it sparingly, it will mean more when we do say it.

As teens grow older, we may have to say no with one form or another of tough love. For example, "These are my simple requirements: do your chores, earn decent grades, and treat me with respect. They're pretty simple. If you can't meet them then I'm sad for you, and you may need to think about that before we can trust you to use our car again or to go out on the weekends on your own."

We have a responsibility as parents and an obligation to our children to expect and require responsible behavior. That's not the same as demanding blind obedience. Also, if we keep teens focused on how they can meet expectations for responsible behavior, they're less likely to be dwelling on how they can get their way.

Whose Problem Is It?

Child psychiatrists stay busy answering the question: Who owns a problem? Is it the teen's problem or is it the parents' problem? Foster will tell you directly as an experienced psychiatrist that if every parent were able to discern whether something is the child's problem or their own problem, the average child psychologist or psychiatrist would soon be out of business.

Parents' problems are those that directly affect them, such as

- chores not being done
- loud music
- teens coming home late or not being home when they're supposed to be

- being awakened by teens in the middle of the night

Teens' problems do not directly affect parents, such as

- losing schoolbooks and clothes. Protective parents goof here because they say, "Well, I'm the one who pays for those things." They don't go the next step and say, "I'm the one who paid for the *first* one of those."
- bad grades in school
- choice of friends—unless those friends cause trouble on the parents' property
- bedtime schedules

This is not a theoretical exercise. If we don't separate out who owns these problems, we'll have rebellious teenagers. And we'll also get mad at them for something they've done to themselves.

Any time somebody gets mad at you for something you've done to yourself, it makes the problem worse. Let's say you're putting up a picture, using a hammer, and by accident you haul off and whack your thumb. Someone else comes along and remarks, "You dummy! You shouldn't have done that! Didn't I warn you about that? That's such a careless thing to do." This does not help. It only makes the problem worse. And you will probably start thinking about what else you would like to hit with the hammer rather than how you can keep from hitting your thumb again.

Joe recently shelled out several months' pay for his daughter Tori's braces. He notices that Tori has not been brushing her teeth.

"Tori, I've become aware that you're not brushing your teeth," says Joe. He does *not* say, "I paid a lot of money for those braces. You'd better brush your teeth! Look at what you're doing to your gums." Joe knows that would only make the problem worse.

So he continues, "The nice thing about braces, Tori, is they can be put on when you're an adult or when you're thirteen. Right now, as a matter of fact, there are a zillion orthodontists making money on adults, putting the tin in their grin. The advantage of having braces when you're thirteen is that I pay for them. The disadvantage, for you, of having braces when you're an adult is that *you* pay for them."

Joe then turns empathetic, with a dose of humor: "But it will be sad when you go to high school and college, and you want to kiss someone but he says, 'I don't want to kiss you; you're Fang Face!' And every time you'd kiss him, you'd poke him with your incisors. That would be hard on him."

Finally, Joe drives home the consequences of Tori's failure to brush but leaves the decision up to her by saying, "If the brushing doesn't improve, on the next visit to the dentist, your braces come out."

Tori pleads, "Please—I want my braces! I don't want to be Fang Face!"

Joe concludes without anger and with great kindness, "Well, we'll see. But if there's no brushing, the braces come out."

Parenting Perspectives on Real-World Readiness

As you work to apply the above techniques, keep in mind the following perspectives on helping your teens get ready for the real world.

One Month of Love and Logic Covers a Year's Multitude of Sins

Some readers may have been applying Love and Logic principles for years, while others—such as drill sergeants, helicopters, or laissez-faire parents—are being introduced to them for the first time. If these principles are new to you, you may wonder if you will ever be able to apply them before your teen flies the nest.

We've found that when parents start applying Love and Logic principles, it takes about one month of choices and consequences to correct one year of drill sergeant, helicopter, or laissez-faire parenting. We base this calculation of the one-month-to-one-year correction rate on a simple observation of college students.

On average, teenagers are eighteen when they go off to college. We've observed a typical pattern among those who have been protected by helicopters, bossed by drill sergeants, or let run by laissez-faire parents during those eighteen years. They tend to flounder through their freshman year, the following summer, and the first semester of their sophomore year. By the time they reach the second semester of year two, most of them finally start pulling it together.

That's eighteen months to correct eighteen years of poor patterns of personal responsibility. By applying Love and Logic principles as soon as possible, those eighteen months in college will lessen. Think of it as an investment in your teenager's college tuition. The sooner your teens begin to act responsibly, the more they will participate in and benefit from a college education.

United You Stand, Divided You Fall

It's important for parents to present a united front. In essence, here's the rule of thumb: The more irresponsible the teen, the more important it is for the parents to agree on the discipline they use. The healthier the teen, the more the parents can agree to disagree openly in front of the teen by saying, "Well, we have different ideas. This is how your mom feels, and I back her to the hilt." If you have a disturbed child or a difficult child, the united front must be absolute, with no cracks in it: "This is where we stand. Period."

The best way to do this is to agree with your spouse before you address the issue with your son or daughter. Too many make the mistake of doing what they feel is right and then getting angry when the spouse disagrees and says so in front of the child. However, if you discuss it first, then you have already created your effective double team.

Most parents find ways to work through their disagreements over discipline. Sometimes, however, they may reach an impasse. Or they may throw up their hands and say, "We just can't handle this problem." This is a good time to seek help from individuals or organizations who can help identify the issues and suggest approaches that have worked for other parents in similar situations.

If the parents themselves have disturbed personalities and try to enforce inappropriate rules, however, a tough-love approach will fail because they will not have earned the respect of their teens.

Save Punishment

What we're about to say sounds a little strange, because we believe in law and order. But here it is anyway: *There's no room in Love and Logic philosophy for punishment—none at all.*

Of course, this immediately prompts all sorts of protests. "Hey, wait a minute. You expect teens to behave. You expect them to be responsible. Yet you don't believe in punishment?" True, we don't. Then parents say, "You mean you *never* use punishment?" Well, we're human too. We haven't arrived at the point where we can always settle a problem or help a teen without using punishment. The only problem is every time we use punishment, we don't feel very good about ourselves. Stay with us as we try to explain.

There are two ways of hurting: from the outside in, and from the inside out. Hurting from the outside in only goes skin deep. It occurs when someone else is angry or when teens can't make a connection between the infraction and the parent's response. It just doesn't sink in. This occurs when the response is not something that would happen to an adult in the real world.

Instead of punishment, we use "the concept of hurting from the inside out." We allow children to suffer the consequences of their decisions so that every time they ask themselves the question "Who's making me hurt like that?" they have to turn around and say, "Oh, me."

For example, Tyler's parents get angry about his report card and ground him, but it doesn't sink in because he makes no logical connection. Jack's parents say, "Wow, no more good student discount for your car insurance. You'll probably want to pay the difference so you can still drive."

Tyler knows that grounding is punishment. Yet how many adults in the last two years have been grounded? It doesn't happen in the adult world. And it doesn't work with teens. Tyler simply hurts from the outside in. No lessons, no change, no growth.

The same principle goes for washing out your children's mouths with soap when they swear. Neither your boss nor your spouse will wash out your mouth with soap when you swear. But they may avoid you or tell you politely to clean up your language, which will make you hurt from the inside out. There's a good chance you'll learn a lesson here.

Whenever we lay something on teenagers that doesn't happen in the real world, it's almost bound to be a punishment and not a consequence. But we all operate by consequences. If we do a lousy job, we get fired. If we don't make our car payments, the bank repossesses the car.

We oppose punishment because it doesn't lead to self-examination. Instead it leads to resentment. When teens hurt from the inside out by correctly suffering the consequences of their actions, they examine their actions. This takes some thought, because laying down consequences is not always a natural thing for us. We may have to stop and reflect on what would happen in the real world in order for us to identify what the consequences should be for our teen.

As an alternative to punishment, give a lot of thought to how you can reinforce positive behavior, look for solutions, help your children reach their own conclusions, and allow the natural consequences to occur.

Angry? Bite Your Tongue

Many of us want to know, "How do I learn to come across without the booming voice, the anger, and the threats?" Some of us tell ourselves, "I'm not going to yell anymore." And then we find ourselves right back there again, that awful voice coming out of our mouths that we hate to hear. Our children hate to hear it too.

The nice thing about teenagers is that if we don't properly apply a Love and Logic principle today, they're certain to give us another opportunity tomorrow. Sometimes it helps to say to yourself over and over just before you fall asleep at night, *When I get angry, I'm going to whisper. When I get angry, I'm going to whisper.* You can mentally rehearse as well. You may find that, lo and behold, when your teen gives you another opportunity to react, you're able to handle it much more calmly.

Here are three principles that may help you bite your tongue instead of lash out with it when you're angry:

> *Principle 1.* If it's not an emergency, it doesn't have to be handled right then. So we can say to our teens, "Unlucky for you, I'm angry. Lucky for you, I'm not going to talk to you about it until tomorrow."
>
> *Principle 2.* Generally speaking, the angrier you are, the more important it is to lower your voice.
>
> *Principle 3.* Talk it over with other people before you decide what to do. The consequence is usually better if it comes after

both you and the teen have entered the "thinking state" after leaving the "emotional state."

Parents don't consult each other as much as those in earlier decades who were surrounded by extended family or a close-knit community. Instead of going to a professional, many parents don't realize they can look up someone in the neighborhood who has really great teens and ask them for advice. A mom could say to another mom, "You know, yesterday Susan said she would be in at midnight. She didn't come in until 1:30. She gave a lame reason, and I haven't done anything or said anything about it. You seem to have really neat kids. If your kids did that, what would you do?" Most of us would feel pleased and privileged if someone in our community asked us what we would do with our teens because they like the way our teens behave. This kind of networking is a good way to get advice and make new friends in the process.

The most appropriate time to reason with teenagers is when they're not in an emotional state. Even though they may act flippant and say, "I don't care," they still harbor plenty of emotion in controversial situations. If we try to communicate in the midst of a heated exchange, however, chances are they'll never hear the words we say. And we'll probably end up wishing we could take those words back anyway.

Another caution about anger is to avoid handing down a consequence to your teen while you're angry, because it may be too strong and you'll want to change your mind once you've cooled down later on. If this happens very often, your teen may lose respect for you. Once that respect is lost, everything is a downhill slide from there.

If we've come down on our teens too hard, we can say, "I'm sorry I did that. I've given it more thought, and I'm thinking maybe I made a mistake. Here's what I think might be better. . . ." That can only be done a few times, however, or we will form a pattern of being inconsistent.

When parents are inconsistent, teens usually respond in one of three ways: (1) they get the impression that their parents shoot from the hip without thinking things through; (2) they wonder if their parents are basically pushovers; and (3) they doubt whether their parents have their best interests at heart.

If you're concerned about being inconsistent with your teen, you might try this approach: "I'm wondering if I've come across inconsistently with you, telling you something one day and changing my mind the next. I don't think that helps you very much, so I'm going to try to do less of that. If you notice that I'm being inconsistent, you may want to remind me about it in a thoughtful way." But keep in mind that your teen may bring it up only when it's in his or her favor to do so.

Air Out Your Disagreements

As parents, most of us have learned by now that we're not always right. If we have a responsible teenager who is bent out of shape about something we've done or said, he or she probably has a legitimate grievance.

When I (Foster) have seen teens really hacked off at parents, they're usually right. I ask them, "Are you seeing red? Why are you feeling this way?"

When something's going on in the family that family members are trying to keep secret—telling the teen that this shouldn't be talked about with *anyone*—it's a red flag that it should be talked about with *someone*. That's the issue that's crippling the family, so that's the issue that should be dealt with.

When we tell our teens not to talk about something, we're ensuring that they're not going to be able to work it through. Then they lose no matter what: If they don't talk, they don't resolve it; if they do talk, they suffer guilt over violating a parental injunction. A mandate of secrecy cripples our teens.

When parents and teens have a disagreement, it's best to air it out by getting an outside opinion both parties respect. The best person is someone who's raised great teens, a youth counselor, or a professional counselor.

Keep Some of Your Curiosity to Yourself

Parents naturally want to know everything about what's going on with their teen. Interest can become inordinate curiosity, however, and questions can quickly turn into interrogations.

If you feel uncomfortable that you're questioning an awful lot, perhaps you should keep some of your curiosity under wraps. Ask yourself,

"Is it really any of my business? Would I be better off not knowing everything about my teen?"

There are a lot of things we'd like to find out from our teens that would devastate us if we learned the answer to them. Why not just let teens have a certain amount of their lives that's private? We can probably live happily for the rest of our lives in ignorance of some of those things.

There are probably several reasons why your teens don't share everything with you. First, they figure you might not be able to handle what they tell you. Second, they may feel that what they say would be too different from the way you see things. Third, they probably don't have a real good handle on how they feel or how to express themselves. All in all, they most likely feel a little inadequate sharing some things with you.

Our rule of thumb is to give incomplete sentences (which is a form of questioning), or to ask questions when we truly want that teen to think, not when *we* want the information. There's a big difference between the two. It's pretty obvious to teens whether we're truly trying to help them think something through or just prying to satisfy our curiosity.

Questioning can be more comfortable if you start with an open-ended question, thank them for sharing their response, and clarify whether you understand their responses correctly—for example, "Is this the way you're really feeling?" Other suggestions for opening conversations include:

- "It seems to me that . . ."
- "I've noticed . . . Do you have any thoughts on that?"
- "I'm pleased that you did well on . . . What did you think about it?"

Often parents are afraid to comment on what they're seeing or hearing because they're afraid they will chase their teens away. If your teens are hesitant to talk, don't force it. Show that you trust them, and allow them to talk on their own. Your conversations will be much more meaningful.

An understanding counselor or Father in a confessional can explore with questions how a person chose to mess up his or her life. On the witness stand, a cross-examining attorney can ask almost the same questions. One is loved, the other hated.

Only curiosity and interest, listening with love and acceptance (not necessarily approval) to things you'd rather not hear, keep the lines of communication open with your kids.

Say No Thanks to Guilt
Too often parents feel like failures if their teens don't measure up. They shouldn't. When teens have trouble, it doesn't necessarily mean the fault belongs to the parent.

Matters aren't helped if communities that should provide support cut parents down in their efforts. We know of a church that denied a man the opportunity to become a deacon because his daughter became pregnant out of wedlock. He hadn't been a lousy father. The daughter got pregnant, not the father. That church wasn't being fair about where the lines of responsibility are. It should have been supportive of the man.

Getting ready for and living in the real world means that we learn to take responsibility for our own actions. If you've done all you can for your child, and the child still makes harmful decisions, you should rest in the knowledge that you did your job. You're not a failure. Your child made those decisions. When guilt comes calling through this door, say, "Thanks, but no thanks."

What Love and Logic Is Not

Over the years since we started the research that led to this book, and through the seminars and research that have followed, we have discovered how good ideas and practices can be misconstrued, misrepresented, and taken out of context. It's been said that the road to hell is paved with good intentions. Perhaps on the way down, one might meet teens raised by parents who read books on how to raise little angels. What went wrong?

Love and Logic does not guarantee angelic children and teens, but we do know that these concepts, tools, and techniques provide the best chance for parental success. Love and Logic material is filled with beautiful constructs that can be misapplied even by well-meaning parents, especially if their background is one of dysfunction, abuse, and pain.

One of the interesting things about the Love and Logic method is that it is somewhat self-regulating. If you don't do it exactly right, it simply won't work. For instance, we place a great deal of emphasis on modeling. This is one of the Es of Love and Logic—*example*—which, along with *experience* and *empathy,* form the backbone of effective parenting. But when we encourage parents to use themselves in setting the example, we assume that the parent understands how to set a healthy, win-win example. For parents with poor self-image, it's hard to set the example that they want their children to emulate.

Since writing the first edition, we have discovered some common confusions that are unique to Love and Logic newbies. We would like to help you avoid some of the pitfalls by exploring a few of these sad, if understandable, confusions.

Using Insincere Empathy
Love and Logic emphasizes empathy. Because so many adults raising children were raised without empathy, we often give examples of empathetic statements such as

- "How sad."
- "What a bummer."
- "Hope things go better for you."
- "If anyone can learn from this mistake, it's you."
- "I'm sure it's hard to be you at times."
- "If anyone can cope with this, it's you."
- "When the going gets tough, the tough get going."
- "That's a problem for you, that's for sure."
- "With a little deeper figuring, you'll probably come up with good answers."

These statements, which are meant to be expressed dripping with kindness and understanding, can be uttered with the warmth of an icicle. Every so often we have heard parents say, "Bummer for you," with such callousness that it would freeze a river in summer. And here's why. Some parents are used to being angry and frustrated. So, while trying to remember and use new statements while also feeling unsure of themselves and perhaps insecure with the new knowledge, they use the right words but with the wrong meaning. Their old disappointment leaks through with an unhappy, angry, critical, or sarcastic tone.

True empathetic statements are generated not from the head but from the heart. Also, any empathetic statement overused becomes meaningless, for while the head can respond with rote comments, the heart always finds new ways of expressing itself.

Rob failed a test for lack of study. His mom, who was learning not to be a helicopter parent, said blandly, "Too bad for you that you didn't put more effort into studying for that test," and experienced an icy response from her son. If she had put her arm around her son's shoulder and say, "Honey, that makes me sad. It's hard to study when it seems at times like other things are more important, isn't it?" the sun would have shone on mother and son.

The delivery, and the heart behind it, can make all the difference in the world.

Using Consequences as Threats

Sometimes when a consequence is uttered as a threat, it's pretty obvious, such as when you say to a small child, "Aidan, if you can't sit still, I am going to send you to your room." Threat is equally obvious when a parent says, "If you don't know how to behave properly, I don't want you around me at all."

It's a win-win when the adults impose consequences to take care of themselves and are still able to offer a choice of how it might be imposed: "Tom, when you smoke in the house, your second-hand smoke endangers the health of the rest of the family. Where else would you feel comfortable doing that?"

Giving Choices That Do Not Give Reasonable or Acceptable Alternatives

Some choices just aren't good, honest, and true choices. For example, Zach was giving his sister Rebecca a hard time in the back seat. His mom, who had been growing more and more enraged by Zach's behavior, screamed from behind the steering wheel, "Zach, when I pull over, do you want me to allow Rebecca to hit you, or do you want me to do it myself?"

Love and Logic parents give their children choices within acceptable limits that follow a few key guidelines:

1. The child is expected to willingly pick one of the choices, and is therefore given at least one choice that is appealing.
2. The parent can live with whatever choice is picked.
3. If the choice is refused, the parent can lovingly take his or her turn at deciding and knows that the outcome is enforceable.

Interpreting and Enforcing Love and Logic Metaphors Literally

In our first book, *Parenting with Love and Logic*, we taught that by age two children should have "Basic German Shepherd" down pat. That is, come, sit, go, no, and stay are all commands that a two-year-old should be able to follow just as a trained German Shepherd would. Imagine our surprise when one of us heard a mom saying to her child in a grocery store, "Sit!" "No!" "Come!" "Stay!" While we attempt to help parents understand that sentient beings of all kinds need to honor basic requests, this mom had taken us much too literally.

Love and Logic uses many metaphors, such as Basic German Shepherd, which are shorthand for truths that are complicated and need to be worked though.

In another case a woman told Jim he was the meanest man she had ever heard when he suggested "holding the kids' feet to the fire" as a metaphor for holding them accountable for their actions.

Using "Taking Care of Yourself" as an Excuse for Selfishness

Selfishness; selflessness; self-centered; centered with self. These can be confusing terms with many nuances. When parents come from difficult backgrounds, the important nuances can be lost. For instance, it's considered good to be selfless, but to have no sense of self is bad. It's good to be centered in yourself, but to be self-centered is bad.

Love and Logic stresses the importance of parents taking good care of themselves to set the model for their children. If parents take good care of themselves, their children have a good chance of growing up to be people who take good care of themselves too. When parents always put the children first, they often put themselves last and raise entitled, demanding children, better known as spoiled brats.

Love and Logic parents need to put themselves first in a "centered in self" way that is not selfish but insists on a win-win relationship. Toddlers don't naturally put their parents first. They're not supposed to. So parents must teach children, in the first few years of life, "I love you so much. First, I win, and then look how well it works out for you. When I'm happy, you're happy too." Of course that grows to be reciprocal, and when our children are happy, we're happy too.

Children who haven't learned the win-win message at two or soon thereafter often carefully manipulate rebellious win-lose situations when they grow into adolescence. These are actually lose-lose—upsetting for everyone. Therefore, Love and Logic parents insist on respect and insist on it in a healthy way: that their children not pollute their life with controlling demands and outrageous expectations. They take good care of themselves, even if it means their offspring may suffer unhappy consequences in the short run.

The important point is, if someone has to be unhappy and frustrated with the way things are going, it is *not* going to be the loving, giving parents who prefer win-win relationships and who refuse to give up their win in the face of the other side insisting on a lose-win situation.

Using Love and Logic Statements as a Means of Manipulating

As the old saying goes, "Kids don't care how much you know until they know how much you care." We provide Love and Logic techniques so that you can win key power struggles with your kids so that they learn to be responsible, not so that you can control every aspect of their lives. In truth, Love and Logic is about gradually giving up control to your kids over the years, not gaining more. Kids need to know you are doing this because you love them and want them to grow into great adults, not because you are constantly on a control trip.

Using Love and Logic Techniques in Lieu of Relationships

As we started researching Love and Logic, we took for granted that all parents love their children and want the best for them. We still believe this is true, though some parents have more difficulty expressing love than others. Some juggle an incredible number of plates to keep up with the demands they put on themselves, leaving little time for their children. Still others didn't have good models for building relationships and aren't sure where to begin with their own kids, so rather than confront the issue, they flee into hobbies, television, or other forms of avoiding their children.

One of the primary benefits of using Love and Logic is that it eliminates many of the factors that traditionally divide children from their parents, namely anger, lectures, threats, and warnings. As Love and Logic is used successfully, there should actually be less need to "hold the kid's feet to the fire" and more time to enjoy the relationship. This doesn't necessarily mean kids mess up any less, but they become better at handling those problems without us and better at making decisions that keep them away from "bummer" consequences. That leaves more time for parents to do things with their kids that range from coaching their soccer team, to taking walks, to going to art classes together, to exploring whatever interests you happen to share.

Love and Logic is about spending quantities of quality time with your kids and having that time be enjoyable, not about having to deal with them less.

Love and Logic Cannot Change the Child Before It Changes the Parent
One of the reasons we emphasize over and over that we parents need to take care of ourselves first is that if we are stressed, on edge, angry, or simply not taking care of ourselves in a healthy way, Love and Logic will not work for us. Unless parents who have continually dealt with their kids in anger in the past deal with defusing that anger first, they are liable to fall back in it every time they try to explore consequences with their kids.

In Love and Logic, parents lead. If we want our teens to have self-control, we must model it. If we want our teens to be responsible, we must be responsible. If we want our teens to treat us and speak to us with respect, we must treat and speak to them with respect. This is the parenting with Love and Logic two-step: first the parent, then the child.

Ready, Set, Go!

Our children are the most precious and valuable gifts
give us. We have eighteen short years to prepare them f(
they're teens, the window of time is even smaller, but it's a window
nonetheless.

Let's spend more time thinking about how we're going to parent
our teenagers and what we can learn from them, and less time thinking
about what might go wrong.

Ready, set, off into the real world! Parenting achieves its major goal
when teens leave home and go out into the world able to cope with it
and make productive contributions. If your teen can exercise his or her
judgment, make decisions, and live with the consequences, rest assured
that you've done your part.

Over time, your children will love and respect you more and more
for teaching them how to think and how to live. As their maturity
catches up to yours, you will discover that you can meet on common
ground as adults and that you have become friends. This is the greatest
reward any parent can hope for.

The following section will examine specific issues. In dealing with
them all, remember the essential tools you have learned in the first two
sections of this book. Show love and affection while empathetically providing consequences that make parenting effective for you and your
children.

Best wishes on your journey through life together.

Part Three

Love and Logic
Parenting Pearls

How to Use Love and Logic Pearls

Knowing some basic concepts on parenting teens is a good beginning; they offer a foundation on which to build a system of discipline. But putting those ideas into practice in individual situations sets us on ground decidedly more treacherous.

How do we handle a child who pulls a Mount St. Helens whenever he or she doesn't win a struggle of wills? What about curfews, using the family car, and learning to budget money wisely? How about the child who won't do chores, or homework, or feed the pets, or whatever?

We don't want philosophy. *We want answers!* How does empathy with the consequences play itself out in real, practical, down-to-earth parenting?

This part of the book consists of thirty-nine pearls offering practical advice for handling some of the more common disciplinary problems parents meet during their children's adolescent years. In these pearls, we explore and discuss individual topics and give advice on each. Many of the pearls also contain a sample dialogue that shows how you might discuss the issue with your teen.

But, reader, beware: Do not try these pearls until you've read part 1 and part 2 of this book. Don't try to build the house until you have the foundation laid first.

Aggressive Behavior

B ill and Pam always had been proud of their son Cody. As a child, he grew like a weed, ate like a horse, and appeared to be a natural leader. Cody played sports aggressively and won the respect of his playmates—or so Bill and Pam thought.

By the time Cody turned twelve, he was taller than Pam. At fifteen, he towered above Bill. His younger brother and sister cowered around him, especially when he was angry, which was most of the time. Cody was stronger than all of them put together, and he knew it.

Cody had already earned a reputation at school as an antisocial bully. Now he took his aggressiveness out on his family. He learned that he could ignore his parents when it suited him. He treated simple chores, such as taking out the trash or raking the yard, as big productions, and he made sure that Bill and Pam knew his displeasure in no uncertain terms.

When Bill or Pam confronted Cody about his unwillingness to do chores, he would just as soon flip them off as ignore them.

By sixteen, Cody turned abusive—verbally as well as physically. When his frustrated parents yelled at him to straighten up, he screamed back a string of profanities. Then he started pushing his mother away and shoving his father up against the wall. To make a point, Cody also threw plates and even furniture.

This was no ordinary disrespect. This was violence by a child against his family.

At first, Bill tried to reason with Cody. He chose to talk to him when family matters were quiet, and said, "Son, we know that adolescence is a tough time, but you have no right to treat your mother that way."

"Shove it, Dad. I'm sick of your bull." Bill dropped the conversation there.

He and Pam then found a family counselor who was willing to meet with them and Cody and talk it over.

Cody would have none of it. "I'm not wasting my time to talk to a f— shrink!" he shouted, slamming around what was close at hand to drive home his point. They met with the therapist without Cody. They needed professional advice. Most of what they learned was painful to hear.

Immediately upon returning home they removed knives and other possible weapons from the house in case his aggressiveness increased. Their first responsibility was to protect the family members.

So Bill and Pam had a decision to make. Although it was a painful decision, they made the right one. They gave Cody the choice of enrolling in a military academy or finding a place to live where his behavior would be more accepted. Either way, they no longer permitted him to live at home.

Cody chose to live on the street.

Bill and Pam told him that they loved him and would consider admitting him to the household again if he decided to change his ways and seek counseling. But until such time, they told him that he was not permitted inside the house, and if he tried to violate that rule they would call the police.

Parents rarely face such a hard choice. It is a shattered dream. Bill and Pam didn't do this because they were mean or selfish. They did it to protect themselves and their other children from physical harm. Their concern for Cody had to be balanced with their need to ensure family safety and protection.

Pearl 2

Appearance: Clothing, Hairstyle, and Other Surprises

In adolescence, for better or worse, children show their autonomy and independence from adults by their appearance. Actually, considering all the other ways kids can show autonomy and independence, most appearance issues are really fairly harmless. It's not worth the trouble to engage in control battles over them.

Clothes and the Need to Fit In

We all like to know that we "fit" within one group or another. Teens are no different.

I (Foster) remember when, long ago, as a younger parent, I would find out that *weird* meant "different," and *different* meant "special," and *special* meant "awesome"—as long as the "in group" dressed different, special, and awesome.

One morning, as I waited to drive my eighth-grade daughter to school, she came down dressed like a cheerleader—in a short, flouncy dress that barely reached to mid-thigh. Had she been a cheerleader going to practice, this would have been wonderful.

Now, don't get me wrong—for the most part, I was a fairly "easy" dad. Nevertheless, even I could not think of any real good reason for her to walk into school in a dress that looked like it had come to a bad end in the dryer. By that time in my parenting career, however, I had learned that the first things I tended to say were often wrong. So if Dad says anything, Dad had better give it some thought first.

After mulling over various possibilities on the way to school, I said, "Robin, have you given the way you dress a lot of thought? I'm wondering if you set yourself up as being a little different when you dress like that?"

She smiled at me and quickly replied, "Oh, Dad, all the girls dress like this."

I thought, *I'm sure. All the girls? No pants? Give me a break!* But, luckily, I kept my mouth closed.

When we got to school, I pulled up behind all the buses with their red lights flashing, students streaming out of them. I noticed with a shock that *all* the girls *did* wear cheerleader outfits—but they weren't cheerleaders! Again I learned that my child often knew what she was talking about. Yet no matter how often I learn that, it always comes as a surprise.

Today it is everything from short skirts to bare midriffs and shoulders. That is, of course, just the style, but if it bothers you, it is not a problem to say something like, "Oh, honey, you have such pretty eyes! I think more people should notice them. Of course, that probably won't happen when they are looking at your belly button. Do you ever think it would be better to accent your face instead?"

Clothes and the Need to Stand Out

Teens' desire to fit in with their peers is often at odds with what adults think is "normal" dress. Paradoxically, teens struggle with the need to fit in at the same time they're struggling with the need to stand out.

Teens will sometimes go to great lengths to make their exterior unavoidably apparent. Why would anyone who wants to be accepted dress so unacceptably, we wonder? The answer is fairly easy. The teen reasons: "If anyone accepts me, they'll have to accept the real me—and they'll have to handle (or ignore!) the way I look."

We regrettably undermine our teen's self-respect when we insist that they look "normal," even though what's normal changes from year to year.

For example, when you go to Aunt Hilda's funeral and you're about to see all these family members you haven't seen in a while—and you know everybody's judging how well your family has turned out—you show up with your teenage girl who, in your eyes, looks like a fright. You want to tell her, "Why can't you, just this one time, put on a regular dress and comb your hair nicely. What's wrong with looking normal?"

But using the phrase "look normal" is devastating to a teenager. To get your point across without alienating your daughter, you might say instead, "If you go dressed like that, luckily for me, I know what a neat kid you are. I don't judge you by how you look. But there will be a few relatives there who will probably stay on the other side of the coffin. So please give it some thought." That way, your daughter knows that what she wears reflects on her, not on you.

Also, teens may dress atrociously as a statement of identity. "I am not my dad or mom! Since my parents can't stand the way I look, this has to be the real me, because I know I'm different from them." Teens create their own identities by imitating the styles of their athletic, music, or media heroes, and in turn adapt them to their own bodies.

Hairstyle, Makeup, Piercings, and Tattoos

The same holds true for hairstyles. Teens have expressed their personalities by their hairstyles with flattops in the fifties, afros and long hair in the sixties, punk cuts in the seventies, and the intricate razor cuts in the eighties and early nineties. Parents can't control what a hairstylist will do to their teens' heads. If Mom and Dad really disapprove of how their teens wear their hair, they can refuse to pay the extra money it might cost for a new style.

Makeup can be an issue too. The age at which girls use makeup largely depends on where they live and the value system in their peer group. Most girls start wearing makeup when they're in junior high or middle school. The rule of thumb for appearance in general and makeup in particular is that your girl should not stick out like a sore thumb. Some parents can unconsciously set their daughters up to be socially isolated, however, by forbidding them to wear makeup when it's a common practice among their peers.

Even more problematic than makeup on girls are earrings on boys—or any other kinds of piercing on both boys and girls for that matter. In the past decade, increasing numbers of young people have shocked their parents by piercing their ears, nose, belly buttons, tongue, eyebrows, and the list goes on. Earrings on males was once considered a fashion statement by homosexual men, but that identification has long faded. If we find a pierced ear on our teenage son objectionable, we can ask that he not wear the earring in the house. The same can go with other piercings, or we can ask them to at least keep them covered.

With this in mind, however, there is recent evidence that such piercing, especially in the tongue, can add unwanted metals to the body that can cause long-term health problems. Similar findings are being made about the inks used in tattoos. Finding Internet articles on such topics and sharing them with your teens before they decide to follow this trend can go a long way in helping them make the right decision when considering getting a piercing or tattoo.

Sometimes teens' attire and apparent rebelliousness reflects what they see at home rather than what they see on television or in school.

Donald Sr., a well-known and well-respected lawyer, came to see Foster because he was upset about the way Don Jr. dressed. "The way that kid dresses, nobody's going to want to see hide nor hair of him, let alone hire him," groused Don Sr.

One day Foster saw Don Sr. at the courthouse and was somewhat shocked to see him wearing jeans (albeit nice jeans) with a white shirt and tie. Foster questioned him about the way he was dressed. "Well, I'm just here in court doin' my thing," Donald Sr. said. "If people don't like the way I'm dressed, that's their problem. I think they can figure out that I know my stuff."

No wonder Don Jr. was rebellious about his attire!

Three Rules of Thumb

Here are some suggestions for handling an adolescent's appearance:

- *If you can, say something nice.* If it isn't stretching the truth too much, comment favorably on almost every change in dress or haircut that your child chooses. This has one great advantage: If your teen is very rebellious, it might drive him or her back to an appearance that's more to your liking.

- *If you can't say something nice, don't say anything.* If it's stretching the truth too much to make a positive comment, then mum's the word.
- *If it's offensive, draw your own line.* If your teen's appearance is completely beyond the laws of decorum and good taste, you can simply say, "I know you appreciate that style of dress, but it is beyond my limits and I don't want you to be dressed like that when you're with me. I'm a little old-fashioned, as are most of my friends, and unfortunately we have our limits."

In summary, above all, try to avoid control battles over appearance. Schools and parents have lost plenty of those conflicts. Give yourself a break. Remember that wise parents don't pay for clothes, hairstyles, and other appearance modifiers they don't like.

PEARL 3

Arguments

Raising teens is a risky business. No matter how parents play them, most situations are still risky. You are about to read a conversation between a basically responsible teen and a very loving mother. Before rejecting this mother's response as uncaring, unsympathetic, or dangerous remember that prohibiting that a child sell drugs has a track record of *not* working. Many drug dealers were ordered as children to stop all sorts of antisocial and negative behavior. Such orders are simply not effective.

Jesse is basically a responsible youth. If he were mostly irresponsible, the approach would have to be modified. Notice how this wise mom keeps her cool and avoids a major-league argument about not having enough money to buy concert tickets.

JESSE: Okay, if you guys don't love me enough to give me more
   allowance, I'll just have to start selling drugs.
MOM: Well, I guess that's an option.
JESSE: That's an option? What do you mean that's an option?
MOM (shrugs): That could be one way to solve your problem.
JESSE: You've got to be crazy! What's wrong with you?
MOM: Nothing. Even though I love you more than anything
   in the world, the time has come when you have to decide for
   yourself how you are going to live your life.
JESSE: No way. You're on something. Otherwise you'd be giving
   me a lot of grief about this. Do you know that I could get caught

for dealing? I could go to jail!

MOM: True. But maybe you'll make enough money dealing that you can hire some good lawyers to get you some light time. I'm sure you've thought it all out. Anyway, just think, if you get caught, the state will take care of you. You won't have to worry about allowance, room and board, or anything.

JESSE: Wait a minute! How am I supposed to go to college?

MOM (relaxed, reclining on the couch): Oh, you won't be in the slammer forever. With good behavior you'll get out and go to college later. You might even be better prepared because you'll have more life experiences.

JESSE: This is weird, man! Are you just going to sit there and let me ruin my life? Don't you even care about what happens to me? I can't listen to this! (Stomps out of the room.)

As farfetched as this sounds, it is an actual conversation with a parent who had learned to keep the monkey on the back of the teen who owned the problem. She had learned that teens love to "hit" us, like Jesse did in this situation.

Jesse hoped to engage his mom in defending herself and making demands on him. When teens such as Jesse are successful at getting this far, they switch into their judge role with statements such as "That's not fair" or "I can't do *that*." Before long the parent totally owns a problem the teen actually needs to learn to solve.

First, Mom refused to engage. She did not criticize Jesse's thinking by saying, "That's stupid. Don't you dare do that!" Nor did she tell him what to do, with a comment like, "If you want to go to that concert badly enough, you'll go out and get yourself an honest job." And Mom did not use anger, guilt, intimidation, or orders, such as, "As long as you live in my house you're not going to talk like that!"

Mom remembered that the magic response, "That's an option," will apply regardless of the brilliance or foolishness of a teen's suggestion. She refused to take Jesse's bait by doing his thinking for him and ultimately taking over ownership of his problem.

The second skill Mom used was to think of all the advantages to Jesse's solution of selling drugs. However, she stated them in negative—yet enthusiastic—terms. As you can tell from the dialogue, it blew Jesse's mind. So he switched into the role of telling her what was wrong with dealing drugs.

The third thing Mom knew was that Jesse could learn from this type of dialogue because she had a reasonably good relationship with him and things had gone well during his childhood.

Clear thinking and calm emotions go far in defusing otherwise explosive arguments. And remember, if you lose your cool the first time you apply these Love and Logic principles, you can count on your teen to give you another opportunity to practice. Take heart!

Back in the Nest: If an Older Child Needs to Move Home

"**M**om, can I come home?" For some parents, this question was once a plea from a teenager who had strayed, recognized the dead-end of that lifestyle, and wanted to make a new start. Today, this question is often a cry for economic rescue. And parents are often caught in the middle between their child's plight and their own needs.

Increasing numbers of young people in their late teens to mid-thirties are going through the experience of losing a job or splitting up with a spouse. The only way they can make ends meet after such financial hardships is to move in with their parents, even if they had just moved out only a few years before.

Parents often want to help. But we should keep a few things in mind.

First, the primary rule when older children want to move home is that *we now wear two hats: parent and landlord.* Parents should require whatever a landlord would require, but perhaps not as strictly.

Second, *adult children need to have an appropriately thankful attitude* for the opportunity to return home. Parents need to be grateful too—yet firm. However, home is not a place for the child to come and "hang out." After all, landlords don't allow people to "hang out" at property they own.

You can say, "I know what a good deal it is for you to be here. Now I want you to tell me what benefits are in this for me?"

You hope your grown-up child will say, "I'll do the laundry," "I'll mow the lawn," and/or "I'll paint the garage." If he or she doesn't, then you must decide whether you should allow your child to stay with you or how much a month they need to pay while "renting" from you.

The bottom line: If it's not a win-win situation, it's a lose-lose situation. It's a two-way street or it's a no-way street.

Back Talk

"This stinks!" It probably does. The question for you as a parent, however, is how you deal with your teen's back talk.

There are three possible reasons why adolescents mouth off to us:

1. They back talk because we are threatening their autonomy and independence.
2. They back talk because they, like the rest of us, have the inalienable right to protest.
3. Back talk may be a part of other issues, including poor school behavior, use of drugs, mood swings, or basic irresponsibility.

The Threat to Their Independence

The first reason is the healthiest and easiest to deal with. If your child was a basically good and loving child through the fifth or sixth grade, then almost certainly you can help your child clean up the back talk.

First, *listen* to your child's ideas.

Second, *offer your ideas* without trying to make your child do it your way.

If you have had a good relationship with your children, they will love and respect you and realize that you are usually right.

Our children will test us to see whether or not we will rescue them by feeling sorry for them when they talk back to us, but after they find out that we continue in a loving way to give our point of view, refuse to rescue, and—without being angry—allow them to suffer the consequences of their behavior, they will stop most of their back talk.

Here's a scenario showing how a parent can deal with this first category of back talk. This dad has picked a moment when his daughter is in a relatively good mood. He mainly asks questions; he doesn't lecture. And he starts out by focusing on Sarah's feelings, not on her back talk or tacky behavior. He knows that teens need to be understood before they are willing to talk about actions.

> DAD: Sarah, sometimes you and I have a pretty hard time together. I would really appreciate our talking about that for a few minutes. What do you think the problem could be?
>
> SARAH: You're always on my case.
>
> DAD: Like how?
>
> SARAH: Like everything. You try to choose my friends and tell me what I have to do all the time. Everything.
>
> DAD: Then how do you feel?
>
> SARAH: Like nuthin' I do is right.
>
> DAD: And then how do you act toward me?
>
> SARAH: I get mad, Dad.
>
> DAD: I know you do. I've been realizing, Sarah, that I've been always trying to make sure you do the right thing and see that you don't get in trouble. I've been trying to help you live a happy life. I realize that I'm not giving you the right to make your own mistakes. And I just want to apologize. Everyone has the right to make mistakes. I'm sorry, Sarah.
>
> SARAH (stunned): Well—that's okay, Dad.
>
> DAD: No, it isn't okay. It robs you of deciding for yourself when you come in or how important school is.
>
> SARAH: Well, you should worry about some things, like if I drink or do drugs or other bad stuff.
>
> DAD: I know, and that may not be a real big deal. Of course, if I think you're drinking and driving, I'll just give the license plate number to the cops. No big deal.
>
> SARAH: Dad, get serious!

DAD: I am serious. I love you too much to keep messing around trying to save you and make sure everything goes okay. Thanks for talking.

SARAH: Thanks—I guess.

The Right to Protest

When you're dealing with back talk, remember that all of us—including our children—have the right to protest. We may not like paying taxes, and we may gripe, but we pay them. When we accept our children's protest, they usually feel understood—and that's often enough to satisfy their need, so they don't have to up the ante to outright disrespect.

Here's an example of how to handle the second type of back talk:

MOM: Jason, would you please empty the trash?

JASON: I hate emptying the trash. I do everything around here.

MOM: I know, honey. It's a bummer when there are always jobs to do. Thanks for doing it anyway.

This smart parent was thanking the child in advance. It works with "Thanks for not smoking" signs in public places and it may work for your child. Society often thanks us for our cooperation before we actually give it.

Humor can often defuse back talk or even disrespect. Sometimes when a child makes a common obscene comment, we can simply say, "Rich, you always have sex on your mind."

If the back talk and disrespect is extreme, it is sometimes best simply to let them know that they may need to leave and come back when they can talk differently. The wise parent says, "I'm having trouble listening to this," rather than, "Don't you dare talk that way to me!"

When Back Talk Is Part of a Bigger Problem

When back talk is part of a bigger problem, such as a symptom of drug abuse, it requires a much firmer tack. Instead of allowing more freedom with its consequences, parental structure may need to be tightened. Consequences may need to be imposed, rather than simply being allowed to occur. These problems are deeper than just establishing independence or protesting. It is usually best to confer with a professional before attempting to deal with these serious issues.

In summary, if back talk starts in adolescence, it is almost always because we have not allowed the child enough opportunity to suffer and learn from mistakes. Teens who back talk often have parents who get angry and then rescue the child from the results of their mistakes. It is almost guaranteed to bring the worst out of a teen.

Cars, Driving, and Catching Rides

Teenage transportation is a thought-provoking issue for parents. All we have to do is imagine other teens driving our kids around, or our kids driving themselves and their friends around, and plenty of thoughts come to mind.

We want to handle car responsibilities with our teens the way the real world does. Having wheels is a great privilege as well as a great responsibility.

Before teens learn to drive, we should explore with them the new dangers they're going to face. Some parents handle the transportation issue by laying down the law. Other parents handle it by getting their teens to think about life in the fast lane. Effective parents might hold a conversation like this:

> DAD: Kyle, if you were to die before you were twenty-one—and I hope you don't—how, statistically, would you die?
>
> KYLE: I don't know.
>
> DAD: Oh, I bet you do. What are the two major ways teens die?
>
> KYLE: Suicide?
>
> DAD: Well, that's third on the list. Do you think you're the suicidal type?
>
> KYLE: No.
>
> DAD: I don't either. So you probably won't die by suicide. How else would you die early?
>
> KYLE: Car accident?

DAD: Right! If you were to die before you were twenty-one, it would probably be in a car accident. And generally, in these car accidents, there is something else involved. What's that?

KYLE: Alcohol?

DAD: You're right. Do you think about this very often, or don't you think about it much?

KYLE: I don't think about it much.

DAD: I see. Now, considering the kids who die, do you think they think about it a lot, or do you think they probably don't?

KYLE: They probably don't.

DAD: Right. So you fit the profile. Anyway, I just want you to know that I love you and would miss you if you were killed before you're twenty-one.

KYLE: I know, Dad. I'll be careful.

DAD: Thanks.

This dad has placed the responsibility of driving squarely in Kyle's lap. He guides his son in realizing that driving is a life-and-death issue, but he doesn't threaten or cajole him. Future conversations along these lines can help Kyle spell out how he will be careful in other driving situations.

There are other general strategies for handling teenage transportation issues.

First, *wise parents consider offering their teens "good guy" auto insurance.* "Good guy" auto insurance means you pay the premium based on teens maintaining a B average in school, achieving a flawless driving record, and in most states, having completed driver's education. Then, if your teen gets a ticket or declining grades, you can respond with sorrow, not anger, as you say, "Gee, what a bummer for you. Your insurance is going to go up now. How do you think you'll pay for the increase?"

Second, *wise parents do not buy cars for their teens unless their teens are responsible, nose-to-the grindstone young adults.* Many teens own their own cars—and many more want to. In most cases, the parents are the ones who buy them. However, we believe that parents should buy a car for their teen only if the teen has demonstrated that he or she can handle the responsibility. And then the car they buy should be an old one. If the teen has an accident, the parents don't have to get bent out of shape—only the car is bent out of shape.

When Jim was a principal, the teacher's room of my grade school used to look down on the high school parking lot. One day he was talking with a teacher at that window and commented, "Boy, there are sure some fancy-looking cars down there."

"Yeah," the teacher responded, "that one is a Ferrari and that other is a Lotus."

"Boy, they must pay those high school teachers a lot more than they pay us to be able to afford cars like that!"

"Oh, those aren't the teachers' cars; those belong to the students."

That school had some fairly wealthy families that sent their kids there, and it was really only pocket change for those parents to buy their kids such nice sports cars. It was practically a school tradition.

That school also had another tradition: Every year at graduation there would be a bouquet of flowers in the chair for each kid who had died in a car accident and not made it to the ceremony as a result. Guess what kind of cars those kids often had? Well, we will give you a hint: It usually wasn't the kids who had had to slave to fix up a beater they'd bought with their own money just so that they had their own set of wheels.

Third, *parents have the right to restrict who rides with their teen when the teen is driving.* After all, most of the time it's their car. However, we ought to set reasonable restrictions by carefully explaining why certain people should not ride with our teens.

Finally, a word of caution. Most states allow teens to get their driver's license when they reach age sixteen. However, many teens who are chronologically sixteen are socially and emotionally age fourteen or younger. Some children, who may have repeated several grades, are still in junior high school at sixteen. Wise parents will discourage their teens from obtaining a license until they are socially and emotionally sixteen years of age. Generally speaking, this means the teen is functioning on an eleventh-grade level.

We are strong advocates for teens making a deposit in the parents' savings account, equal to the amount of the insurance deductible, prior to driving. The parent-teen understanding is that in the event of an accident the money will go to repair the car. The youngster will then be able to drive again once a new deposit is made. Teens who drive under these conditions are usually much safer drivers. Here's a sample conversation between Mom and teen on car insurance.

> TAMI: Mom, am I going to get to use the family car when I get my driver's license?
>
> MOM: Sure. All you'll need to do is make a deposit in my savings account for the amount of the insurance deductible: five hundred dollars.
>
> TAMI: How come?
>
> MOM: That way if you're unfortunate enough to have an accident, I won't have to worry about getting the car fixed.
>
> TAMI: I don't have that much money.
>
> MOM: Oh, I might consider holding something of yours for the deposit as long as it's valuable enough for me to sell quickly to get the five hundred dollars. Or maybe you'd like to call the agent and do some cost comparisons on lowering the deductible? Then you could make up the difference in the premiums. Either is fine with me.

Tami makes a call to the agent and comes back for another talk with Mom.

> TAMI: Geez, Mom, if we lower the deductible, the premiums go out of sight. I can't afford that.
>
> MOM: Now you know why we have a higher deductible. What are you going to do?
>
> TAMI: If I let you hold some of my stuff, do I still get to use it?
>
> MOM: No, banks don't operate that way.
>
> TAMI: Well, what happens if I have an accident and you sell my stuff to pay the deductible? Do I still get to drive?
>
> MOM: Oh, you'll get to drive again as soon as you come up with another deposit. But don't worry about it. I'm sure you'll be careful. Let me know when you've decided what you're going to do.

Church and Synagogue: When Teens Don't Want to Go

The battles about going to church are generally unnecessary. Why?

- The most effective method for raising faithful children is for parents to model their faith.
- There is an urge of the soul to turn to God. In times of trial, even committed atheists often find faith.
- One of the most common reasons given for rebelling against religion is a childhood history of tight rules of forced religion.
- If kids are raised with love and understanding—and that love and understanding is deeply rooted in the faith of their parents, even though kids will rebel against going to services for a time, most return stronger to their faith later in life, making it work in their own belief system rather than that of their parents.

There is an old hymn with the line, "I have returned to the faith of my fathers." Generally *faith-filled* parents have children who will model after them and become *faithful*. Overtly religious but controlling parents tend to have the most trouble with children who refuse to go to church.

Many teens start slacking off on youth group and church attendance. If faithful responses have been a part of the child's life growing up, then, barring obviously self-destructive behavior, most parents best handle the refusal with a relaxed but encouraging attitude. By encouraging their children to go to church without demanding it, they are recognizing that *a kiss demanded is not a kiss received, and church commanded is not a church believed.*

Even when children attend youth group faithfully in high school, they often forgo church in college or when they move out of the home. As one pastor said, laughing, "Some stay active by becoming leaders of youth. That way they can stay in youth group."

If a child appears to be making poor decisions in choice of friends or is behaving in a way that is of concern to the parents, then a church youth group with good leadership should be encouraged and generally the best method of encouragement is not going down the road that emphasizes how it would be *good* for the child, but how much the parent would appreciate the teen trying it out. As one mother wrote to her son:

Paul,
    I would really appreciate it if you would attend youth group four times.

Mom

Marci and Jack had an interesting solution that met their needs. They told their son that they would be happy for him to choose to stay home on Sunday to prepare a special meal for the family. He felt great about contributing to the quality of family life, but soon tired of the task and decided it was easier just to go to church with the rest of the family.

Of course, there are always ways to force adolescents to go to worship or youth group—tactics we don't advise. When parents do this, they do not allow their children to appreciate and value the experience on their own volition. We can exert our power and feel in control, or we can look for a creative long-term solution.

The important thing to remember is that parental demands will probably come to fruition in rebellion. Teens will fight parents who insist that "you have to believe what I believe."

But have faith. Disliking church is most likely a stage.

As little kids, they loved Sunday school. Then came the phase when they didn't want to go. However, if we haven't made church attendance the spiritual issue during the early years — presenting a good role model instead — our kids will almost always see value in going to church as they get older.

PEARL 8

College Expenses: Who Pays?

One of the best gifts we can give our teens is an education. If God has given us enough resources to help them obtain a college education, we should do it. The development of the mind is something permanent that we can do for our children, because neither hard economic times nor physical illness can take away an education.

But like all gifts and privileges, a college education can be abused. Teenagers are much more prone to be careless and drop out when someone else is paying for it.

Colleges themselves can abuse the education process because it's better for them financially if students take five or six years instead of four to graduate. Sometimes, the encouragement subtly creeps in for students to meander through school and "find themselves." The question is, whose dime is that done on?

Sometimes parents will fall into the trap of paying for college to "encourage" teens, falsely reasoning, "If I don't pay, he'll never get an education." Teens, of course, will use that argument too, to hook Mom and Dad into a guilt trip: "If you don't shell out for tuition, room and board, and books for Behemoth U, I'll have to beg for a living, and then what will your friends say?"

In roughly five decades of working with children, we have never seen a teen flunk out of college on his or her own dime. Allowing your son or daughter to finance a college education is one of the best (and last!) ways you can teach your teen fiscal and intellectual responsibility.

There are several options parents and their teens can use to pay for college:

- You can pay a percentage of college expenses, from none of them to all of them. If you are also going to pay for books, lodging, and incidentals, those should be covered in some sort of allowance that your student has responsibility over rather than you. Just giving a child a credit card whose bill is sent to you is not only dangerous, but also teaches the child nothing about fiscal management.
- The more responsible the teenager, the safer it is for you to pay more.
- The safest plan is for you to tell your teens, "You pay for the first semester of college. After you get through the first semester, send me a report card with average or above-average grades, and I'll reimburse you to help with the second semester."
- Some wise parents say, "I will pay for four years of under-graduate State U tuition. If you want to go out of state, fine: I'll pay the same amount as in-state tuition, and you pay for the difference."
- Some teens are really industrious and want to help pay for their own tuition, room and board, and books by working at often low-paying jobs. Their parents may want to reward their industriousness by matching their wages on a percentage basis to be agreed on by the teens and their parents.

Regardless of the financial plan you agree on, remember that college is the final transition from childhood to adulthood for teens. You can help them on their journey (and even inspire them to study harder) by discussing their classes, ideas, and adventures with them. This will help you monitor their progress while you build the kind of friendship you want to have with your adult children.

PEARL 9

Crisis Situations

A car wreck. A drug overdose. A suicide. A runaway teen. Families struggle with different kinds of crises, but every one carries its unique trauma and pain. When a crisis hits our lives or the lives of our teens, it can send us reeling. Guilt, worry, anxiety, anger, and inconsolable grief are some of the emotions that can stagger us.

When a crisis hits, the first thing to remember is, don't panic. Most of us think that something has to be done *right now*. This is seldom true. The Chinese language has an intriguing character for *crisis*, combining the symbols for *danger* and *opportunity*. We see the danger all too well, but we often miss the opportunity.

Use these four thoughts to help you deal with a crisis:

1. Crises, by their very nature, are generally temporary. Knowing that better times lie ahead can help you guard against overinvolvement and overreaction.
2. Almost no crisis must be dealt with immediately. You will usually have time to pray and think and act rationally.
3. Cope with the what-ifs by asking yourself what the worst possible outcome of the crisis would be. Often you'll find that you can actually cope with that.
4. As much as you can, keep the monkey on the back of the person(s) responsible for the problems related to the crisis.

The knowledge that every crisis is temporary helps us to avoid becoming overinvolved. Generally, in every crisis there is time to seek advice from others who have had similar experiences or who are professionally capable of dealing with the situation.

Sometimes what we might perceive as a crisis is certainly a serious issue but not really a crisis. The problem—such as illicit sexual activity, a life-threatening illness, or drug use—may have been going on for months or years. Then it comes to the attention of the parents, and *that's* what makes it a crisis! Sometimes we need to stop, take some time, and evaluate the situation in order to decide how best to respond appropriately.

You may find it helpful to ask yourself, "What would happen if I did nothing at all?" That may not be a good solution, but it might clarify things enough so that you'll get a better idea of what you *are* able to do. When you're up against a crisis, don't just react. First sit down and write out all your options. Then talk over those options with a person you respect.

Good resources at this time are people you respect at your place of worship, at school, or at county social services, or friends and neighbors who have a good track record with raising their own children. Many local sheriffs' offices and police departments have a chaplain. They are familiar with the resources available.

Don't pass up this opportunity to solidify your relationship with your teen. We often get some great help and understanding from teens when we ask, "How can I best help you through this?"

The appealing thing about acting hastily is that you can almost always "do something." But once you do something—such as moving a person with a broken back—it may be difficult to undo what you've done. What's more important is doing the *right thing*—not just *something*.

A general rule is that the more sincere questions a parent asks, the better the results. The more orders, accusations, and demands, the worse we mess up the situation.

Finally, it's important that you acknowledge the worst possible outcome. Often that outcome is simply death. Once you look it in the face, you won't be spending valuable energy trying to deny that possibility. The acceptance will free you to focus your energies in positive directions. Keep the faith; it's your best weapon.

Curfews

The real world doesn't have curfews, except during civil emergencies. If we're raising our teens to live in the real world, we shouldn't have curfews either. Instead we should negotiate when they will come home.

I (Jim) remember how my wife, Shirley, and I negotiated with our teenagers. We would start when they were thirteen and ask, "Where are you going to be? How long? Is that enough time? Can you get home by then? Will you let us know if it's a problem?" And they continued negotiating with us as they got older.

The rule in our household was, "We'll know where you are and you'll know where we are. So if we go away, we'll let you know. If there's an emergency, we always want to be able to get in touch with you. You need to be able to contact us."

That worked pretty well until I came home two hours late one night, and Charlie, our youngest, started yelling at me that he'd been worrying about his father for two hours. Then I found out that it was a two-way street.

I (Foster) didn't have firm curfews with my kids either. We'd say, "What time do you expect to be home?"

Our son would respond, "Well, the dance is over at twelve, and we may go out to get something to eat afterwards. I'll be home at one"

"Well, if you're not going to be home at one, will you phone?"

"Yes."

Later we'd have to make sure that when he did phone us, we didn't say, "Now look, you said you were going to be home at one." Then he'd never phone again. Instead we took a deep breath and said, "Gee, thanks for phoning. What are the new plans?"

"We're popping corn at Jeanne's."

"Is that all you're popping?"

"Yes, Dad!"

"Thank you. Okay, just checking. Now, when do you think you'll be home?"

"Well, we thought we'd stay here another hour, and then we'll be home."

"Okay. Thanks."

I (Jim) also had to be up front with my teens when they came in late. I'd say something like, "You didn't get home on time. I missed a lot of sleep. I was really concerned for you. We'll talk about it another time." Then I went off to bed. I would keep my mouth shut until the next time they said they were going to go out, then I'd say, "Oh gee, I'm just not up to worrying tonight. Why don't you stick around?" or "I'm sorry. You can't go out tonight, honey. I need my sleep."

When teenagers don't come home at a reasonable hour, most parents react first by getting scared and then by getting angry. We can't do anything by getting scared, so we get mad. But in this case, anger is an ineffective emotion.

If we can show our teenagers that their coming home late frightens us, it will have more power and impact than our anger. We don't want to worry; that's why we would appreciate knowing where they are and hearing from them by phone when they're late. We want them to come home when they're supposed to, whatever the agreed-upon time.

Here's a conversation in which a Love and Logic parent helps her teen see that phoning home if she's going to be late is a sensible agreement:

MOM: We're not the type of parents who are always worrying. Let's say you're supposed to be home by midnight, but you show up at two instead. If we don't have an agreement that you will call to tell us where you are and how much later you're going to be, we'll just figure that you're out there somewhere, doing fine. But you could be lying beside the road. And fifteen minutes could be the difference in saving your life.

BRITTANY: Gee, Mom, don't make it sound so dramatic. I'm not going out to look for trouble and wind up in a gang fight.

MOM: I didn't think so. You see, if we have an agreement that you will give me a phone call if you're going to be later than you're supposed to be, then I know what to do when 12:01 a.m. rolls around and you were supposed to be in by midnight but you haven't called. I'll phone the police and tell them, 'I'm not an overprotective parent. My kid is always responsible about phoning. This is the license plate on her car. She's in trouble somewhere.' Then I can get you help real quick.

BRITTANY: Well, that seems reasonable. But why make such a big deal about it?

MOM: Because if we make a decision that you can come in anytime and you're not going to phone me when you're late, then my decision is to figure that you're probably okay somewhere. Maybe you're not, but you won't be getting any help. So give it some thought.

BRITTANY: Okay, I can live with that.

We can put faith in people to act in their own best interests. We act on this faith when we say, "If you operate in this way, your life is likely to be more happy. So please give it some thought."

Another way to handle this is to have your sons or daughters leave a list of numbers where they will be and then let them know that you will be setting your alarm for the time they are expected home. You trust them, so it is no problem to go to sleep when they are out; however, should that alarm wake you and they haven't called to let you know they will be home later, then you know something is wrong and you will start calling everyone on that list, ending with the police. However, if they are home on time, they can simply slip into your room and turn the alarm off before it wakes you. If you are worried about them drinking, then having them lean over you to turn the alarm off also gives you a good chance to smell their breath.

We're often most effective when we simply let our teens know what our concerns are. For example, when our teen comes home late, we could say, "I hope this doesn't happen again because I think it stresses our relationship. And you're way ahead if our relationship is good. I think that when you do things that stress me out a lot, it doesn't work out well for you in the long run. So I hope you give these things some thought."

PEARL 11

Dating

Brooke's parents were proud of her. She was in the ninth grade, but she was so mentally advanced for her age that she was taking eleventh-grade math. But math wasn't the only thing Brooke liked. She was maturing physically and liked the guys. Several juniors had already asked her out.

Her parents didn't feel the same way about junior guys. They firmly said no, telling her, "Well, you're not *that* mature." Brooke and her mom couldn't resolve the issue, so they came to Foster for advice. Mom stood her ground and stated flatly that no way would her daughter date boys two years older than she was.

Brooke wailed, "Mom, if you knew those ninth-grade boys, you wouldn't want to date them either."

There is no hard-and-fast "right" age to begin dating, nor is there an appropriate limit to the age difference between your teen and the teen he or she wants to date (notice we said *teen*, not twenty-some-year-old who works at one of the shops in the mall).

Such rules about dating, like most other rules, create their own problems. As soon as you come up with a hard-and-fast rule, your teen will bring up an exception to that rule. In turn, dating becomes another control battle that the parent will lose, and they consequently will lose respect in the eyes of the child.

For example, Gretchen's mom told her that she was forbidden to date that no-good biker, Bill. As far as her mom knew, Gretchen never dated Bill, but because Gretchen's every move could not be monitored,

Bill did become the father of her baby. Mom was unwise to ignore Gretchen's emerging independence.

We might think it's hard to avoid such rules like the ones Gretchen's mom set for her, especially when our children are about to begin dating. We've been used to our children's behavior within our families and with their friends. But now dating comes along and seems to be the springboard that launches our children into adolescence and adulthood as they interact with the opposite sex. We worry about them taking the plunge.

We should be excited for our teens at this time. It helps to remember that girls and boys mature at different rates. Although there are exceptions, girls like Brooke mature earlier than boys and usually begin dating earlier than boys too. We can invite our teens to talk to us about kids they're interested in or about who's interested in them. But we should cut them some slack if they don't want to talk about dating.

Inevitably, some dates are diamonds and some dates are lumps of coal. Teens' egos tend to be fragile at this time, especially in boys when girls turn them down for dates. We need to befriend our children when they go through times that seem overwhelmingly traumatic.

Discuss with your teens who they will date, the activities they will engage in, and the hours they will keep. You might want to offer some suggestions for activities and how to behave toward their dates so that they will want to go out with them again (though, of course, that opens other issues). After all, you dated once too! These discussions can go a long way in enhancing your friendship with your teens.

You should also let them know the true purpose of dating: having fun and getting to be more comfortable and better friends with members of the opposite sex. Teens aren't courting to find the person they will marry, so they should treat this as an opportunity to learn how to build healthy relationships and friendships. Certainly, physical intimacy is wonderful, but that is why it is saved for later in life. The real hurts come not from being unable to connect physically, but from failures in relating mentally, emotionally, socially, and spiritually. Dating is the opportunity to explore those types of connections and relationships in those areas; the physical should wait until our teens have met that someone they have committed to spend the rest of their life with.

When your teens date, it's important to know who their friends are. Show interest in your teen's friends, even if you don't approve of everything about them. After all, you wouldn't want your teen to judge *your* friends.

Have faith that you've taught your child some lessons about how to make decisions. And have faith in your child to make the right decisions and live with the consequences.

A girl once told Foster, "Up until midnight, I'm a princess. But at one minute past twelve, I turn into a pumpkin." Her parents, ordering her to "be back at midnight and not one minute later!" had not yet learned to have faith in their daughter or her ability to make decisions.

We shouldn't jump to the assumption that an otherwise responsible son or daughter will act irresponsibly while dating. On the other hand, it's foolish to assume that an irresponsible teen will behave responsibly.

Those assumptions about teens' responsibilities (or lack of them) in dating hit closest to home when parents deal with their teens' dating and possible sexual activity. Parents like to warn their teens of all the dangers of premarital intimacy, but we need to realize that behind every warning lies a hidden expectation.

Wise parents don't send the message to their children that they will engage in early sex by saying something irresponsible like, "You better watch out! Your emotions will get the best of you and before you know it you'll have sex." Such a pessimistic comment appears to make sexually responsible behavior nearly impossible for teens. So if they engage in sex, teens will then reason, "It's something we couldn't help!"

Much better is for you to share clearly both good sexual values as well as basic information. You might say, "Dating and intimacy can lead to sexual involvement. Before you take such a step, you need to decide for yourself if having sex before marriage is a wise choice. You already know how I feel about that. But if it does happen I'm sure you will talk to me about it. Act responsibly, and the consequences of your decision will be easier to live with." Such a discussion shows your teen that you're not as ignorant about his or her behavior as your teen might assume. It also fosters mutual respect between parents and teens.

Keep discussions matter-of-fact. With responsible teens, we don't have to elaborate on what the consequences of a pregnancy or an STI might be. With irresponsible teens, however, we must ask appropriate questions: "How would you pay for an obstetrician?" "How would you care for a baby?" "What kind of job would you get to support a family?" "How would you explain to your future dates and spouse that you have herpes or are sterile because you had sex as a teen?" These are not flippant questions. They have lifelong implications.

If your teen has not yet shown that he or she is responsible, you need to bring a jolt of reality by telling him or her that dating could be a rough road. You might say, "This is a two-generation home, where parents and children live; not a three-generation home of parents, children, and grandchildren. This is not a group home for children." For most teens, that's a nice way of saying, "If you have children, you won't live here," and communicating the expectation that they will make good choices and conduct themselves responsibly.

Since there is no fixed rule about when a teen is old enough to date, our emphasis should be on the teen's decision making and what you both have agreed on through conversation. A teen is ready when he or she can describe a plan for handling the situations that concern the parent.

PEARL 12

Disrespect

Sometimes our teens' problems become our problems as well. These problems often revolve around the issue of their disrespect for us. But in order to gain our teens' respect, we must first learn to respect ourselves.

One of my (Jim's) friends had teenagers who were just impossible. She told me, "I couldn't drive anywhere without them hanging out the windows, yelling at other motorists, telling other people how to drive, flipping the bird, the whole works. It was so embarrassing, I couldn't stand it."

She resolved the problem by applying Love and Logic principles — first, to herself. The next time her teens started acting up, she pulled over, got out of the car, and said, "Okay, everybody. *Out*."

But she had a problem with this order. She was staring at two teen-agers twice her size who responded, "No way. You can't make us get out." And she thought to herself, *At this point, they're right.*

Like all good consultant parents, she started to buy time. In other words, she started backpedaling. The first thing she said was, "Did I forget to ask in a nice way?"

They said, "You asked in a nice way."

She said, "And you're not going to do it?"

And they said, "No way. You can't make us get out."

"Oh boy, I thought it would work."

"It won't work on us."

"Well, I'd better think this over."

"Yeah, you'd better think it over a whole bunch."

"Would you guys mind if I walked across the street to that restaurant and got a cup of coffee while I'm thinking this over?"

And these smart-alecky teens said, "Mom, whatever turns you on. You've just got to go for it."

So she said, "Thank you," and walked across the street. They immediately started playing their radios, having a wonderful time to show her that it didn't bother them. After a while, they noticed she'd been gone fifteen minutes, then twenty minutes. Pretty soon they were saying, "Wait a minute! What's going on here?"

Suddenly something very strange happened across the street. Mom's best friend drove up to the front of the restaurant. Mom came out, got in the car, and off she went with a little wave on the way.

This mom later recalled that she thought they would be madder than hornets when they got home. But she was ready for them. She watched them get out of the taxi and walk to the front door. When they walked in, they did not say one word. Months went by, and they never said a word. She thinks they'll bring it up at some family reunion: "Oh, Mom, remember that day you ditched us?"

This mom gained respect. How? By taking good care of herself first. "The bigger my kids get, the more I have to fall back on that," she said.

"Up until that day, I was a doormat for them. They wiped their feet on me all the time. They had no respect whatsoever. I used to beg for it. I used to demand it. I used to yell at my husband, 'What are you going to do to make those kids show me some respect?!' I finally discovered something: You never ever get respect by demanding or pleading for it; you get respect when you start treating yourself with respect."

And you know what her teens had been saying to themselves all that time? "Well, it's my mom, and she knows herself better than anybody else. She knows whether or not she deserves any respect." They now say, "My mom knows herself better than anybody else. She knows she deserves respect."

"Life is a whole lot better just after that one time," this mom reflected. "We don't have to do it over and over. Isn't that funny? The consequences of winning respect came like a bolt out of the blue — with no anger, with no lectures, and with words at a minimum. I feel a whole lot more powerful now than I ever did before because I'm learning how to take care of myself. I used to think it would hurt my kids if I did that. But I'm finding out that they're more capable and fun to be around."

Teens' respect for their parents is a critical issue for how families function. But paradoxically, we win others' respect only after we demonstrate respect for ourselves.

In extreme cases when disrespectful teens refuse to change no matter how much we model respect for ourselves, we may want to seek professional help. But for most conflicts, our self-respect will cancel out our teens' disrespect.

PEARL 13

Divorce and Visitation

When parents divorce, the casualty list includes the kids too. They may experience mood swings, defensiveness about being touched, general problems with schoolwork, lack of interest, and laziness.

Luckily, such behavior is often part of a normal grieving process and can be alleviated by following these ten guidelines for divorced or divorcing parents. Remember that there is no way to make it good for the kids. In their eyes divorce is a disaster. These guidelines are offered as a way to make a bad situation a little better.

1. Expect teens to handle the divorce as well as the adults handle it. If a divorce is marked by bitterness, lack of communication, and anger, the children will probably behave in much the same way as the parents.

2. Let the children know that the divorce is not their fault. Some children may think, "If I had been a better kid, my parents wouldn't be divorcing." A parent can say, "Michael, you know that some kids are friends and then decide they can't get along. Well, that's kind of what has happened with Dad and me. But we both still love you."

3. Be honest about feelings and observations. Parents need to tell their teens, without giving details, how they feel about the ex-spouse and why. It is also helpful to give the other parent's point of view. While it is important to let children know our concerns, it is equally important to let them know that the ex-spouse continues to love them (if that is true). Bad-mouthing the ex-spouse backfires.

4. Understand children's misbehavior without excusing it. Encourage your kids to express their feelings, but continue to give consequences for misbehavior. Parents must never tolerate disrespect.

5. Give children a support group. Teens need someone outside the family to talk with: school counselors, teachers, peer groups, or friends of the family.

6. Post-divorce counseling for parents and children may help. When communication is poor and distrust rampant between the adults, counseling is almost always helpful, especially if both adults would really like things to improve.

7. Remain available without prying. Children sometimes give answers their parent wants to hear. They can figure out what the parent is looking for. If one parent is looking for evidence that the other is a jerk, the kids will feed that desire. The parental attitude must be, "Tell me your thoughts; I can handle them," regardless of what those thoughts may be.

8. Handle visitation issues directly with the ex-spouse. It is never wise to send messages to the ex-partner through the kids. If you want that person to know something, contact him or her directly.

9. Children need moms and dads. Generally, it is best to encourage children to call a stepparent "Mom" or "Dad." Kids won't forget who the "real" parent is.

10. The birth parent must back the stepparent in discipline completely. The parent must let the child know that his or her new spouse is a lifetime partner.

Sometimes parents worry about *when* to tell their children about an impending divorce, but *when* is not nearly as important as *how* the child is told. Hand-wringing and overdoing apologies indicate guilt. Understandably, many children take advantage of guilt-ridden adults. A guilty-sounding parent may covertly be saying, "If it weren't for my problems, you wouldn't be acting this way, so you have every reason to complain, treat me with disrespect, and behave inappropriately." So, wise parents, while admitting their humanness, are not overly apologetic. They might handle such a situation something like this:

> Guys, Mom and I have figured out a plan that we think will help us all live much happier lives. I know you know we have had a good deal of disagreements—maybe you didn't—but we have decided to get a divorce and that it is best if we live in different houses for now. I know you love your sister (or brother), but can you imagine spending a whole lifetime with her (him)? We have decided that we don't want to live a whole lifetime together either.

Here are some other basic things to keep in mind when talking with your children:

> *1. Do not blame one parent or the other:* If the child starts crying, it's okay to hug them and hold them. A lot doesn't need to be said. If the parents handle the situation calmly and factually, the teens probably will too.
>
> *2. Do not be a Pollyanna,* putting a nice spin on everything, but stress that there could be benefits: getting to see new places, meeting new people, helping to pick out pictures for a parent's new apartment, etcetera.

In talking with our kids about divorce, we might take note of how this mother counseled her thirteen-year-old, Alyssa:

> MOM: So, Alyssa, do you think you'll be affected by Dad's and my divorce, or will it have no effect on you, or what?
> ALYSSA: I think it's pretty bad.
> MOM: Oh, really? Why's that?
> ALYSSA: I don't want you to get divorced from Dad.
> MOM: Oh, why is that? You know we fought all the time.
> ALYSSA: Yeah, but I try to be good so you won't fight.

MOM: Do you think we're fighting over your not being good, or do we fight over other things?

ALYSSA: I don't know.

MOM: Well, I want you to know that your dad and I do fight a lot, but frankly, most of it isn't over you. I think we'd be getting a divorce even if we'd never had children. You know this divorce makes me feel troubled. But just because it upsets me, does that mean it has to upset you too? Or are you going to decide by yourself how much it upsets you?

ALYSSA: I don't want you to be upset.

MOM: Well, I am, honey. I thought I would be married to your dad for life. But you'll still get to see him a lot anyway. So you don't have to be upset just because I'm upset. Because who was going to live with him his whole life? I was, right? That was never the plan for you. So I should be more upset about it.

ALYSSA: I was only going to live with him until I was eighteen?

MOM: Right. So the main thing is, I don't want you to feel troubled just because I'm upset. You can decide for yourself how you're going to feel. What should you think about more—the divorce or your schoolwork?

ALYSSA: My schoolwork.

MOM: That would be great.

The message divorcing parents should send to their kids is, "This isn't going to wreck your lives. I know you can handle it. It might be hard, but now you may have three or four adults who love you instead of only two." Kids whose parents divorce have a much easier time if the parents are positive.

Using Love and Logic Between Two Homes

Unfortunately, when kids have two homes because of divorce, discussions like the following happen all too often:

CHERYL: Sam, how could you let me down like this again? I think you do these things just to undermine what I'm trying to do with our daughter. You said you would support me by not letting her drive, and then you turn around and give her your extra car to drive. How are we supposed to make her responsible if you reverse every decision we make?

SAM: Now, Cheryl, you don't have to be so upset. I was going to call you and tell you that I think you're just overreacting on this. What she's doing is just typical teenage stuff. Maybe if you'd lighten up a little, you'd both be a lot happier.

CHERYL: Wait just a minute, Sam! That kind of behavior might be typical for some teenagers, but it's not how all teens act. She's gone way over the line lately. She doesn't feel that she has any limits at all, and I can see why. Every time she misbehaves, you're there to excuse it away and turn me into the bad guy for trying to hold her accountable for her actions.

Here we see two divorced parents embroiled in a classic struggle. It may have been a competition for Sara's love on Sam's part. But it probably went deeper than that. Sam was a caring man who didn't like conflict. He lived to make sure his daughter is always happy. Playing the role of the good guy was easy for him. It fit right into his lifelong pattern of conflict avoidance. It also helped him deal with his fear of losing Sara to her mother.

Cheryl, on the other hand, was left with the responsibility of helping their daughter grow into a responsible person. She knew that this could happen only if she set limits and held Sara accountable for her actions. But it often put her in the role of the bad guy in her daughter's eyes. In spite of this dilemma, she tried to hold the line with Sara, even in the face of unintentional but very damaging acts of sabotage by her ex-husband.

Trying to be a good parent, Cheryl was making several mistakes that continue to lock all three into a vicious cycle: Sara misbehaved, Cheryl punished, and Sam overturned the punishment.

Sam's mistakes: Sam was willing to sacrifice Sara's long-term happiness and quality of life in exchange for her short-term happiness. He feared the loss of Sara's love and lives with the mistaken idea that she would appreciate and respect him in the role of her protector. Overturning his ex-wife's discipline also gave him a chance to make

Mom look bad in his daughter's eyes. He didn't realize that Sara may eventually view him with contempt for sabotaging her relationship with Mom.

Cheryl's mistakes: Cheryl held on to a fantasy that she and Sam were a team. If she couldn't get him to cooperate when they were married, what were the chances that this would happen after they'd lived through the pain of divorce?

Based on this mistaken idea, Cheryl imposed consequences that she insisted be upheld when her daughter was at Sam's house. This gave Sam both the opportunity and the power to rescind the punishment and place himself in the role of Sara's hero.

Cheryl's next mistake was believing that she could make both homes work the same. All the energy she used trying to make this happen was energy that could have been spent on things she could actually control.

Her next mistake was trying to reason with Sam about this problem. All her discussions accomplished was to give her ex-husband yet another opportunity to go on the offensive and to attack her parenting attempts. The more she reasoned with and begged him, the worse the problem gets.

Cheryl's solution: Once she decided to take control of the situation, Cheryl imposed consequences that applied only while Sara was with her. If her daughter tried to get Sam to intervene, Cheryl would not allow him to change her mind.

Her next step was to share her love and her thoughts with Sara. Because their relationship was strained, it was very unlikely that Cheryl could get all of her thoughts out without facing a counterattack. At times like this, teens are experts at taking parents on "bird walks," arguing each point until both are totally off the subject at hand. What starts out as a discussion, soon becomes a fight. Neither person has heard the other.

The solution was for Cheryl to put her thoughts in writing. Notice how her letter begins with a wonderful attention-getting strategy.

Dear Sara,

I need to apologize to you. I'm doing it in writing just in case you want to revisit my thoughts in the future. Please don't feel a need to respond right away. I just want you to think about this for a while.

I have made a big mistake not being open with you about the fact that your dad and I often differ on how to be parents. I have spent too much time trying to make him be the same as I am. That's not fair to you or to him. We both love you very much but have different ways of showing it. By trying to make him do things my way, I have put you in the middle of our unhappiness. This often happens in marriages and especially happens in divorces.

My way of showing my love for you is to work hard to help you become a good person. To do this, I have to hold you accountable for your actions. This means I also have to be prepared for you to be angry with me in the short term.

The mistake I have been making is to ask your dad to discipline you over things that happen in my house. I'm not going to be doing that anymore. You and I will take care of those problems without involving Dad. Dad can deal with any problems that come up at his house without interference from me. I hope that this will be less confusing for you.

You are growing up with two different kinds of parents. As time goes on, you will have plenty of different thoughts and feelings about both of us. Please remember that we both love you very much. I hope you know that the divorce was not your fault. I hope you know that it's okay to love both Dad and me at the same time.

Love,
Mom

This was a tough letter for Cheryl to write. There were many things she wanted to say but knew better. She wanted to share her feelings of anger and hurt toward Sam. She felt a twinge of desire to tell Sara how irresponsible she believed Sam to be. She wanted to scream out, "Your dad is messing up your life! Look at me! I'm the one who *really* cares!"

Instead Cheryl walked the much healthier and nobler path. Why? Because she realized that each time she criticized Sam in front of her daughter, she drove her daughter further away. Even though Sam rescued and excused Sara from her poor decisions, he was an important part of her life. If Cheryl were to bad-mouth him, it would do much more damage than his rescuing behavior. Sara would learn some positive things from Dad and learn how to take good care of herself and be responsible from Mom. Cheryl staying out of the "blame game" would allow Sara to sit back, watch her parents, and gather what's good from each.

After all, isn't that what we all want for our kids?

PEARL 14

Drug or Substance Abuse

Substance or drug abuse is, unfortunately, a common youth problem. There are eight facts to keep in mind when considering teen substance abuse:

1. Alcohol is the most commonly abused substance.
2. Cigarette smoking is a leading cause of death in the United States. It contributes to cancer, heart disease, diabetes, and a number of other long-term and eventually terminal illnesses.
3. Nicotine is the most addictive substance.
4. There are different types of drug use. Some are more dangerous than others.
5. Cocaine and other drugs are distributed to elementary-school-age children in almost all parts of the country and in all socioeconomic groups. Methamphetamines has become the new drug of choice because it is easier to make and cheaper to buy. Unfortunately, new drugs and ways to abuse them are being discovered every day.
6. The best insurance against drug abuse is a loving and open relationship between parent and child.
7. Parents need to know how to talk to their children about substance experimentation, use, and abuse.
8. Parents need to be aware of the signs of drug abuse, while understanding that other problems may mimic drug abuse.

Now let's fill in some information on issues related to the above list.

Types of Drug Abuse

It's important to understand that there are many types of drug use and abuse. Some are more dangerous than others. The largest group of drug abusers is adults. The legal substances of nicotine and alcohol kill more Americans, by far, than illegal drugs. Nicotine is now thought to be the most addictive of all drugs, including cocaine. Awareness of these facts can help us keep things in perspective, which is often lost these days.

Drug use falls into three categories: drug experimentation, drug use, and drug abuse. Most children will experiment with drugs sometime during adolescence. However, of those who experiment, most do not go on to use or abuse drugs, although it is also true that almost all who abuse cocaine and other dangerous drugs started out experimenting with nicotine or alcohol first. But experimentation with nicotine or alcohol does not necessarily lead to experimentation with or abuse of harder drugs.

How to Draw the Line on Drug Use

Parents must take a hard line around drug experimentation and abuse without becoming angry. This may be difficult, but it is essential. Parents who are willing to be consequential and not rescue their children tend to be quieter. Anger, shouting, and ranting all decrease the teen's self-image and put stress on the parent-child relationship. When teens and parents fight, it simply makes drug use more likely.

Substance abuse does not happen in a vacuum. It is directly related to the parent-child bond of love and good communication. We can't order our teens not to take drugs. As a matter of fact, drug use is often a sign of rebellion; therefore, orders are bound to make the problem worse. Instead of orders, we should offer our thoughts and opinions on drug experimentation and abuse, and then allow consequences, without jumping in to rescue our teens.

We have an obligation to take care of ourselves and make that commitment clear to the teen. Therefore, we need to let our teens know, calmly and clearly, that if illegal drugs are in the home, we are accessories to crime. We should communicate to our teens that, if necessary in order to protect ourselves, we will call the police and grant them permission to search the premises.

Similarly, if the teen is drinking and driving, the parent will simply phone the sheriff or highway patrol, give them the license plate number of the car, and tell them that teens in the car may be risking their own and others' safety on the highway.

We should state these realities to our teens in a loving, matter-of-fact way. They need to know that we don't want to live with the guilt we would experience if they killed someone while drinking and driving, and we had suspected the problem but done nothing.

Remember, statements about taking good care of ourselves and refusing to become accessories to crime are much more effective than lecturing teens about what's good for them. We can let our kids know that if we get in trouble for drug use, we won't expect them to hire lawyers and bail us out. Likewise, we won't bail them out. All drug users, we can say, must deal with the law on their own.

Informing Our Teens About Drugs

It's essential for us to obtain fact-based articles about drug abuse and suggest our children read them. If we don't force our teens to read information, they will generally be interested when we provide straightforward and informative evidence.

Girls particularly need to know about the effects of drugs during the first trimester of pregnancy. In Dade County, Florida, for example, currently thousands of infants are born each year to cocaine-addicted mothers. These children are at high risk for having learning disorders and developmental difficulties.

Signs of Drug Use

Socially, signs of drug use and abuse may include a sudden worsening of school grades or sudden changes in friendships at school. Sometimes a drug abuser will experience mood and attitude changes for no apparent reason.

Use of marijuana leads to a red-rimmed appearance of the eyes. Acute signs of drug abuse may include enlarged pupils. Kids on amphetamines may appear overly paranoid, or they seem to have a chip on their shoulder all the time. Highs may be followed by depressive lows. Perhaps the major symptom following even infrequent methamphetamine experimentation is a lack of joy in life, or anhedonia. One adolescent told Foster, "Now, since my weekends using meth, it's just as if nothing seems to make life worthwhile. I don't enjoy anything. Everything seems flat." Long-term use leads to weight loss, paranoia, insomnia, and possible cardiac failure.

There are medical problems, however, that closely parallel the symptoms of acute drug abuse. Manic depression is one example. Also, natural physiological changes associated with adolescence can trigger behavioral fluctuations. A child who has previously been doing very well in school may suddenly appear angry, accompanied by an abrupt drop in grades. This shift usually occurs around ages fourteen or fifteen, more often in girls than boys.

What to Do When You Suspect Drug Use
If you suspect drug use, here is what we suggest you do:

1. *Remain calm.* Drug use (besides an overdose) is not an emergency. As with other "crises," drug use may have been going on for a long time, but it only becomes a crisis when we find out about it.
2. *Talk it over with your teen.*
3. *Talk to the school counselor.*
4. *Find out if your teen's friends and siblings are concerned.* This is not an issue of others "ratting" on your teen. True friends and family members shouldn't maintain silence if your teen is engaged in self-destructive behavior.

Confronting substance abuse provides an excellent opportunity to open lines of communication between parent and teen. But remember that if you respond by getting upset and angry over your teen's drug use, you will most likely worsen the problem.

Don't hesitate to get professional help. These types of problems are not solved with a parenting book.

Pearl 15

Eating Disorders

M andy looked in the mirror for the twentieth time that day and cursed. "I can't seem to lose any weight," she sobbed softly.

Actually, Mandy had lost a lot of weight in the past six months. Her clothes hung loosely around her bony figure. But it still wasn't good enough for her. She still looked fat, or so she thought.

She rarely hung around for dinner, and when she did, she just picked at her food. Afterward she would often head directly to the bathroom, put a finger down her throat, and throw up what she had eaten only a few minutes before.

Mandy's eating disorder can kill her if she doesn't get help. Approximately 10 percent of teens with anorexia die, even with treatment.

No one is really sure what causes anorexia. It may be linked to depression in the family, especially the mother's depression. Studies indicate that it occurs in one of every twenty-five thousand females. The average woman who becomes anorexic starts out weighing between 140 to 150 pounds and may drop to as little as 70 pounds, apparently unaware of the physical consequences of such drastic weight loss. But there are no "typical" cases of anorexia; they vary from person to person.

Although there are cases of boys becoming anorexic, the disease has primarily affected females. Almost always, those females are in the young reproductive phase of their lives. Anorexia usually starts when a girl feels insecure, is made fun of, or feels that her femininity is threatened. It accelerates with vomiting (bulimia), constipation, and the cessation of menstruation. The girl aggravates the problem with intense physical activity.

Some girls who turn anorexic are deluded into thinking that they can ward off pregnancy by staying thin. Other young women are fast-track professionals who believe the only way they can compete in a "man's world" is to be thin.

As the girl gets thinner, she becomes the center of attention. This traps parents who recognize their daughter has a problem but don't want to draw attention to it. Parents make her anorexia worse by encouraging her to eat more.

Because the circumstances surrounding anorexia and other eating disorders vary so much, the best recourse for parents is to seek professional help for their child.

Entitlement

COUNSELOR: So, Haley, what's happening in your life that brings you into counseling with me?

HALEY: It's my parents. They're clueless! All they can do is bitch and moan about my credit cards and phone bills. They are so living in the past. They don't get it. There's lots more important things than grades. And they don't have a clue about what kids need. My dad bought me this stupid four-door car. He knows I was supposed to get a convertible.

COUNSELOR: When your dad called to set up these sessions, he told me that money is really tight and that if things don't change, he will have to consider bankruptcy. Given the situation, do you feel any guilt about the amount of money you spend?

HALEY: Of course not! I didn't ask to be born into this stupid family. Besides, that's what parents are supposed to do. They're supposed to buy great stuff for their kids.

We're not sure who to feel sorry for in situations like this: Haley, her parents, or all America. As outrageous as Haley seemed, we all know kids like her. She and her counselor are real people. Haley is suffering from the belief of entitlement. Once she started to believe that it is her birthright to have everything she wants as soon as she wants it, she was doomed. She will never have enough to satisfy her. Her happiness will not be based on what she can attain through effort, but will depend on how others serve or provide for her. She will enter the adult world expecting far too much from others and far too little from herself.

Haley's parents tore up their parent license early in her life. By treating her like an honored guest in the home, they became product and service providers instead of parents. As the years went by, they stripped her of the need to act responsibly.

As Haley enters the adult world, what her parents once provided will become society's responsibility. And that will never be enough to satisfy her. Entitled people see themselves as victims. Once this sets in, all unhappiness and all disappointments are the fault of others.

Haley's parents, in their efforts to create a perfect life for their child, failed to teach her that adulthood requires personal restraints regarding personal behavior. Her discussion with the counselor indicates that she has no ability to see how her behavior impacts others, both in her home and in society.

Unfortunately, parents who try to teach responsibility are consistently faced with the fact that it is not reinforced in other parts of their children's lives. What is reinforced is a belief in limitless entitlement.

Many kids arrive at college with wealth that they have not earned. They have no idea how to attain or maintain their lifestyle other than demanding it from their parents. They have lots of money to spend, but no idea how to earn it.

As the authors of the Love and Logic approach, we have major concerns about the rapid growth of entitlement in our young people and its threat to society. As we study this problem we have become aware of the beliefs that entitled people harbor. Following are what we call the "Highs and Lows of Entitlement."

HIGH: High need for goods and services.
LOW: Low pressure to succeed or to hold down a job.

HIGH: High amount of time to party.
LOW: Low amount of time to devote to effort toward accomplishment.

HIGH: High expectations of others.

LOW: Low ambition.

HIGH: High resentment for those who would require them to achieve through study and effort.
LOW: Low appreciation for the opportunity for an education.

HIGH: High demand for entertainment and excitement.
LOW: Low awareness of the sacrifices made by their parents.

HIGH: High willingness to defy society's traditional rules and values.
LOW: Low respect for adults and leaders.

HIGH: High inclination to find substitute highs such as alcohol and drugs.
LOW: Low respect for society's traditional rules.

The foundation for these beliefs is created in early life. Actually, this problem is not started by kids, but by parents who fail to set reasonable limits for behavior. It is normal for kids to want what they see advertised. However, many parents don't do a good job of helping their kids distinguish between a want and a need. Young children don't naturally place limits on themselves. This is the parent's job.

Faced with society's pressures and the fact that personal responsibility is not reinforced in many parts of our lives, we need to do three things:

1. Hold tight to our belief that kids need to learn how to get what they want through their own effort and struggle. After all, it is only finding success after such efforts that builds positive self-esteem.
2. Acquire skills for setting and enforcing limits and boundaries.
3. Surround ourselves with like-minded friends so that we don't have to listen to the mistaken beliefs of those who are busy raising entitled children.

Your Kids Can Be the Fortunate Ones

Obviously, until universities, high schools, community leaders, and particularly parents work together to provide a culture that encourages coping skills by allowing children to experience the fruits of their good and poor decisions, the culture of self-indulgence will be hard to overcome. Thankfully, though, we have seen many parents who are successful at helping their kids avoid the infliction of entitlement. Parents who study and use Love and Logic parenting techniques increase the odds of raising kids who do not show symptoms of entitlement.

Fortunate are the children whose parents are willing to let them struggle for, and earn, the goods and services they want.

Fortunate are the children whose parents subscribe to the "matching funds" approach. These parents help their children buy goods and services with money after the kids earn and save a portion of the cost.

Fortunate are the children whose parents expect them to do their fair share of the work required to maintain a household.

Fortunate are the children whose parents set loving limits, give their children reasonable choices, and allow consequences of those choices to prepare them for the adult world.[14]

PEARL 17

Friends and Peer Pressure

Parents worry a lot about who their teens' friends are. In general, they worry too much.

First, your teen's choice of friends is potentially a control battle that you can't win. It's just like the unwinnable control battle parents try to fight over what kinds of clothes their teen wears.

Second, teens learn to make their own decisions about how they'll live when they interact with their friends. As they make those decisions, they also learn to live with the consequences of those decisions.

Third, peer pressure is a two-way street. We know that peers pressure our teens. But we often forget that our teens can be redemptive and influence their peers.

To the chagrin of most parents, teenagers often want to hang around other teens who walk on the wild side. Good teenagers often have thoughts that they'd like to be a little bit wilder, a little bit more exciting. But they also know they're not going to. So how do they live out these fantasies? They pick friends who are like that. That doesn't mean they're going to be that way. It just means they've found a substitute for being so wild and outrageous themselves.

When my (Jim's) son, Charlie, was in high school, I used to say, "Charlie, with friends like yours, you get to make more decisions than anybody in the whole school."

One of his friends was a druggie; another was an alcoholic. I used to think to myself, *Boy, why does he need those kids for friends?* The only thing that saved a control battle with him was that I had had enough psychological training and enough work with teens that I was able to finally bite the bullet and say to Charlie, "You really like those guys, don't you?"

"Yeah, they're kind of exciting," responded Charlie.

"You know, they're probably lucky to have a friend like you," I said. "My guess is that more of you rubs off on them than they rub off on you."

"Yeah, they're better when they're around me because they don't do their drugs and they don't drink."

"Charlie, I knew it would be that way, and I feel happy for those guys that they have you for a friend."

But I still had my doubts. My wife and I would go in the other room and express our many misgivings. It was just horrible. There were times when I even said, "I know I'm wrong. I know I'm wrong. I've got to stop this."

But there were other times when I'd say, "I know I'm right. I know I'm right." I didn't want to indicate to Charlie that I thought his friends would rub off on him and drag him down. And the way we say those friends will rub off on our teen is to tell him or her very simply, "You're not going to be around those kids."

There is a major exception to this guideline, however. There are times when the law steps in and says your teenager cannot be around other teens because it's a violation of his or her probation. Then it absolutely must be that way, because that's the way the real world operates. When adults commit a crime and are put on probation, the law limits most of their civil rights. And it's better for a teen to learn that early in life. If your teen is put on probation, you should be sad for him or her. "Well, I'm really sad it's happened to you. That would really be too bad if you violated your probation."

Other than this exception, we should tell our teens, "You know, you get to make a lot of tough decisions when you're with friends like those. But I guess if anybody can make those decisions, it's you, right? And not only that, but if anybody can make some bad decisions and live with the consequences, I'll bet you can do it. So best of luck around those friends."

Then, when your teen leaves the house, you can rest assured that he or she at least has this idea in mind: "I'm in charge of me, not other kids."

Giving Gifts to Our Adolescents

We may generate problems with the best of intentions when we give money to "bail out" our children. Some parents give thoughtfully and joyfully, and generally have children who receive gratefully. Other parents give resentfully or thoughtlessly and raise children who feel entitled. We have found that when loving parents have very disrespectful teens, it is generally because the children are entitled and the parents have been giving and bailing out far too much.

How much to give becomes an issue because there is a natural tendency to want to give to our children, especially if we have the means. Giving to others and helping them out makes the human heart sing. Giving, self-sacrifice, and altruism are all traits that demonstrate character. For instance, if we are talking to someone and he or she drops a pencil, our natural tendency is to pick it up. So giving to others—be it our child, our place of worship, or a worthy cause—can be rewarding.

On the other hand, when giving leads to a feeling of entitlement in the child, everyone loses. Most adults recognize the danger of well-off parents ruining their children by giving them money for the wrong reasons, in the wrong way, at the wrong age, with terrible results. The term "trust-fund baby" is sometimes used for those unfortunate children—even when they are forty years old—who received too much, too soon, and live wasted and often self-destructive lives.

Be it a car, college tuition, gas money, date money, or almost any gift, three essential rules must be observed if the gift-giving is to be healthy and an enhancement of your life and the life of your child. The gift must be given freely with the following expectations:

1. The child doesn't demand or expect it.
2. The child smiles and says a variation of "Gee, thanks!"
3. The child uses the gift in a responsible manner approved by the giver.

Let's look at these rules one at a time.

First, when a child demands or expects a gift, rather than hopes for a gift, it means the child feels the gift is owed. This is the first step toward entitlement. If the gift is not given, then the child feels cheated and victimized, and the adult feels guilty. When gifts are owed, they become bribes, and the joy of giving and receiving is lost.

Second, one way of determining when giving a gift or helping out is healthy for your child is to pay attention to the response when the gift or help is given. The *only* correct response is a variation on "thanks." Any variation like "About time!" or "Why have I had to wait so long?!" means entitlement is present, and while the help may bring the child short-term relief, it is short-term gain for long-term pain. Ultimately, the child will continue the behavior that obligated the adult to bail the child out in the first place.

Third, does your child use your gifts in a way that you feel is responsible? This is very important. Remember, children who abuse their parents' generosity feel justified in how they use up the dollars. Few children say, "I've wasted my parent's resources." Most feel it is *essential* to spend bucks on whatever clothes or causes they deem necessary. The more responsible the child, the more necessary the expenditure may actually be, and the more likely the resource base (the parent) will agree to the way the money was used.

Some parents might ask, "Why is it necessary for my child to spend my money in the way I approve? Isn't that expecting too much?" Not at all! That's the way the real world works. Banks insist when individuals or companies are bailed out, they spend the money wisely, determined often by a bankruptcy court. Few sources of funds in the real world — be it government, bank, or foundation — say to the beneficiaries: "Here's a pile of money. Spend it however you wish."

A Love and Logic father once decided to cut off family funds to his son, who was spending both time and dollars during his sophomore year on a political cause the father deemed inappropriate. When the angry son accosted his father for "trying to control my life," the father used questions, with empathy and love, to communicate to his son that he could spend money on such causes only if he earned that money himself. But the father's money was to be spent in ways that were in line with the father's wishes.

Love and Logic parents enjoy helping their children and giving them things that bring joy, but they are aware of the dangers in raising entitled children, which inappropriate giving can produce. Parents can furnish resources to young adults to help them succeed in life, but they need to beware allowing a child to self-destruct on the family dime.[15]

Grades

Parents are understandably concerned and frustrated when their teens have trouble motivating themselves to take school seriously or work for good grades. There are, however, levels of concern. The more responsible the teen, the less involved the parent ought to be.

But when teens aren't responsible—constantly failing to bring books home or losing homework—and parents try to get involved in making them do homework, it becomes a control battle that only the teen can win. The parents get indignant and give lectures, which in turn play into their teens' hands. Teens love to see their parents all worked up.

Instead, it is vital that we explore the situation from a teen's point of view and try to elicit their feelings in the process. The best guarantee of graduation—or, more strategically, the best route to helping our teens maintain a healthy self-image—is to keep the doors of communication open by taking interest in our teens' lives without rescuing them.

Why Teens Lack Motivation

Each case of poor school motivation is an individual issue, so we will review only the main causes.

Teens get tired of keeping up with the demands. High school is a time of intense competition, academically and socially. Few teens are not tired of the high school routine before it is completed. The most common mistake parents make is to try to shove children into graduation. This almost always fails. Or, when it is successful, the children often fail their first semester of college or their first job.

There comes a time when no adult can push another to success. It's often best simply to let our kids know that we hope they will graduate, but if they reach the point where school is unimportant, then they are really saying by their actions that they are ready for life and employment.

Depression or learning disorders: If parents suspect that their teens are depressed or hampered by a learning disorder, they should seek competent professional testing and counseling. Berating a student who is suffering from problems like these will only make high school underachievement worse.

Peer pressure: When teens are running with a peer group that does not value school, it may help if we let them know that we hope some of them rubs off on their friends. We should let our teens know that we're concerned, but it hardly ever does any good to forbid them from seeing their friends.

Preoccupation with other interests: Some teens do poorly because they have a specific consuming interest in something else. Some of America's great entrepreneurs dropped out of high school to start their own businesses. This is not to say that dropping out should be encouraged, but it's not the end of the world either. If your child maintains a good self-image, it's a good bet that later he or she will obtain a GED or high school equivalency degree and perhaps attend college as an adult.

Substance abuse: If a teen's low motivation is related to drug abuse, then the issue is drugs, not poor school achievement.

Letting Teens Own Their Grades

You can head off a lot of control battles at the pass by allowing your teen to own his or her grades. As a helpful perspective, remember that a C is a satisfactory grade, and most of us in life get Cs in almost everything we do. Most of us drive C, eat C, and clean house C. A little understanding about average grades can go a long way.

For most high-achieving individuals, C is not acceptable in the major areas of vocation and avocation. But ultimately that has to be an individual decision. Teenagers must be taught to view their own success or failure in school as belonging directly to them. Many children have problems in school out of conscious or unconscious rebellion, thinking that if they fail, their parents—not they themselves—will suffer. The important issue is to maintain a good parent-child relationship through non-accusing questions, maintaining interest without anger, and letting the consequences naturally fall.

Watch how this Love and Logic parent handles this situation.

DAD: Hey, Nathan, how goes school these days?

NATHAN: Great. Laura and I are hitting the class party tonight.

DAD: Super! I hope you have a good time. How are the mid-quarter grades?

NATHAN: I have some English and math assignments that the teacher wouldn't even look at because they were a day late. School's a drag!

DAD: That's disappointing. So what are the grades?

NATHAN: About a C, two Ds, and two Fs.

DAD: Um . . . what's your thought on that?

NATHAN: I can pull them up . . . if I try.

DAD: Trying can be hard sometimes. I was thinking you might be happier if you were out of school and it wouldn't be so much of a drag.

NATHAN (shocked): You mean just quit?

DAD: Well, isn't that sort of where you're at now?

NATHAN: Yeah, but . . .

DAD: See, Nathan, here's what I'm thinking. I love you and want to provide for you, but all the stuff you enjoy around here—the TV, the heat, all the food—is because I do an average to good job at work. Since you're not into doing an average job in school right now, I find myself becoming a little resentful, and I love you too much to let that continue. So I'm wondering if it isn't time for you to make your way in the world, or if you choose to stay here, start working and pay room and board, or whatever. You know? I just don't want to have bad feelings about you.

NATHAN: Gee, Dad, I'm going to graduate—I'll work harder.

DAD: Well, why don't we give it one last quarter, and if you get a C in school, and I'm continuing to get a C at work, we're even.

But if next quarter, the grades are still low and things are still a drag at school, I'll expect you to start a job and start paying room and board within three weeks. You're a great worker, and you'd be great at McDonald's.

NATHAN: Well, I'm not leaving here!

DAD: Well, good luck, son. How do you think it will work out?

NATHAN: The math teacher said I could get the late papers in tomorrow, but I'd have to miss the party. . . .

DAD: That would be a bummer. Tough bind! Hope you work it out. Love ya, Nathan.

Another way of handling this with children is in writing, especially if a dialogue with them is bound to turn explosive. The following is a letter a parent might write to the child as a way of responding effectively. The advantage of putting it in writing is that the teen has an opportunity to get the parent's complete thoughts before having the opportunity to argue or defend. It usually works best to give the letter with a suggestion that the child think about it for a while before responding.

Dear Son,

Why do I set expectations for school achievement?

Why do I want to know where you are and when you will be home?

Why do I expect you to respect me the way I respect you?

Why do I expect you to do your share of the work around the house?

Why do I expect you at family meals?

Why do I set limits for you?

I do these things because it is the best way I know to prove to you that you are important to me and that I love you.

Having expectations for you is not easy. It makes a lot of extra work for me to hold you accountable. You test me frequently to see if I really do love you and believe in you.

You came home late to see what I would do, and you found that I limited your going out for a while. You talked back to me to see if I really loved you, and you ended up giving your sassy words a lot of thought while you were doing some of my chores to make up for the energy drain you caused me.

You "forgot" to do your chores and were very surprised when I woke you up that night from a sound sleep to finish the chores. You tested me by being slow getting ready for school and missing the bus. What a long walk that was to school that day. You threw a fit one day at the shopping center and had to pay for a sitter the next time the rest of us went to the center.

Each time I laid down some consequences for you it broke my heart. I truly believe that it hurt me as much as it did you. And it was not easy to listen to you tell me that I did what I did because I was mean. Oh, how much easier it would have been to just yell at you or spank you or even excuse your behavior in some way. My love for you and my belief in what you can become was all that gave me strength to do what I needed to do.

I know that adults who lead happy lives were once children who tested the limits of their parents and did not get their parents to wilt under the pressure. They grew up to be educated and responsible and therefore equipped with what they need to have the freedom to achieve their dreams.

I also know that the world is filled with people who did not have limits as children. You have seen these people yourself. The only life they will ever live is filled with disappointment.

Yesterday you brought home a report card with grades far below your ability level. Please understand that it would be so much easier for me to make excuses for your behavior than to hold you accountable. It might even make me feel better if I could blame your poor grades on your age, your friends, or even your teacher.

But I love you too much to let you down that way.

Please give your school performance some serious thought and be ready to share your plans for solving this problem and getting your academic life back on track.

Your father and I will be available to discuss this with you on Friday evening. We want you to be prepared to tell us what you plan to do and also to explain to us what kind of support or help you need from us.

I understand that you were hoping to go out Friday evening. Your father and I were planning to do the same. However, we are willing to stay home for this because you are so important to us and we care about the kind of person you become.

In the meantime, we understand you are probably hurting a great deal about your report card. It must be a great disappointment. Please tell your teachers you have our love and support.

Sincerely,
Mom

There are several advantages to approaching the problem in this manner. First, it gives both the parents and the child time to cool down and put the situation into proper perspective. It gives the parents time to consult with teachers and counselors.

Second, this approach gives the parents time to rehearse how they want to come across to the teen when they finally meet on the subject, and it greatly reduces the emotions and power struggle aspects of the problem.

Finally, an important factor in dealing with a problem in this manner is that the child gets to learn—especially that the parents' love and support are the most important issues at hand. Warnings, threats, and arguments often cause both parents and children to forget their love and commitment to each other.[16]

PEARL 20

Grounding

The real world doesn't ground people, except in jail. Expressing your concerns with your teenager works better than grounding. A lot of parents who may be grounding their teens would be surprised to find out that they don't have to do it at all. Discipline works just as well without it. In fact, grounding teenagers is about as silly as trying to ground a spouse.

Say you were driving home a little too fast and the police pulled you over and gave you a ticket. You'd probably arrive home upset and tell your spouse, "Gee, I was doing seventy under the bridge on I-70, and I got a ticket." How would you feel if your spouse responded, "What! So you thought you were going skiing next weekend, did you? Well, guess what? You're not. You're grounded!" Can you imagine the irritation you would feel?

Of course, if you've tried all other methods for discipline, and grounding works, then by all means give it a shot. But do it reluctantly, because your teen's future spouse isn't going to be able to use it on him or her.

Jim didn't ground any of his children. He found that talking over a problem and letting them live with the consequences of their decisions worked much better.

We've noticed that the people who seem to use grounding most effectively are parents who already have a really good relationship with their kids. Their teens will do almost anything for them, so the kids will put up with the grounding. The parents who can never make it work are usually struggling with poor relationships with their teens and are hoping to overpower them.

We suggest that grounding should be used on a once-per-child-per-lifetime basis. Save it for the worst thing your teen is ever going to do. It very quickly loses its effectiveness after the first time.

PEARL 21

The Internet

At the time of this writing, one third of websites contain explicit sexual content. In addition to porn, all across the Internet, pedophiles, identity thieves, and other miscreants are able to troll through chat rooms to strike up conversations with unsuspecting children who are encouraged to provide addresses, telephone numbers, and other personal information.

Internet providers offer electronic filters to screen content, but it is impossible for any filter to adequately screen the thousands of websites and chat rooms that spring up like mushrooms around the Internet trunks. And by simply checking the box that affirms that the user is over eighteen, anyone can access any chat room.

One in five U.S. children aged ten to seventeen who regularly log on to the Internet said he or she had received an unwanted sexual solicitation via the Web, according to a recent survey. Solicitations were defined as requests to engage in sexual activities or sexual talk, or to give personal sexual information.

Parents may filter their home machines; however, they shouldn't rely on the filters alone to prevent self-destructive viewing of sexually explicit sites or Internet chats. There are problems with relying on filters:

- Obviously, filters have a hard time catching every site.
- Computer-savvy teens easily circumvent filters.
- Unfiltered machines somewhere, someplace are available to all children who seek them out.

- Filters may prevent research on legitimate content. For instance, those based on keywords may prevent research on breast or prostate cancers.
- Most important, filters say to your child, "You don't have the self-discipline to thoughtfully choose what content to view or how to participate in Internet chats."

Love and Logic emphasizes raising children who control their own behavior. Internet filters are essentially like locking children in the bedroom because they won't stay on their own. It isn't long before the child says, "You think you can control me from the outside, but you can't," and then breaks the bedroom door or climbs out the window.

There is always a way around external control. Most external control simply provides resistant and rebellious children with a challenge. Even prisons, the strongest of external control programs, experience breakouts. So Love and Logic places greater reliance on internal control and in the self-discipline that grows as children model after loving parents who give factual information.

Children who are parented well gradually develop an internal voice that says, "I wonder how my next decision is going to affect me and those around me?" This voice comes from having made bad decisions and living with the consequences while experiencing the love and empathy of their parents. This voice is far more important than all the external controls parents can think up.

So why use filters at all? We believe filters are a wise first defense, because children may accidentally access some sites. At present, popups, redirects, and malware surreptitiously display content that the user never requested or expected.

The following is an abbreviated conversation between a parent and his son. It shows that before wise parents take any action, they empower their child to be a participant in decision making and the choices that follow.

DAD: Derek, what's your take on filtering some of the Internet content on your computer?

DEREK: Why, don't you trust me? I don't need a filter!

DAD: It's not a matter of trust. At the office, the business filters content, not because they don't trust us, but simply as a way to prevent material that we don't want from sneaking into our machines.

DEREK: Oh.

DAD: There are a number of different types of filters. Some are tighter than others. Some filter all pictures that are sent through e-mail, some are based on sight and some on words. I was thinking we might have some fun exploring those options together. It's important to me for you to feel good about whatever we decide.

DEREK: Okay.

Let's listen in on an abbreviated conversation a mom might have with her daughter about Internet chat:

MOM: Honey, you've been doing some chatting on some of the Internet forums, right?

HEATHER: Yeah, Mom, it's fun. I've been getting ideas for prom decoration from lots of other kids. There's a whole forum just on prom themes and it's really fun.

MOM: And you're talking with other girls about prom stuff?

HEATHER: Yeah, I'm so happy I found it. Janice told me about the site.

MOM: How do you know you are talking to another girl?

HEATHER: What do you mean?

MOM: I mean, how do you know you are not talking to a thirty-year-old man pretending to be a teen girl just to get to know you?

HEATHER: Well . . .

MOM: Sites like the prom site would be a perfect place for a sexual predator to troll around for his next little victim.

HEATHER: Oh, Mom, you always worry! That won't happen!

MOM: Well, it's something to think about. (Mom continues to ask questions, not in a witness-stand or cross-examine-your-kid way, but with an attitude that reflects curiosity and interest.)

What kind of information do you give the other girls that you get to know?

HEATHER: Nothing.

MOM: Nothing, honey? Not even about your school?

HEATHER: Well, maybe the school and stuff like that.

MOM: Do you think that if some sneaky, very nasty guy pretended to be your friend and knew your school and any of your classes, what you might look like, or what you are wearing to a prom, he could identify you on prom night, sort of hang around after that and nab you?

HEATHER: Well . . .

MOM: I have some thoughts and observations. Can I share them with you?

HEATHER: Sure.

MOM: I'm thinking that if I were you, I'd sleep a lot better at night if I never sent one little bit of information about myself to anyone, and I mean anyone, that I hadn't met face to face, because the more dangerous the man, the more he can sound fun, sincere, friendly, caring, and like a great teen and would wheedle information out of me.

HEATHER: Oh . . .

MOM: So, what's your take on this, honey?

HEATHER: You're right, Mom. (Wanting to sleep well herself) I'm not going to even talk about my school or anything from now on.

MOM: That's a wise decision. (then, with a laugh) I'd be pretty broken up if you were raped and cut up.

HEATHER: Mom!

MOM: (Giving her daughter a hug) I love you, darlin'.

HEATHER: I love you too. Thanks.

Jobs

Until recently, working at a part-time job was a sign of teenage maturity. Teens learned responsibility and time management, and they made some money for college or vocational training on top of it all.

Those motives for holding down a part-time job have changed, however. Studies have shown that many teens work not to save money for the future but to maintain a materialistic lifestyle of consumption in the present. They often spend their money on clothes, music, food, and other items that are discarded in a few months.

What should parents do when their teen wants to get a part-time job? Wise parents know they can't control whether their teen works outside the home, just as they can't control who the teen's friends are. However, they can control their own expectations of their teen. Those expectations, as we have outlined previously, are: maintain a C average or above at school, do the household chores, and respect Mom and Dad.

Here's a scenario of how a mom dealt with her daughter and her excitement over a job.

LYNDSAY: Hey, Mom, I got the job at the restaurant. The boss wants me to start this Saturday.

MOM: That's great, Lyndsay. How many hours a week are you going to work?

LYNDSAY: The boss said fifteen, but if I do a good job he'll increase them to twenty.

MOM: I'm glad he believes in you. But how are you planning to maintain your grades and do your chores around the house? You got a D in math last term, and I've had to lean on you as it is to do the dishes after dinner. Besides, what do you plan to do with the money you'll earn?

LYNDSAY (whining): Aw, Mom. Aren't you proud of me that I'm working?

MOM: Answer my questions, please.

LYNDSAY: Well, my clothes are so old, and I need to buy those new CDs that just came out.

MOM: Are you planning on saving any of that money for college?

LYNDSAY: Well, I don't know. You're paying for college, aren't you?

MOM: Well, I don't know either, Lyndsay. We agreed that we'd pay for your tuition and other expenses at the state university. But you'll need to raise your grades if you have any hope of even getting accepted. If you don't get in, our paying for college is a dead issue, isn't it? And if you keep slacking off in doing your chores, we may have to come to some sort of agreement about your paying for room and board.

LYNDSAY: Gee, Mom, you make it all sound so harsh.

MOM: Well, Lyndsay, that's how the real working world is. You see, Dad and I work because it's financially better for us to do that than it is to stay home. But working to get ahead involves sacrificing some things such as buying the latest clothes or cars. And it also means that we all need to pay the bills and do our chores.

LYNDSAY (crestfallen): Well, if you don't want me to have the job, I'll call the boss and tell him I can't work.

MOM: I'm not saying you can't have the job, Lyndsay. But I am asking you how you plan to balance the responsibilities of your job with your responsibilities at home.

LYNDSAY: Well, I can ask the boss to give me only one shift one day a week. I think I can arrange my time better to get my schoolwork and chores done. Is that okay, Mom?

MOM: That sounds fine to me. But if your grades drop any

further in the next six weeks, what do you think should happen
with the job?

LYNDSAY: I guess I'd have to quit.

Part-time employment by teens can still be a good experience for
them. Many teens learn valuable lessons about life and responsibility by
working, not to mention reaping the monetary rewards of their labors.
But parents and teens need to keep the lines of communication open so
the responsibility of a job doesn't become an area of conflict.

Leadership: Prepare Your Teen to Be a Leader

The world is focused on leadership right now. Tough times are ahead for our nation and for the world. We'd better get serious about preparing our children for leadership. Some little eight-year-old running around the playground right now could control three-fourths of the world's armaments in the future.

What are the characteristics of great leaders? If we can figure that out, there is hope for us to instill those traits in our children.

Great leaders use group consensus in data gathering, but not in decision making. Leaders, by definition, aren't in the group. They are either at the edge of the group or outside it altogether. They encourage others to their point of view, pick the direction, and lead toward a goal. By definition, no one can lead by being inside the herd and part of the "group think." Thus leadership is often lonely. Only a real leader will have legions of critics. As we celebrate the great leaders of the past, it is easy to forget that in their day, Washington, Lincoln, Churchill, and King were all excoriated by large segments of the public. I believe it was Lincoln who said, "Leadership is known by the enemies it makes."

Leadership is the opposite of bowing to peer pressure. Churchill alone stood up to Hitler when the rest of the world attempted appeasement.

That being said, how do we encourage leadership in our children?

- Encourage your child to stand up to you by respectfully giving good counter-proposals and thoughtful disagreements. We're not talking rebellious disrespect; we're talking parents who encourage their children to express different ideas and different beliefs, and parents who listen respectfully, while not necessarily agreeing with their children.

- Let your children know how proud you are of them when they don't give in to group pressure around clothes, music, and choice of friends. (Every parent and teen should watch the movie *A Walk to Remember* together.) We've seen many a little kid stand a bit straighter when parents have been taught to say, "Yeah, it looks like you are pretty alone on this idea. Perhaps it's preparation for leadership one day."

- Encourage respectful competition in the area of your child's strengths. Be it sports or chess, it's great if your child wants to be the best. Don't stifle it; encourage it.

- Great leaders have internal compasses. Encourage your child to self-evaluate rather than rely on your praise. It's okay to say, "Good job, son," but it may be more effective to say, "How do you think you did?" "How did you figure that one out?" "How do you feel about your self now?" or "Would you do it any different next time?"

The possibility of leadership is cooked into kids by parental expectations. Often leadership runs in families. It's probably not genetics, but instead found in the atmosphere of the home. It may be unspoken, or expressed in terms similar to "You may be born to do great things." It's a great dad who says to his teen, "That foul language may work for the group you are with now, but someday, when you are a leader, you'll have to talk differently. Mom and I would certainly appreciate a little early practice."

Of course, the hard part for all of us is modeling. We'd better make sure we don't drive one car or another because it is the popular thing to do. Or live in one home or another because everyone wants to live there. Or hold opinions just because they are popular.

PEARL 24

Money

There is really no clearer indicator of responsibility and self-control than how teens handle their money. Does it burn a hole in their pocket, do they hoard it, do they give to charities, do they budget, do they save to buy big things, do they save to build a future for themselves and their family, or do they call home and ask you for yet another extension on their inheritance? Do they shop for bargains, do they buy on impulse, or do they buy what they need when they need it at retail prices?

In an age when many students are offered credit cards before they even think of looking for a job, can they wait and save to buy what they want or are they the perfect target for those offering "no money down, no interest, and no payments until next January."

Here are some startling statistics:

- Nearly one-fifth of all people who filed for bankruptcy in 2002 were college students.
- Ninety percent of people in the United States buy things they don't have the cash to pay for.
- Three-fifths of all Americans don't pay off their credit-card balances every month. Because of this, the average cost of something purchased with a credit card is 112 percent higher (more than twice as much!) than if they had paid cash for the same item.
- Nearly half of all Americans have reserves and savings equal to less than one month's expenses. If they lost their jobs, they

would be in immediate trouble and probably live off of their credit cards exclusively until they either found a new job or went bankrupt.

• Near the beginning of the 1990s, the typical American family saved just under 8 percent of its income. By the beginning of the 2000s, that same household spent a tenth of a percent more than it earned.

It is much better for a twelve-year-old to go bankrupt than it is for a twenty-seven-year-old whose first baby is on the way. Therefore, we advise parents to start giving their children allowances around the age of five or six. As with other areas, facing the consequences of their decisions with money early in life can teach them a great deal that they will need to know to be healthy, responsible adults.

Here are some helpful thoughts on allowances that will help your kids make the most of this terrific learning opportunity.

1. Children do not earn their allowances. That means we do not pay them to do their chores. Being paid for chores robs them of the dignity of holding up their fair share of the family workload. The only time we'd pay them for chores is when they do our chores if we don't want to do them.

2. Provide the allowance at the same time every week. This can be done with pay envelopes. Place the cash, plus a small invoice indicating the breakdown of the funds (for example, for a child in first grade: "$1 allowance, $6 lunch money") inside an envelope with the child's name on it. Sign the invoice, "Because we love you. Spend it wisely and make it last." The child must then tend to the envelope.

3. Never insist that children save the allowance. They can't learn to handle money if they stash their allowance in a shoebox at the back of their closet, saving it for when they get big. Kids must go through their own economic depression—wasting money, then not having any when they need it—to learn about money. In general, people—including kids—learn best to save only after they've learned how to be broke.

4. As long as they're not engaged in illegal activity, ***allow children to spend, save, give, or waste the money any way they see fit.*** They can use it to hire others to do their chores.

5. *A teen's allowance should be enough to cover most regular activities, but not much more than that.* Not only should weekly expenses be covered—enough for school lunches and activities like movies and snacks after school with friends—but also irregular expenses like birthday presents for friends and relatives, Christmas presents, field trips, and whatever other expenses they may face. If you need to, make a list of what you as the parent will cover when needed (school clothes, a place to live, meals, etcetera) and the rest (concert tickets; that new jacket that is so cool; the latest, smallest, handheld portable music player; the latest, greatest video game, etcetera) is their responsibility to cover out of their allowance or the money they earn on their own.

6. This may be the most important: ***When it's gone, it's gone.*** No more allowance until the next week's envelope.

My (Jim's) son, Charlie, learned a powerful lesson in money management the very first week he got on the allowance payroll. Our family visited a carnival, and the midway barkers had their way with the boy. He came home flat broke.

"Dad, what am I going to do for lunch?" Charlie said when reality struck him on Monday morning.

"Go over to your pay envelope and get your lunch money out," I replied.

"But it's all gone," Charlie said.

"Oh no, that's really too bad. What are you going to do?" I said.

"I don't know," Charlie said. "Can I get some food out of the refrigerator and make a lunch?"

"Sure, if you can afford to pay for it," I said. "Mom and I have already paid for lunches once, and we don't want to pay for them again."

It was a tough week for Charlie. But surviving for five days on two meals a day (we made sure they were good ones) taught him a big lesson in money management.

There will be times, however, when kids are more persistent—and more psychologically devious—than Charlie. When they blow their bankroll early and shuffle up to us begging for more money before the appointed allowance time, we must become as tight as a Depression-era banker. There will be more money, sure—on the next allowance day. Even when our kids push the powerful guilt button, we must make sure nothing moves out of our pockets.

Observe how this dad handles his daughter's midweek crisis:

STEFFI: Dad, I need more allowance.

DAD: Yeah, that's kind of how it is for me. I always need more money in my paycheck than I get. Have you got any ideas about what you're going to do?

STEFFI: Yeah. I'm asking you. Dad, could you give me more allowance?

DAD: Well, I'll be happy to give you your allowance on Saturday. But for now, maybe you'll consider bidding on someone else's chores around the house so you can earn some money that way.

STEFFI: But I need it now!

DAD: Boy, I bet you do. But don't worry. You'll get more on Saturday.

STEFFI: That's not fair!

DAD: That could be true, and there will be more on Saturday.

STEFFI: My friends don't have this problem because their parents love them and give them more money.

DAD: I bet that's true too, *and* there will be more on Saturday.

If Steffi keeps it up, Dad could put a finishing touch to the discussion by saying, "If I kept carrying on like that to my boss, how do you suppose he'd feel about my job? He'd feel like paying me less, wouldn't he? So do your best to solve this, Steffi. We'll see you later."

As kids get older it is not a bad idea to let them know how you save and invest for the future, what you are doing so that they can go to college, what expenses their future will hold that they may not even be thinking of yet: Want to buy your own car? Do you have money for gas? Insurance? Changing the oil every three thousand miles? What if it breaks down?—and about how they can get more interest for the money in their savings account and can earn even more interest through CDs, money market accounts, and so on.

This may sound complicated, but the inevitable day is coming when your child receives his or her first solicitation for a credit card in the mail. We need to make sure our children are ready for it.[17]

Mood Swings

Remember the central figure in Robert Louis Stevenson's story *The Strange Case of Dr. Jekyll and Mr. Hyde*? Dr. Jekyll discovered drugs that transformed him into a vicious, brutal creature named Mr. Hyde. As the effects wore off, he reverted back to the kindly Jekyll.

Sometimes our teens seem like modern versions of Jekyll and Hyde. When they're in a particularly bad mood, we may wonder if they're on drugs or are facing some other awful crisis.

If your teen's mood swings are making you dizzy, keep these helpful hints in mind:

Mood swings are typical in adolescence. During the period of about five years when teens are hurtling through the physical changes that transition them from childhood to adulthood, Jekyll-and-Hyde behavior comes with the territory. The intense physical and emotional changes of adolescence are usually responsible for drastic mood swings.

Don't interrogate your teen. The worst thing we can do to depressed teens is fire questions at them: "What's the matter with you?" or "Why don't you snap out of it?" To them, that's like putting them on the witness stand while the prosecutor launches a courtroom attack.

Instead we should acknowledge what we see and let our teen know we're available to talk. We can try caring words such as, "I wonder if you're hurting right now?" Then wait to hear what our teen says. If our teen doesn't want to talk, it's time for us to back off.

Encourage your teen to share feelings. It's okay to ask your teen, "Are you mad at me right now?" or "Have I done something to hurt you?" It will help both of you if your teen shares his or her feelings with you.

One father learned a valuable but difficult lesson from his son Jeremy. Ron and his wife sought counseling for Jeremy because he was depressed for a long time. It took many sessions with a therapist to coax Jeremy into talking about what was going on inside him.

It turned out that Jeremy thought his dad was mad at him all the time. Jeremy finally asked Ron, "Are you mad at me today?"

Surprised, Ron answered, "No."

"Then why are you frowning at me?" Jeremy asked.

Ron answered that he frowns when he thinks hard. He learned from his son that it makes others think he is angry. Ron had thought he had a great relationship with Jeremy, while for years Jeremy suffered under the impression that his father was always angry with him.

Most bad moods don't require a counselor. Unless your teen's depression continues over a long period for no apparent reason, there is usually no reason to seek professional counseling. Your teen's bad moods may have nothing to do with you. If you have approached your teen about the sadness or depression, and it lasts no more than about two weeks, it's usually better to let the matter rest.

PEARL 26

Music

Don't criticize. It will not make you a more effective parent. Tell yourself, "There are four things I absolutely must not criticize: my teen's clothes, hair, friends, and music."

And this means we shouldn't try to slide our opinions in under cover by criticizing the clothes, hair, friends, or music of our teens' peers. Despite our occasional feelings to the contrary, our teens weren't born yesterday. They'll immediately know that we're really criticizing *them*.

Quarrels over music, like quarrels over television, may be more destructive to relationships and the ability to show love than the actual content of the music or TV show merits. It is very easy for parents to become destructive about things they believe might be destructive.

Parents can avoid a lot of arguments simply by accepting these facts: (1) to most teens, music is very important, and (2) most adolescents go through a phase in which they like the beat and the volume. It's hard for most of us to realize how much teens want to feel that their opinions are respected.

Since the fifties, music has been so intertwined with teen culture that it's impossible to separate the two. You can get great insights into your teen's way of thinking and relating to others by understanding his or her music. It wouldn't take that much effort for you to become conversant about musicians and bands by reading the paper and watching television. If you feel really daring, ask their permission to listen to their albums.

Although pop music trends change rapidly, the central role of music in our culture tends to remain steady. Many of the popular musicians from our teen years have found new audiences today. Even the Big Band sounds from the thirties and forties have found new life among some teens. The best way to get your teen to accept and enjoy other kinds of music is for you to enjoy listening to other kinds of music and to talk about why you like them.

How should we respond to our teen's music preferences? Blanket approval from a distance is certainly naive, because much of today's popular music is saturated with violent or sexually explicit themes. However, blanket condemnation is not the answer either. Even bands notorious for their immoral lifestyles have created beautiful love songs and insightful social commentary. Teens no more appreciate parents roundly castigating their music and its creators as immoral than parents like teens knocking all business as corrupt.

Some of us find it awkward to talk with our teens about their music. We can ease the awkwardness by asking them questions instead of just telling them what we think. If they don't want to talk about the subject, it's best to politely drop the conversation. Our graciousness at this point may come back in a blessing later on when they feel free to talk to us about their music.

If your teen pumps up the volume so loud that it disturbs you or other family members, make a deal like this one: "Hey, you're free to listen to your music, and we're free to listen to our music. Neither one of us pushes our music on the other. Try to keep it down—or could you try wearing headphones?"

This approach will get the best results. If we just criticize our teen's preferences, we might pay dearly later when the damage of the criticism outweighs the effects of those often temporary listening habits.

PEARL 27

Orders: To Give or Not to Give

Ordering a teenager to do something (or *not* to do something) is essentially an irrevocable act. Once you've handed down that order, you've burned a bridge behind you. If you change your mind, you can't cross back to where you were, because recalling an order breeds disrespect.

Another liability in giving orders is that it tends to lower teens' self-image. Maybe this is why most of us don't like taking orders! The armed services have to *train* people to be good order-takers. Telling a person what to do covertly says, "Even if you had adequate information, you could not figure out the situation for yourself."

Of course, giving orders is sometimes justified in emergency situations where, correctly, one person must say to another, "There isn't time to give you the facts of the situation now, so just do it my way!"

Giving orders works only when there is agreement on two points:

1. Order-givers must be in unquestioned authority. The Army works very hard to make sure troops do not question the authority figure. But teens thrive on questioning authority figures.

2. Order-takers must accept the idea that they could not make a wise decision on their own. The Army works very hard at this as well. When Foster went into basic training, his training sergeant immediately told the soldiers, "Okay, you men, you is not here to *think*. You is here to *do*. *I* is here to think. *I* says, and *you* does. Do you get the picture?" But teenagers struggle with this because they tend to think they know everything.

It's evident that when loving parents share their concerns and thoughts, children learn to respect and consider their opinions, especially when parents are right. Of course, when parents are not right or express concerns and thoughts about issues that never occurred, teens rightly learn that their parents' thoughts and opinions are sometimes fallible. That, of course, is good thinking too: either way, the teen learns.

Why We Should Hardly Ever Give Orders

So when should we give orders? Ideally, only on rare occasions. Usually, we should be giving our children covert messages that they will respect our ideas and our thoughts and will be able to figure out answers for themselves. However, when our kids are in danger, it's reasonable for us to say, "You can't do that."

This brings us to a second important guideline for giving orders: We should give orders *only if we can reasonably expect our child to obey and only if we're able to apply meaningful consequences to disobedience.* By definition, once an order is given it has to be followed "or else."

The next question, of course, is, *or else what?* This "or else" is very important. Every week in psychotherapy, Foster dealt with very unhappy parents who used "or else." They gave their children orders and then usually could not even check whether the orders were obeyed. On top of that, they couldn't effectively apply consequences to the misbehavior. Remember, never give an order until you have first thought of a consequence if your teen fails to comply. Such orders include

- "Turn in all your homework."
- "Don't smoke when you're away from home."
- "Don't hang out with those friends."
- "Don't drink at the party."
- "Don't try drugs."
- "Behave yourself, the way we taught you."

Good luck on those! We grown-ups sometimes have trouble making *ourselves* behave, let alone making our teenagers do what we tell them.

Here are a few examples of orders given with consequences that are available to most parents to apply to disobedience:

- "Don't smoke in the house (or else I'll ask you to step outside)."
- "Don't have drugs in your room (or else I'll call the police)."
- "Don't be disrespectful to me (or else I'll ask you to leave)."

Alternatives to Giving Orders

What's our alternative to giving orders? We'll put ourselves in the best position by sharing our own concerns and thoughts, because that's what we have control over.

In place of orders, thoughtful parents might use phrases like these:

- "I would appreciate it if . . . "
- "I would really like you to . . . "
- "I'm hoping that . . . "

With this approach, it's not such a big deal when our teen disregards our thoughts, opinions, wishes, and hopes. We can handle that, and it does not increase our child's disrespect. As we pointed out, if our teen directly disobeys an order and we can't thoughtfully apply consequences to the disobedience, he or she will lose respect for us. This occurs because every parent is a part of the child's own self-image: *a disobedient child loses self-respect.*

Most parents tend to give orders to their teens around "very important" issues. But it's not the importance of the issue that matters; it's these variables:

1. Will the teen obey the order?
2. If not, will we know if he or she has disobeyed?
3. If he or she has disobeyed, can we effectively apply consequences to the disobedience?

PEARL 28

Parties

Many teens dream about the fun parties they'll attend or host when their parents are away. And while they dream, their parents try to think of ways to restrict their party activities—often with unsuccessful results. The following guidelines can be helpful to parents faced with these kinds of situations.

Never give an order you can't enforce. Parents' orders often backfire. This is because the teens who need orders also disobey them, while those who follow them probably don't need them.

It's far more effective to say, "I don't want you to host a party while we're away," or "I'm hoping you'll avoid parties where drugs are present." Then, if your teen disobeys your expectations, you have not lost as much as if your teen disobeys a direct order.

Wise parents get serious, not angry, about party behavior. They get serious by letting consequences unfold.

When Brent's parents were out of town, he threw a party that resulted in damage to the family's new stereo system. In a calm manner, Brent's father let him know that repairs were totally his responsibility. After several time-consuming trips to the repair shop and a 370-dollar bill, Brent appeared less interested in being a host. "Parties can be real expensive," he said.

Wise parents keep lines of communication open without rescuing. They listen (even to information they don't want to hear), remain loving, and never confuse acceptance of party behavior with approval.

Prohibit attendance at parties only when a teen will obey the order and truly can't cope with the setting. Make sure both criteria of this rule are met before prohibiting your teen from going to a party.

For example, Aaron attended a party where alcohol was served, despite his father's warning. His father had decided that no matter what happened, Aaron would be able to cope. Later, after breaking up the party, police contacted Aaron's father and asked him to pick up his son. Despite accusations of negligence, he refused.

Instead Aaron spent the night in detention, learning some valuable lessons. "I should have listened to my dad," he said, adding, "I can handle detention once, but never again!"

Require your teen to tell you where he or she is and when he or she will return. Why should teens let us know where they are going and when they will return? Most parents answer, "Because we worry!" But that response usually leads to even less responsible behavior by teens. Parents *do* need to know their teens' whereabouts, because they promise *not* to worry.

An effective thing to say is, "As long as we know where you are and when you'll return, we promise not to worry. It is only when we don't know that we find ourselves worrying. We appreciate your help on this."

Parties in *Your* House

Erin responded this way when her dad said he would be chaperoning her party at their house: "There's no way you can be at the party. My social life will be ruined if you're supervising my party."

How many parents do you know who have given in to this kind of teenage logic and allowed their kids to have unsupervised parties? Some parents give in because they are desperate for their teens to be popular. Some give in because they are afraid of alienating their kids and have a history of allowing their kids to hold them hostage. When parents allow unsupervised parties, they leave themselves vulnerable to

- lawsuits resulting from teen drinking or drug use
- having their house destroyed by uninvited guests
- raising kids who are used to getting their way through manipulation

- missing opportunities to share and enforce values and principles

Here is how Erin's dad handled the conversation:

DAD: Why is it important to you that I not be there?
ERIN: If you are spying on us, how can we have any fun?
DAD: Are you going to be doing stuff I don't approve of?
ERIN: Of course not, but none of my friends have their parents
    at their parties. Everybody will think I'm weird. You don't want
    other kids to think I'm weird, do you? You don't realize what it'll
    do to my social life.
DAD: This is pretty important to you then?
ERIN: Yeah, I don't want everybody to see you treating me like
    a baby. I'm not a baby. I'm sixteen. A lot of girls have babies by
    then, and I can't even have a party without my dad breathing
    down my neck. All I want is one little party. It's not like I'm
    drinking and drugging like a lot of kids. You should appreciate
    that I'm not like that.
DAD: I can see you really want to have an unsupervised party. I'm
    not sure how to react to that. I need some time to think it over
    and see if there are any choices I can live with. I'll let you know
    by Friday. Thanks for letting me know how important this is to
    you.

Dad and Mom talk this over in private and agree there is no way
they can allow this unsupervised party. They brainstorm some choices
and decide to have another talk with their daughter:

DAD: Erin, we've been thinking about your unsupervised party.
    And we've also been thinking about our legal responsibilities.
ERIN: So?
DAD: We've thought of three choices. You can decide.
ERIN: Okay, what?
DAD: The first choice is to have the party with me in the house.
    I'll try to stay out of the way.
ERIN: No way! I already told you that's no good!

DAD: The second choice is that you hire a professional chaperone. You can call the police department and they will give you some referrals. Or you may know some adults who would meet our approval.

ERIN: Oh fine! That's even worse.

DAD: The third choice is that you can wait and have that unsupervised party at your own home after you go out on your own.

ERIN: This is stupid. Can't you think of anything better?

DAD: That's the best we can do. Maybe you can think of something better. Let us know what you decide.

ERIN: No! I told you what I want!

DAD: You know the choices. Let us know what you decide.

ERIN: This house is a police state. I can't wait to move out.

DAD: We love you too much to argue with you about it. Let us know what you decide.

Professional Help: When to Seek It

A delicate question often comes up for parents of troubled teenagers: "When should we decide to seek professional help?"

Seeking professional help is not an admission of failure. In our complex society, with its countless social problems, our teens quite naturally face dilemmas that we never had to cope with during our childhood.

For example, overwhelming societal pressures for success are filtering down even to the lower grades. Peer pressure prompts even kindergartners to insist on designer clothes. More children than ever before are having severe problems, and the causes of those problems stand apart from the method or intent of parental discipline.

There are two basic reasons for considering the option of professional help:

1. *A steadily deteriorating situation* for at least a three-month period with no improvement in sight. In this case, professional help may be necessary to reverse the downward trend.
2. *An abrupt, dramatic change* in mood or behavior. If your basically responsible and responsive teen suddenly changes his or her overall demeanor (grades go down dramatically, friendships drop off), you may want to seek professional help immediately.

Don't assume that professional care has to involve a long, drawn-out series of counseling sessions. One session with a trained and competent counselor may be enough to straighten out the problem.

Here are some guidelines for finding the right professional care:

- Find a therapist who has a busy schedule. A busy professional with many clients is most likely on the right track.
- Seek out satisfied clients. Ask the therapist to give you a list of a few satisfied clients you can talk with.
- A good therapist should be willing to give you a free half-hour session to discuss your situation.
- Look at what's going on in the professional's life. Does this person have a good marriage? Are the counselor's children well adjusted?
- Get professional recommendations. Talk with pediatricians, school counselors, and psychiatric or pediatric nurses. Pick the person whose name comes up three times. If hospitalization is recommended, make sure the person recommending it is working outside that hospital system.

PEARL 30

Runaways

Parents are rightly terrified when their children run away from home. But they can turn such an incident into a significant learning opportunity.

Take a case I (Foster) once had with two adolescent girls, Debbie and Connie. Both had overprotective parents. Both got tired of it and ran away together one summer to Vancouver, which is a very pretty city, especially during the summer.

The parents came into my office. They were angry and upset about their children running away from home. I offered some advice. One set of parents listened. One set didn't.

Summer drifted into fall, then winter. It was getting cold in Vancouver.

Debbie's Parents Got Angry

When Debbie phoned home, her parents started getting angry. They wanted to punish their daughter, but they wouldn't allow the consequences of her actions to take place. They demanded to know where she was.

"Vancouver," Debbie told them.

"Well, that really makes us mad!" They blew up on the phone. "You should have been phoning us. We haven't heard from you! Who do you think we are? You get home right now!"

"I don't have any money," complained Debbie.

"Well, we'll send you money to get home, but when you get home—we're telling you right now—you're going to be grounded for three months! Do you understand?"

"Yes," said Debbie.

"All right! You stay right there; we'll send you the money."

Debbie's parents sent her the money with the warning that she would be grounded when she got home. Debbie came home for about two weeks, and then she ran away again.

Connie's Parents Stayed Calm

When Connie phoned home, her mom and dad showed no anger. Rebellious teens love anger, but there wasn't any to react to.

"Well, hi, honey." They low-keyed it. "Where have you been?"

"Vancouver," answered Connie.

"That's a nice city. You been having fun up there?"

"Oh yeah."

"What have you been doing?" they inquired politely.

"Waiting tables and bumming around," Connie said.

"That's good! When do you think you're coming home?"

"Now?" asked Connie.

Then Mom said, "Well, that would be wonderful! We'd be glad to see you again. Let us know when you're coming in, and we'll be here."

"How will I get home?" Connie pressed.

"Well, honey, how did you get there?"

"I thumbed it," Connie replied, waiting for her mother to gasp in horror and rush in to rescue her from doing it again. (Connie's mom knew Connie was going to say that, because we had already rehearsed this conversation in my office. You know what rebellious teens are going to say long before they say it. They're often not very creative.)

"Well, Connie, how do you plan to get home?" her mom said.

"I don't know," came a little tremulous voice.

"Is there something we can do?"

"I'd like you to help."

"Hmmm, Connie," Mom answered. "I've always felt that if you got yourself somewhere you should get yourself back. However, I would be willing to send you half the fare for a bus trip home if you found out how much it would cost and how we could mail the money to the bus company. Of course, you'd have to pay us back with interest after you returned home and got a job here."

A moment of silence.

Then Connie said, "Okay, I'll find a job, and then I'll come home on the bus."

"Hey, good thinking!" Connie's dad chimed in. "It probably beats thumbing home in the winter. It's cold! And of course, it's better than taking the risks of getting beat up or raped."

"Debbie's already gone because her parents paid airfare for her return," Connie said, with some resentment.

"I know, dear," Mom said. "That probably was convenient. But this is what we are willing to do, and we'd love to see you. You got yourself there by thumbing. The bus trip probably should be better than that, right?"

Acquiescing, "I guess you're right."

See how these parents handled it? No anger, no punishment, just pure questions and consequences.

What's Harder At First Is Easier Later On

Both girls eventually pulled their lives together and became responsible adults, but Connie did it sooner. And unlike Debbie, Connie never ran away again.

We realize that the approach used by Connie's parents may seem harsh. We believe, though, that teens are more resilient than we give them credit for. As a parent, you must take the long view on what is best for your teen. If your goal is to help your teen become a responsible, productive, self-sufficient adult, you may have to take some difficult steps along the way. But what's harder at first is easier later on — for you and your teen.

Satanism and Religious Cults

Black clothes, jewelry with inverted pentacles, black candles, books describing satanic rituals—all of these can suggest involvement in satanic activity. Of all the kinds of trouble that teens can get into, and of all the ways that they may express rebellion, probably nothing frightens parents more than when their children flirt with satanism or join religious cults.

Parental attitudes of fright and overreaction make it more likely to be a problem. In many cases we're dealing with a lot of hype. We're not saying satanic activity doesn't occur or can't involve long-term emotional and spiritual damage, but it also involves hype.

Let's say police find two teens who have disemboweled squirrels. Given a choice between "Here are two psychopathic kids cutting open squirrels," or "Here are two kids in a cult," it's easier for society to say, "We've got a cult" instead of "We've got a lot of disturbed people." We look for simplistic, flashy answers.

There is a regrettable outlook in a lot of Christian literature that satanism and religious cults are everywhere. It's our opinion, based on what the Bible says, only God is everywhere.

Why Faith-Filled Families Are Especially at Risk

Faith-filled families who have been very authoritarian are at risk for two reasons. First, these parents are likely to get more emotionally involved about their teens flirting with satanism than about anything else. When teens stray from the faith, they draw more parental emotion. Children like emotion, even if it's negative.

This apparent involvement works extra well for teens who have a poor relationship with their parents, because it's such an effective way to get back at them. It's a great channel for a teen going through a bit of rebellion. As parents react more, teens go into it deeper. It becomes a vicious cycle.

Second, some religious families tend to be rigid about what children should and should not believe. A satanic or religious cult is going to be as doctrinaire, rigid, authoritarian, and demanding as hyper-religious parents. Nothing really changes for teens in this case, because someone is still telling them what to do. It remains somewhat familiar, but has the added bonus of driving their parents nuts.

What Parents Should Do

So, what can parents do? We recommend these six steps:

1. Parents should first assess their own parenting techniques. Children will go where they feel most loved. If they are rejected at home, they will go elsewhere, even if that elsewhere is a religious cult. Parents should ask themselves if they will love their children unconditionally, regardless of their religious persuasion.

Sometimes parents get upset that a sect teaches satanic rites such as human or animal sacrifice. These parents are worried about the blood and gore of the sect. What they need to wonder is why their teen is interested in blood and gore in the first place. How did they raise their children?

2. Parents should recognize that as distasteful or horrifying as it may appear, teen involvement in satanism or a religious sect is usually a phase, often subtly encouraged by a strict home environment. When teens leave structured homes, they look around for a new structured environment, whether it's the military, a fraternity or sorority, or a strict religious group. Some of these strong groups can be seen as "transitional parents."

3. Parents should get to know and understand the cult. If the teen is being rebellious and parents invite a cult member over for lunch, it takes the fun away. Just be sure not to be judgmental around your teen and the other cult members.

Parents can do themselves a favor by understanding that not all alternative religious movements are alike. For example, satanism and witchcraft are two different religious systems. Also, such religious movements have high dropout rates. If Rob joins a new guru's movement, odds are good he will be out of it in a year.

4. Parents can't control when their teens stop their involvement in a religious or satanic sect. People have tried measures as extreme as kidnapping their teens out of cults and deprogramming them. Such actions are at best marginally effective, and they are often illegal.

When satanic activity violates the law, however, it puts the problem in a whole new category. Criminal behavior is criminal behavior. Parents are taxpayers and should take advantage of their police department.

5. In those instances when the dangers are real and threatening the child, parents should consider moving their teen geographically. If you feel that the potential damage to your teen of involvement with a satanic cult or religious sect is greater than the potential stress on your relationship caused by forcing your teen to move away, then you should move your teen. A reputable psychiatric hospital or the home of a close family member are possible alternatives to the present living situation.

6. Parents need to accept it on faith that God is with their teen. After examining their past and present parenting and making adjustments—if any—they should also have faith in their parenting. And they should have faith that their teens will ultimately make the right decisions about what to believe.

PEARL 32

Sex

Teenage sexual activity is increasing. Recent studies indicate that a high number of girls and boys have been sexually active prior to graduation from high school. Many children, unfortunately, are sexually active even in junior high.

Parental prohibitions will not stop sex. Sex is addictive. Even a religious upbringing does not seem to correlate with whether or not teens decide to become sexually active.

Foster knew a father who was concerned that his daughter was sexually active. Therefore, he personally dropped her off at school in the morning and picked her up in the afternoon. What he hadn't planned on was his daughter's ingenuity. She found an opportunity and became pregnant over the noon hour.

An aggravating factor is the hypocrisy of many parents, who worry about their teen's sexual involvement while failing to handle their own sexual life in an ethical and open manner.

What's most important is keeping open lines of communication between us and our teens. This communication should include parents expressing their religious and moral values on the topic in a clear, sensitive, and straightforward fashion. It should also include what health specialists are telling us about teen sexuality and the effects it has on them physically, mentally, emotionally, and socially.

If we raise children who are honest with us about their hopes, aspirations, dreams, and sexuality, we are in pretty good shape as parents.

However, if we are open about sex, we may get questions we have a hard time answering. For example, we've heard of teens asking, "How old do I have to be to have sex?" or "When did you first have sex?" or as one thirteen-year-old asked her mom at dinner, "Mom, do you have oral sex?" The mom nearly choked to death on her chicken.

When parents are asked questions about their own sexuality, which happens when sexual matters are handled openly in the family, we suggest this: Answer your children in general terms and keep your own specifics to yourself, modeling how to take care of yourself by simply reserving the right to your own privacy.

Often, when kids ask why they should not have sex, some parents don't know what to say except *don't*. This is usually not very helpful. It's better to say something like, "Honey, I want you to really enjoy and love sex for all of your life. If you have sexual experiences that you feel bad or guilty about, it could affect the joy you have later with your spouse. Besides that, many serious diseases—like AIDS—are passed person to person through sex. For centuries many wise books, like the Bible, and various teachers have taught that sex is best saved for one person in marriage. That's why I want you to wait until you meet the person who you feel really good about. But if you ever choose to make a different choice about having sex, I hope the two of you will talk it over first, make a careful decision, and see a physician about contraception."

Because we frankly give our teens facts and thoughts on how to handle their sexual urges does not mean we are implicitly approving of premarital or promiscuous sex. Adolescent sexuality is not an issue by itself, but takes place within a loving or a conflicted parent-child relationship. That relationship—in the parent's love shown to the child and in open dialogue—is the most important aspect of adolescent sexuality. Adolescent sexuality is an area in which "Just say no" will not work.

Some parents worry that talking to their child about contraception will send the wrong message that it's okay to have sex and that the parent approves. We don't believe this is the case. Teens are only a few months or years away from a plunge into adult life. They deserve our best shot at real-world communication. In that communication we do have every right to share—not *preach*—our values. By having straightforward, honest discussions, we are sending the message "I believe you are old enough to think wisely and make responsible choices."

Children also need facts on STIs, AIDS, and the risk of pregnancy. These should be presented in a cool, loving, matter-of-fact manner. When parents are unsure of facts, they can easily obtain articles and books available for teens concerning the risks of premarital sex.

Parents can talk to a child of the opposite sex about sexual issues, as long as they are not asking for details or satisfying sexual needs of their own through the child. Let's listen as a loving father talks to a responsible teenage daughter about sexual issues. The secret is to remain loving, accepting, and nonaccusing.

DAD: It looks like you and Sean have been dating awhile and are really happy together.

CASSANDRA: We are.

DAD: I'm not prying at all, but I'm wondering how you and Sean are going to handle intimacy and sex.

CASSANDRA: I don't know.

DAD: Hmm, is it something you've discussed?

CASSANDRA: Some.

DAD: Well, I think if you and Sean do love each other, the subject will come up. I'm hoping you talk about what it means long term, rather than have something just happen—if you know what I mean.

CASSANDRA: Oh, Dad! . . . Actually, we have discussed it some. I think he's pretty interested in sex. But I just don't know.

DAD: You know what my values are on premarital sex—we've talked about them before.

CASSANDRA: Yeah, Dad! I appreciate your ideas. I'm just not sure yet what I think."

DAD: So, what if you did have sex? Would you plan for it, or do you think it would just happen?

CASSANDRA: I'd want to plan for it.

DAD: Well, that's good thinking. What's your thought on having a baby?

CASSANDRA: I don't want a baby yet.

DAD: Great. Well, if I can be of help in your thinking things through, would you talk to me about it or probably not?

CASSANDRA: I'd talk to you.

DAD: Super. That makes me feel good. I know you'll consider these things carefully and make a good decision. I love you, honey.

CASSANDRA: I love you too, Dad.

Many parents might think that such a conversation would only encourage premarital sex. It's true that there's no guarantee what choice Cassandra will make. However, she now knows that her father is not ignorant and condemning. Chances are good that she will consider her dad "safe" and a source of wisdom. The more they talk in a similar manner, the more opportunity he will have to make an impact on her behavior. If they don't talk, Dad's probably out of Cassandra's decision-making loop.

We can keep the lines of communication open by being nonjudgmental, nonaccusing, providing facts about the values, joys, and dangers of sexual behavior, and modeling a healthy approach to sexuality ourselves.

PEARL 33

The Silent Treatment

I f you're worried because your teen won't talk, don't worry! There's probably more reason to be concerned about a teen who shares everything with you. But many parents, accustomed to talkative youngsters, blame themselves when their children grow up and clam up.

It is absolutely normal for young people to withhold information from adults. Here's why:

Teens don't feel safe sharing certain things with their parents. Teens may not share embarrassing thoughts or problems with us because they think (often correctly) we won't be able to handle what they say. We have a natural tendency to become angry and upset when our teens tell us certain things. For example, it's a rare and wise parent who says when a teen admits lying to a teacher, "That's sad. I'm glad you shared that with me. How can I help you?"

Teens are seeking independence. A teen's thinking goes something like this: "If I tell my parents everything, that means I am not independent."

Teens sometimes lack the right words. Some adolescents don't talk because it may be difficult to find the words that match their feelings.

Teens are going through more changes than at any other time in life. The physical, emotional, and chemical changes taking place in a teen's body are intense. It's understandable why an adolescent behaves differently from the child who told you everything.

Teens often think they're the only ones who have certain thoughts. Intense physiological changes can make adolescents feel strange and confused. They may withdraw in the anxious feeling that "something must be wrong with me."

A few rules for parents can go a long way in encouraging teens to open up:

Don't interrogate. Parents who get the best results don't fire a lot of questions at their teenagers. Instead they say, "Let me tell you about my day!" Sometimes, their own enthusiasm rubs off.

Make it safe for your teen to talk. This means don't criticize. Don't tell your daughter she's wrong—even when she is. A teen who is criticized will talk back or clam up even more. We need to show our teens we can handle without anger what they say.

Don't try to force your teen to talk. It's a natural tendency to keep quiet when someone tries to make us talk. Withholding information also makes some teens feel they are in control. Their silent message is, "You can't make me talk!" Keep in mind that teens will talk when they're ready and only when it's safe.

It's normal and natural for teens to keep some information from adults. We're probably better off not knowing everything about them anyway.

PEARL 34

Social and Extracurricular Activities

Parents and teens often find themselves in the heat of battle over social and extracurricular activities. Parents legitimately expect their teens to maintain at least average grades at school. Teens argue that recreational activities can provide a way for them to socialize with their friends.

Many battles flare up from parents' belief that certain activities are just not acceptable. But here is another area in which we often confuse acceptance with approval. We forget that there is a big difference between the two.

Wise parents are more concerned about their teen's plans for handling undesirable activities than they are about restricting the activities themselves. Whether a social activity is good or bad is not nearly as important as knowing your teen can handle any temptations associated with the event. The following scenario illustrates a Love and Logic approach:

KELSEY: Mom, I'm old enough to go to that concert. Can I go?

MOM: I'll know you're old enough when you can tell me about the possible pressures you're going to face and your plans for handling them.

KELSEY: Gee, Mom. Are you worried I'll do drugs? You know I don't do drugs.

MOM: That's not what I said, Kelsey. I want to know what you're going to say when the other kids are telling you that everybody does drugs at a concert and that you know better than to say you're not going to get hooked if you do some once in a while.

KELSEY: Gee, Mom. Don't you trust me?

MOM: That's not the point. I know how hard it is to be in awkward situations. I also know that once you have thought it out and come up with a plan for handling those situations you'll be ready to take care of yourself. I'll be glad to let you go to the concert when you can describe that plan to me.

This mother knows that the day Kelsey can describe her plan for handling an activity is the day Kelsey is ready for that activity. It's also the day that the mom no longer needs to worry about it.

Many of the arguments over outside activities revolve around whether that involvement will detract from schoolwork. Some extracurricular engagements, such as band and theater, fill educational needs even though they aren't part of a formal curriculum. Others, such as athletics, are beneficial even though they aren't academic.

When teens know their parents are listening, they are more willing to be flexible about their participation in extracurricular activities. Observe how this dad and son deal with the son's desire to run track:

COLIN: Dad, the coach thinks I can make the track team!

DAD: I'm happy for you, Colin. But I wonder if you'll be able to keep up with your studies. You made only a C-plus average last term, and I'm wondering whether that will be enough for you to be accepted to college.

COLIN: I know, Dad. I think I can do both track and school.

DAD: How will you manage that?

COLIN: The coach talked over my grades with me too. We agreed that if I can't keep my average up, I'm off the squad.

DAD: That sounds good to me. I certainly hope you make the team, and I look forward to watching you run. But remember, as I've said before, if the grades go down, paying for college tuition is squarely in your lap.

We hope our teens will discuss with us many of the things that go on in their lives. Like adults, teens make mistakes or find themselves in difficult situations. It's helpful when they can talk with an interested, non-blaming adult about these experiences. Their willingness to talk to us is a good sign. It gives them a chance to relive, in a safe way, what happened and get their own beliefs in order. Effective parents listen without being afraid that their willingness to listen in a non-blaming way means approval.

Sports

J unior wide receiver Patrick went out long. The quarterback stepped back, saw all his receivers were covered, but took his chances anyway. He cocked his arm and fired the pass thirty yards to Patrick.

Patrick jumped, reached, and snared the football. The linebacker then snared Patrick, throwing a ham-sized forearm across Patrick's chest while he was still in mid-air. The hit sent Patrick horizontal, airborne, and down. Patrick didn't hit the frozen ground so much as the ground hit him. The shock knocked the ball from his hands and kicked the air out of his lungs.

The play was over, but the action wasn't. Patrick's mother tied the high school record for the fifty-yard dash as she bolted from the stands and ran across the field toward Patrick. As she took in the sight of her fallen son gasping for breath, she whirled around to the linebacker, pointed her leather-gloved hand in his face, and screamed, "You big jerk! Don't you ever hit my son again!"

Patrick's only real regret about the play was that the ground was too hard to dig a hole in so he could crawl down in it and die.

This is *not* the way parents should encourage their teens in sports. Patrick not only lost the ball on the play, he also lost his self-esteem when his mother took matters into her own hands.

Sports offer a lot for teens. They develop bodies, which we want to encourage teens to continue developing for the rest of their lives. Sports also promote team spirit, good peer relationships, and a feeling of solidarity with the school. Perhaps most importantly, sports teach teens how to handle defeat and become good sports.

Parents can encourage their teens' athletic development by observing a few guidelines:

Guard against parental overinvolvement. Spectators at wrestling matches often see parents yelling to their sons, "Kill him! Kill him!" The wrestler doesn't need to put a hammerlock on his opponent as much as the parents need a hammerlock on their mouths. Parental screaming at sports events tends to be counterproductive as well as silly.

When conflicts arise between teens and coaches, it's usually more helpful for parents to suggest how teens should talk to their coach, rather than for parents to talk to the coach. After all, teens don't call up their parents' boss when their parents have a dispute on the job. Teens learn best when they handle such differences by themselves.

Teens should not engage in certain sports before their bodies have developed properly. Heavy weightlifting, for example, can damage undeveloped spines and certain muscle groups.

If your teen doesn't want you to attend a meet or game, talk to your teen about how your behavior might be making him or her uncomfortable. Respect your teen's wishes; change the behavior or refrain from attending.

Let your teen's interest in sports develop naturally. Teens are most likely to do well in sports when their parents take an interest in athletics but don't force it on their kids. Those who do push their teen into sports will tend to get worked up about their teen's mistakes or judgment errors. Those who encourage their teen properly will tend to get excited about what their teen does right.

Foster once knew a young girl who was training to be a figure skater on her way to the Olympics. She benefited greatly from her mother's encouragement. She told me that her mom constantly encouraged her to "go for it." Her mother spent hours at the rink watching her practice her form and turns, cheering her on with every new move she learned.

This mom was encouraging, not forcing, and her daughter excelled. Her daughter's talent blossomed like a flower, and that blossoming was something that her daughter owned. Her mom told me once, "If she wanted to quit, it would be her decision."

This girl also noticed how other mothers tried to coerce their daughters into becoming the next ice-skating superstar. The other girls hated it. "I see the moms pushing their kids," she said. "They even push the kids who can't skate, and the kids just end up crying." The only things these other girls were learning was that they hated to skate and that they weren't happy with their mothers either.

A father wrote to us relating his experience with his son, Love and Logic, and sports:

> My son and I often had conflicts over his performance on the sporting field. Since he was young, he has always played soccer, and I have coached his baseball team the past three years. Last winter, for a number of reasons, he decided to drop out of basketball because "it just wasn't his game," and he wanted to focus more on his other two sports. This was hard on me, growing up in a time when everybody playing three sports was the norm, but it seems times have changed, so I agreed to help him work more on his baseball and soccer skills.
>
> Last year was especially hard. As his soccer league had grown more competitive, he was playing less and less over the year. We had numerous conflicts about his coach, his effort, and whether or not he would continue the sport. I was also trying to coach him on the way home from games and he wanted to hear less and less of it. I felt a rift growing between us and I didn't know what to do about it. I wouldn't let him quit, but I also knew that if he didn't want to play, it didn't matter what I thought; I couldn't *make* him try harder — he had to want to.
>
> With the beginning of this new school year and fresh soccer season, things seemed better. He had a coach that was playing him more and he was performing better on the field. Then a couple of weeks ago, he had a game where he just seemed dead on the field, and all the old frustrations came back about his efforts and his attitudes. I was so upset as the game finished, I was ready to lay into him with a Vince Lombardi halftime speech about winners and losers.
>
> However, having read *Parenting with Love and Logic* recently, I knew that now that he was eleven, he had to choose to play the

game or else he would soon quit—I couldn't make him play harder. So I decided to do the difficult thing: I kept my mouth shut to let him talk about the game.

As we walked back to the car I was fuming and had to excuse myself to stop at the restrooms to calm down before we drove home. The car was silent on the way home, and I refused to let him turn on the radio, to give him time to think. When we arrived home, we discovered he had left one of the sandals he wears before and after the game at the field, so we drove back. That was also a quiet ride until about halfway back when he asked me, "Why did you yell at me to go when that kid fell down?" While he was fighting for the ball with another boy, the kid had fallen to the turf and the whole sideline yelled for him to take the ball and go toward the goal. I explained to him that I didn't see that the other boy was hurt, but that, if he had been concerned, the correct thing to do was kick the ball out of bounds so that the official could call time out to allow the coach to come and check on him. Then I apologized for getting so excited.

After that, the layers of the onion began to peel as his focus changed from outside—my yelling on the sideline—to inside—how he felt about his performance and how badly he had wanted to play well in front of his mom, whose schedule didn't allow her to come to very many of his games. He talked of how he wanted to show her that he was playing because he liked the game and not just because I wanted him to play. Again I just let him talk, but my emotions had changed from being mad to being proud of him—and even a little choked up.

We finally arrived back at the field, found his sandal, and then I decided to go get some smoothies so we could continue our discussion. Over the smoothies we discussed his performance a bit more, why he had felt sluggish (too much water before the game), and he even listened as I gave him a couple of pointers on what he could do to address some of the problems he felt he had had on the field that day. It was one of the best times I have ever had talking with him.

Since then, I have let him own his sports more, and he has even asked me to go out and play catch with him a couple of times so that he can get ready for baseball season, which is his true love. The old image of a dad playing catch with his son has lost none of its nostalgia.

Letting him own his sporting efforts and not taking them away from him by getting too emotional and telling him how to play the game has made all the difference in the world.

Through sports, teens can learn valuable lessons about their own identity, independence, and skills. As in other areas of teens' lives that concern identity and independence, parents need to give their teens the freedom in sports to try, succeed, and fail, and to pick themselves up to try again.

Suicide Threats

T ragically, suicide is one of the leading causes of death among teenagers. It is a sobering problem that parents must take seriously while
recognizing that some suicidal threats are manipulative in nature. If you
have reason to be concerned or if your teen has indirectly referred to suicide, the thought has probably already entered his or her mind, so it's not
really risky to talk about it. The question is how to bring up the subject.
If you do talk to your teen about suicide, show concern and caring while
remaining matter-of-fact. You can make matters worse with responses
such as, "You don't mean that," or "Don't ever talk like that."

The situation is usually more dangerous if a teenager has already
thought of a specific lethal method and has the means at his or her dis-
posal. Giving away favorite objects is another serious sign. Most authorities
believe the risk is also higher if depression or suicide runs in the family.

A physical injury such as a concussion, loss of limbs, blindness, or
paralysis can lead to severe depression, in which suicide becomes a common thought.

Teens at greatest risk are those who usually achieve without struggle. They often expect success to be automatic and, at times when they
think they are failing, have difficulty believing that the struggle to work
through it will lead to solutions.

Teens who continually struggle and never succeed are also at risk.
They become hopeless and want to give up on life.

Our goal in discussing suicide with our teens should be to help
them pursue other options. At the same time, we should be considering

other avenues of support such as counseling, support groups, and, if necessary, hospitalization.

Here's a conversation that models talking to teens about suicide in a loving manner:

DAD: You seem pretty down these days, Tonya.

TONYA (sighs): I don't want to talk about it.

DAD: Sometimes it seems that things are so bad there's no way out.

TONYA (softening): Yeah.

DAD: You've been so unhappy. I wonder if you feel life just isn't worth living.

TONYA (softer): I do, Dad. It's just that everything turns out wrong. I'd probably be better off dead.

DAD: Are there any other solutions?

TONYA: I probably wouldn't do it. I'm too chicken.

DAD: When I'm feeling really down, it always helps me to talk to someone else.

TONYA: Like a shrink?

DAD: Maybe. The nice thing about seeing a therapist is you can always quit if things don't seem better. I know, because I've been there. I hope you'll think about finding someone to talk with.

TONYA: I will, Dad. Thanks.

During this conversation, Tonya's dad never becomes defensive. Instead he stays with her feelings and lets her know what works for him when he is down. He does not force Tonya into a decision. If he did, she might say no. If he allows her to give it some thought, she might say yes.

Explore alternatives with your teen in a loving, calm, and receptive manner, without moralizing or downplaying the problem, but if the threats escalate or lead to an actual suicide attempt, seek professional help.

The Telephone

The telephone is a wonderful parenting instrument. Like all instruments, it can be used appropriately by parents to help children learn responsibility and develop a consistently cheerful demeanor. On the other hand, it may be used inappropriately and lead to family squabbles.

Family phone hassles typically begin when children are young. They see that when mom is on the phone, they are free to run around the house, cause minor furniture damage, pollute the auditory atmosphere, and generally behave in a way that they could never get away with if she were off the phone.

This control of parents around the phone often continues when childhood years slip into adolescence. Then the parents become frustrated because the child is on the phone "too much." Parents fret because homework isn't getting done. They become frustrated when they can't get their calls because their teen is monopolizing the phone.

Sometimes parents throw in the towel, pay the extra bucks, and get teens their own telephone in their own room. Most parents can't afford that solution, so they muddle through. Today many teens pay for their own cell phone.

Whatever the hassle, the child learns from toddlerhood through adolescence, "Around phone issues, Mom and Dad end up frustrated, and I end up winning!" However, as Love and Logic principles dictate, there is no such thing as a win-lose situation between parent and child. There are only lose-lose situations or win-win situations.

Love and Logic parents use the phone to confirm that they are in loving self-control, which in turn helps the teen learn self-control and responsibility.

With the wide and inexpensive availability of call-waiting service, all parents with teenagers have access to an automatic, inexpensive, and efficient answering machine. As parents of teens know, their "teen phone answering machine" always circles around the phone.

Wise parents set guidelines like these:

PARENT: Robert, you can use the phone as much as you want. Whenever any of us is on the line, we will answer the other line when it clicks and take telephone numbers for the other family member to call back. (Because teens are on the phone for much longer periods than their parents, they, not parents, end up being the phone answering machine.)

ROBERT: Okay, that sounds fair to me.

PARENT: However, there is a difference. When telephone calls come in for you, I always take the number and tell your friends that you will call them back sometime. When a telephone call comes in for an adult who is present in the home, you tell the caller that you are on the phone right now but will get off. Then you summon the adult to the phone. While the adult is coming to pick up the call, within two sentences you tell your friend goodbye and you'll call him back when one of the adults finishes talking, and you hand over the phone. Is the picture clear?

ROBERT: Yeah, it's clear, but that's unfair! How come you get to talk to people immediately and I have to wait?

PARENT: Because I pay the bills. Whoever pays the telephone bill gets to use the phone immediately. It's their phone. If the rule seems unfair to you, you can pay for your own cell phone. (This is based on the supposition that any teen responsible enough to earn his own money is responsible enough to have his own cell phone.)

Most children considering this argument will agree that adults should have immediate access to their phone calls. In return, they get to use the phone, which is a real privilege.

Some teens, unfortunately, need to have the following conversation with their parents:

> PARENT: Erica, how will the rules have to change to ensure that I always get my calls if my business associates or friends try to contact me but all they ever get is a busy signal or just no answer—and I discover that this is occurring while I'm home and you're on the phone?
>
> ERICA: Well, I suppose you could ban me from the telephone so that it would always ring through.
>
> PARENT: What a good idea! Maybe we ought to give that real thought. I appreciate the suggestion. Do you think that we will need that rule?
>
> ERICA (snappish): No, I guess not.
>
> PARENT: Thanks, Erica, you're a jewel!

A loving parent-child relationship, firmness, and high expectations almost always ensure that you will have a pleasant, courteous, effective, and always present "answering machine" in your teen.

PEARL 38

Video and Computer Games

Not so long ago, video games offered a feeble alternative to pin-ball machines. Two players using crude joysticks bounced a tiny white ball back and forth on a black ping-pong table. The action was slow, but for back then it was fun.

How things have changed! Now two, three, four, or more players can search for buried treasure or battle intergalactic aliens. They can even do it with friends across the street, across the country, or on the other side of the planet through the Internet or other gaming systems. With a computer or television set, a gaming system, and a few control-lers, teens can spend hours living a high-tech fantasy.

And they do. The mental intensity generated by playing these games can be a healthy way for teens to develop eye-hand coordination and to learn how to use computers. But the games also can be an unhealthy obsession.

Computer games are perhaps the most popular teen preoccupation. They consume hours of time that might otherwise go into studying, chores, or activities that parents think are more important. But what parents think is important doesn't really matter when it's so much easier and a lot more fun to play games.

Some parents would say that electronic games are an addiction, and this is not without reason (as we will discuss a little later). Their teens won't or can't stop playing. There also is some concern that obsessive playing raises stress levels.

So, what do parents do?

Obviously, we can't prevent our teens from playing electronic games when they are over at their friends' houses or when they are at an arcade at the mall. Remember, parents can't win a battle that they can't control.

But we still have the right to expect that our teens will get average grades and do their chores. We also have the right to insist that our teen treat family members with courtesy and respect.

When teens play their video games, they probably use the family television or computer. Like the telephone or car, the television and computer belong to the parents and the rest of the family. If our teens' use of these appliances interferes with family recreation, home maintenance, or business, we can rightly forbid them from playing their games.

We must also assess how we spend our own recreation time. It's hypocritical to criticize teens for spending too much time playing video games while we're living the life of an unrepentant couch potato glued to TV sitcoms. This hypocritical behavior is a sure way to strip teens of respect for parental authority.

Let's listen in on a dad discussing video games with his son. He follows the Love and Logic steps always recommended when dealing with teens:

1. Confirm that this is a good time for the conversation.
2. Use thoughtful questions, with curiosity and interest to explore with acceptance (not necessarily approval) your child's point of view.
3. Ask if you can share your thoughts and observations.
4. Give your ideas succinctly, with love, without lecturing, often continuing, as possible, with questions.
5. Thank your child for listening and close with the hope that he or she will give your opinion consideration.

Here is their discussion:

DAD: (looking over his son's shoulder as blood of bad guys splatters across the screen and mustering interest in the slaughter) Hey, Rob, looks like you're doing pretty well! How's it going?

ROB: Great, Dad! I'm on level four now, and I've wiped out a whole enemy platoon.

DAD: I can imagine you feel great about that! How long you been fighting here?

ROB: About half an hour so far today, and about two hours yesterday.

DAD: Wow. Lots of time fighting. What do you like best about playing?

ROB: Well, I like outsmarting the enemy. These new games are so realistic. Something that works the first time doesn't work the second. The bad guys learn! It's the artificial intelligence programming.

DAD: Yeah, I can see how that's really exciting. Is it just you, or are you leading a platoon?

ROB: Both. Depends on how I set up the situation.

DAD: Interesting. . . . Do you mind pausing the action while we talk a minute?

ROB: Sure, Dad.

DAD: You know, Rob, I have always thought of you as a person with real leadership qualities and I always kind of thought that you would make a difference in a world of your own creation, and other people would play by your rules.

ROB: What do you mean, Dad?

DAD: Well, as exciting as the combat is, you are living in a world created by very talented and creative computer artists and coders. They've been really good at creating worlds where other people want to spend a lot of time.

ROB: Yeah, but it's not like I'm not making my own decisions—or something."

DAD: I bet you make good ones. Can you make any decision?

ROB: No, not any.

DAD: Right. You can't climb a tree?

ROB: No!

DAD: Or set up possibilities for peace?

ROB: Dad, this game isn't about peace!

DAD: Well, that's kind of my point. It seems a little limiting to me. You get to advance to new levels in a way they have programmed, right?

ROB: Well, yeah, I guess.

DAD: Don't get me wrong, Rob. When I see you here enjoying the game, I really do realize that most people do play the game of life by other people's rules; really living in a world other people create. So join the human race. The more time you spend outside of virtual reality, with real people, the more you gain skills to communicate and create a world of *your own* making, not someone else's.

ROB: I get your drift, Dad.

DAD: Well, good luck, pal! Thanks for giving this some thought.

Game Addiction

Dealing with game addictions can be as challenging as facing a gambling and other type of addiction. The following story can both give us an example, and hope, about such situations:

"How could this happen?" worried Paul's mother. She finally realized that her son had become addicted to Internet computer games. Before today she had been ambivalent about the amount of time he spent in his room playing the games, and she was able to convince herself that it was not all that bad. After all, when he is off in his room they aren't arguing about things and she doesn't have to have him underfoot. His interest in the computer games keeps him out of the way so she can do the things she wants to do and provides an inexpensive babysitter.

Denial has great power over humans. In this case, it helped Mom avoid seeing the real problem. She even had days when she was able to think, "Other kids are out smoking dope. Other kids are out getting into trouble. How can his interest in the games be so bad? He's safe in his room; I know where he is and what he's doing." Of course, this kind of thinking makes about as much sense as, "Other kids rape and murder. My kid's not that bad. He only sells drugs."

Recently, she'd seen a television news show that touted the millions of dollars a local school paid to provide academic instruction through computer games. The news reporter said that the kids loved the games and were actually scoring better on their school tests. This information helped her feel better about Paul's compulsive use of the computer games at home.

Paul's mom actually convinced herself that all the time he spent on the computer games was good for his self-concept. She told her friend, Mary, "You know, Paul isn't good at a lot of things other boys are good at. Now he's found something that he's good at. I just know that his self-concept will grow with his successes with the games."

But alas, Mom's thinking got a jolt. She attended a seminar on addictions. The expert talked about common addictions such as alcohol, drugs, and gambling. It was a shock when the therapist talked about the devastating effects of computer addiction. She learned about the breakdown of family relationships when children or adults became consumed with their computers and lost interest in each other. Depression increased in many of these families as well. To add to her concern she learned about documented changes in the brain experienced by those who became addicted to the games.

Mom developed new resolve to look at what she had done to her son by encouraging his infatuation with the screen and the keyboard instead of learning to relate to the family. She realized that family members had drifted apart since she had allowed the computer to take over raising her children.

It was at this time that she came to grips with the fact that her children were only learning what the computer programmers wanted them to learn, and that was to buy and play more of their games. A review of the report cards gave her another jolt. School grades were on a downhill slide.

Mom now knew that she had to take action. This was going to be difficult, since school and society provide support for children owning and using computers. Her children's high school even suggested that each student have his or her own notebook computer. It seemed that the computers were continually connected to the Internet. It did not help that Dad brought work home each night to do on his computer. How could she restrict her children's use of the computers when they saw Dad spending so much of his time that way?

Doing something about this is not going to be easy, she thought. The seminar expert talked about children who became violent and abusive when their time on the computer was restricted. If she was going to take a stand on this issue, she needed a plan and some support.

Getting Paul's father on board was going to be important. Early in her marriage she had learned that her best chance of doing this was to lay out the facts of what she had learned without telling Dad what to do about it. She hoped that he would see this situation for the disaster that it had become.

Mom and Dad had recently attended a Becoming a Love and Logic Parent class. One of the most important skills they learned was how to create a plan and then shelve the plan until they could share it with others. The purpose of this was to have help identifying the holes in the plan. If other adults could see loopholes in the plan, surely a child could find a way of making the plan fail. The price of failure at this point was too great to take chances. Paul was escaping from the challenges of relating to others by living with his addiction.

Both Mom and Dad sought out the services of an addiction specialist in an attempt to understand the challenges they and their boy were going to face. The therapist helped them understand that they would soon be seeing typical behaviors of addicts. Once Paul realized that they were serious about limiting his time on the computer, the pull of his addiction would drive him to do whatever it took to regain access to the computer games.

"No," said Mom. "Paul is a good kid who has never been prone to being sneaky or defiant. He will understand that we are trying to help him." Months later she told how wrong she was about this. "When we took away his computer, he sneaked time on his dad's computer. When we put a password on Dad's computer, he found a way to break the password. He went to his friend's home, lying that he was there to do homework, but instead was using his friend's machine to continue his gaming."

Paul even found a way to buy a used computer that he hid in his room. Mom and Dad never discovered where he got the money to buy that one. They were equally surprised to learn how he was able to sneak away to the Cyber Café when he was supposed to be in school. Truancy became a major problem.

Like all similar situations, this problem got worse before it started to turn around. Fortunately, with the support of a therapist, and finally, with Paul's determination to rejoin the real world instead of the fantasy world of gaming, there was a happy ending to this story.

As this mom looked back on this problem and how it consumed her family, she told of her disappointment that she hadn't learn about Love and Logic when her children were younger. "I'm sure the fantasy world of the games had a lot to do with the fact that they provided an illusion of control for a boy who had too few choices and consequences in his real life. He was denied the opportunity to feel needed in our family. This happened when we gave up on trying to get him to do his fair share of the work around the house. The reason we gave up was because we didn't know how to get him to do chores without constant reminders and battles."

This much wiser mom continued, "I now know that Paul has an addictive personality that made it easier to slip into the gaming addiction as a way of replacing what he was not getting out of his family life. I'm sure the odds for avoiding this problem would have been much higher if we had known and used the Love and Logic process as we raised him."

Give your children a gift. Limit the time they spend with electronic entertainment to thirty minutes per day. Brain science teaches us that kids who spend more time than this are actually doing damage to brain growth and development. Kids who spend their time doing things become doers. Kids who spend their time watching become watchers. That's how the brain grows.

Violence: Bullies and Gangs

A generation ago, the most a teen had to fear at school or out on the street was being accosted by bullies. In recent years, that concern has been folded into the larger specter of violence from gangs and armed students.

The advice of a generation ago for dealing with bullies is still valid today: give them a wide berth. Bullies are bullies. They don't understand decency or reason. And because they are usually gifted with size and physical strength, they can't easily be beaten on their own turf. Wise parents will not encourage their teens to try to beat up a bully. They will, however, alert school officials to harassment by bullies and let officials know that they will not tolerate such intimidation.

Why do some kids get bullied more than others? Many good, quiet, polite, and intelligent kids are mistreated by their peers, particularly in the zoo called middle—or junior high—school. Generally preteens and young adolescents make fun of almost anyone or anything that is different. All the politically correct "celebrate diversity" speeches tend to fall on deaf ears in middle school and aren't going to change behavior that may be simply a normal response at this developmental stage.

Unfortunately, depending on the school, being very pretty, very responsible, very kind, or very sweet leads to standing out like a punching dummy, especially if the child doesn't know how to roll with the teen nonsense. Some children who relate well to adults and who are more mature simply struggle with coping with and understanding the immaturity of their peers.

Here are the things parents do to deal with bullying that often don't work:

- trying to make the environment more accepting (although if a child is being truly threatened, school officials must step in and remove the offenders)
- trying to "build the child up" with false affirmation or phoney praise
- giving unasked-for advice and suggestions on behavior
- showing how "hurt" you are for the child and how frustrated and helpless you feel in the situation

Many parents attempt to make the situation better for their child, and sometimes it works A mom with a special-needs child can talk to a classroom, telling them how much she and her child appreciate their understanding and how hard it is for the child to understand what is socially appropriate. The more challenged the child, the more important it is to try to modify the environment in this way.

However, if the child is able to learn how to cope, it is better to help him or her learn to do so rather than intervening yourself. Instead of trying to change what goes on outside the child, the parent can help the child grow on the inside.

We might encourage our child by saying, "Kids who are awful now often grow up to be good men and women. Someday they'll be almost as mature as you. Luckily, this is just a stage in their lives. I sure am proud of the way you handle it." Wise parents let the child know that teasing doesn't mean there is something wrong with him or her, but it's a problem the other child has.

The more children learn to handle bullying with an unshakable appreciation of their own goodness, the stronger men and women they will be. Early teasing provides children with an opportunity to learn not to internalize the problems of others. A parent might say, "Honey, all your life you are going to be around miserable people. Lucky for you, you are learning to handle that now; some don't really understand this until they are adults. I expect that you'll come out of this wiser, more thoughtful, and more understanding of others."

Of course, if it is a case in which a child is in physical danger, the environment itself has to be modified. Drive-by shootings and other violence associated with gang and drug culture are a more serious matter than normal bullying. In a world in which schools install metal detectors at the doors to apprehend students carrying guns, knives, and other weapons, we need to intervene if our children are in real danger.

Gangs offer a way for teens to find security and a family that they may not have at home. Solidarity is reinforced through secret gestures, language, drugs, and often brutal initiation rites. The danger—regardless of the shocking and senseless violence—draws teens to a lifestyle that brings the movies and the evening news right to their doorstep.

For some young people, the attraction of gang involvement is hard to resist, especially the idea of standing out from peers as a member of an alluring and darkly romantic group. Even a strong and stable family life with both birth parents at home is no guarantee that a teen will steer clear of joining a gang.

With many of the issues facing teens, we can offer choices, point out the results of those choices, let teens make their own decision, and then allow them to learn how to live with the consequences of that decision. But a decision to join a gang—right and wrong issues aside—can be fatal.

Parents who find that their teens may be pressured or attracted to join a gang will probably find that they need to remove their child from the school or community. This is extremely hard for both parents and teens, but gang violence may make such a decision imperative.

If your teens insist on joining a gang, however, you may have no other recourse than to ask them to leave home. You need to stress that your teens are marking themselves as a target for other gangs, which unacceptably places the family in a position of risk as targets for violence. Yet at the same time, your teens need to be told that your family loves them and wants them more than the gang wants them.

Many families have learned to take back their communities from gangs through political or community action and church leadership. Parents have learned to band together and become a source of strength for those teens who are trying to resist the temptation to join a gang.

Notes

1. Chapter 1: Teenagers 101: Welcome to Parenting Graduate School. U.S. Census Bureau, "Households and Families: 2000," http://www.census.gov/prod/2001pubs/c2kbr01-8.pdf (published September 2001; accessed October 3, 2005).

2. This and previous statistics in this list are from the 2003 Youth Risk Behavior Survey done biennially by the U.S. Center for Disease Control. More information available at http://www.cdc.gov.

3. National Highway Traffic Safety Administration, "Traffic safety facts 2002: Young drivers," http://www-nrd.nhtsa.dot.gov/pdf/nrd-30/NCSA/TSF2002/2002ydrfacts.pdf (published August 2003; accessed October 3, 2005).

4. National Survey of Drug Use and Health, "Driving Under the Influence (DUI) among Young Persons." *The NSDUH Report,* December 31, 2004. http://www.oas.samhsa.gov/2k4/youthDUI/youthDUI.htm (accessed October 3, 2005).

5. This and previous statistics in this list are from the 2003 Youth Risk Behavior Survey done biennially by the U.S. Center for Disease Control. More information on these is available at www.cdc.gov.

6. Weinstock, H., Berman, S., and Cates, W., "Sexually transmitted diseases among American youth: Incidence and prevalence estimates, 2000," *Perspectives on Sexual and Reproductive Health* 2004, 36(1):6-10.

7. Chapter 4: Back to the Basics, Part 2: Treating Teenagers as Responsible Adults. Sylvia B. Rimm, PhD, *How to Parent So Children Will Learn* (Watertown, WI: Apple Publishing, 1990).

8. Chapter 6: Understanding Teens from the Inside Out: Internal Changes in Adolescence. Geidd et al., 1999.

9. The following articles are a good place to start: H. Chugani, "Biological Basis of Emotions: Brain Systems and Brain Development," *Pediatrics* 102 (1998):1225-1229; P. Huttenlocher, "Synaptic density in human frontal cortex—developmental changes and effects of aging," *Brain Research* 163 (1979):195-205; M. Lidow, P. Goldman-Rakic, P. Rakic, "Synchronized overproduction of neurotransmitter receptors in diverse regions of the primate cerebral cortex," Proceedings of the National Academy of Sciences of the United States of America 88 (1991):10218-10221; L. P. Spear, "The adolescent brain and the college drinker: biological basis of propensity to use and misuse alcohol." *Journal of studies on alcohol,* supplement 14 (2002):71-81; and P. Seeman, "Images in neuroscience. Brain development, X: pruning during development." *American Journal of Psychiatry* 156 (1999):168.

10. *Whatever Happened to Childhood? The Problem of Teen Pregnancy in the United States* (Washington, DC: The National Campaign to Prevent Teen Pregnancy, 1997), 3.

11. Maggie Fox, "Sex Map Shows Chain of Almost 300 High School Lovers," *Reuters News Service*, January 24, 2005. http://www.pphouston.org/site/News2?JServSessionIdr011=j9b8r644z1.app6a&page=NewsArticle&id=9013 (accessed October 6, 2005).

12. Endnote authority: Robert E. Rector, Kirk A. Johnson, PhD, and Lauren R. Noyes (Center for Data Analysis, Report #303-04).

13. For more about how to talk with your kids about relationships and sex, see pearl 11, "Dating," and pearl 32, "Sex."

14. Pearl 16: Entitlement. For more information and advice on this topic, see *From Innocence to Entitlement* from The Love and Logic Institute. Available at www.loveandlogic.com. In Love and Logic tradition, it offers specific and practical techniques for parents to combat childhood entitlement.

15. Pearl 18: Giving Gifts to Our Adolescents. For more on teaching your children to be fiscally responsible, see pearl 24, "Money."

16. Pearl 19: Grades. For more help on this subject, a video entitled "Hope for Underachieving Kids" is available through the Love and Logic Institute at www.loveandlogic.com.

17. Pearl 24: Money. See also pearl 18, "Giving Gifts to our Adolescents" for a discussion of buying gifts for teens and helping them out of financial hardships.

Index

Authors

Foster Cline, MD, is an internationally renowned child and adult psychiatrist. He is a cofounder, with Jim Fay, of the Love and Logic Institute and specializes in the attachment and bonding of children, dealing with gifted and talented children, parenting and child management, classroom behavior management, and communications systems and patterns.

His love of children and his passion for changing lives give him a unique sense of clarity as he turns difficult and often confusing child development concepts into straight talk and answers for adults. He has served as a consultant to school systems, pupil personnel teams, and hospitals around the world.

Dr. Cline is also a grandparent and the father of three biological children, one adopted child, and several foster children.

Jim Fay has more than fifty years of experience working with children and families. During thirty-one years in education as an educator, principal, and administrator, he served in public, private, and parochial schools. He is a cofounder of the Love and Logic Institute as well as the founder of School Consultant Services, which he began in 1977.

Fay has become one of America's most sought-after presenters in the field of parenting, positive discipline, and classroom management. He has been a consultant to schools, parents, mental health organizations, and the U.S. military. He is also recognized as one of America's top educational experts and has won many awards in the education field.

Fay is a grandparent and the father of three children. His youngest, Charles Fay, PhD, is a school psychologist and has joined the Love and Logic Institute as a presenter, writer, and consultant.

Love and Logic Materials and Seminars

Foster Cline, MD, and Jim Fay present Love and Logic seminars for both parents and educators in many cities each year. For more information on their books, CDs, seminars, or other helpful materials, contact:

The Love and Logic Institute, Inc.
2207 Jackson St., Suite 102
Golden, Colorado 80401-2300
(800) LUV-LOGIC
(800) 588-5644
(303) 278-7552
Fax: (800) 455-7557

Or visit our website at:
www.loveandlogic.com